AGAINST SYMBOLIC LIBERALISM

AGAINST SYMBOLIC LIBERALISM

LIBERALISM

A Plea for Dialogical Sociology

SARI HANAFI

LIVERPOOL UNIVERSITY PRESS

First published 2025 by
Liverpool University Press
4 Cambridge Street
Liverpool
L69 7ZU

British Library Cataloguing-in-Publication data
A British Library CIP record is available

ISBN 978-1-83624-466-0 hardback
ISBN 978-1-83624-467-7 paperback

Typeset by Carnegie Book Production, Lancaster

To Michael Burawoy
A guide, a force, a mentor, a friend

"Sari Hanafi's book offers an original analysis and critique of Western sociology, as well as a diagnosis and therapy for polarized societies. The book resembles its author. It is both powerful and generous, global and local, critical and dialogical. The analysis comes straight from Beirut but will appeal to a larger audience interested in the prospects of sociological theory, post-colonialism, political liberalism and democratic alternatives."
–Frédéric Vandenberghe, Federal University of Rio de Janeiro

"Hanafi's brilliant presentation of his Dialogical Political Liberal Project offers a relevant account of how dialogic sociology is the most lucid tool that we have today to provide eloquent analysis and accomplished solutions. Building on a sound theoretical review of liberalism, he has delved into the study of challenging realities in different contexts to resume demonstrating how the sociology that places dialogue at the core of its analyses is able to engage diversity and offer transformative possibilities. Hanafi's dialogical proposal is an invitation to orient sociology towards improving the lives of citizens, recovering the original purpose for which it was created."
–Marta Soler, University of Barcelona and Vice-president for Publications, International Sociological Association

"In this powerful and timely book, Sari Hanafi takes on one of liberalism's deepest flaws: the gap between lofty ideals and concrete realities, between the universal and the particular, theory and praxis. With clarity and conviction, he calls for a radical, self-reflective renewal of liberalism – one that resists the drift toward cynicism and authoritarian compromise. Rejecting tired dichotomies between fact and norm, Hanafi urges an interdisciplinary and dialogical approach rooted in the complexities of our time. This is a bold, rigorous and essential contribution to the urgent task of aligning liberal values with democratic action."
–Mounir Kchaou, Université de Tunis

"While the world burns and crumbles, and sociology risks becoming self-referential or dissolving into a soulless technocracy, Sari Hanafi breaks through by opening a broad and generative horizon. With thoughtful passion and insight, this book commits to renewing Michael Burawoy's call for a public sociology that is both critical and committed. Grounded in an approach that engages with plural epistemologies, marginalized communities and social conflict, Hanafi redefines knowledge as a dialogic practice where one can be truly 'traversed by the other.'"
–Silvia Cataldi, Sapienza University of Rome

Preface

Michael Burawoy

It was 2010. Sari Hanafi had invited me to Lebanon to participate in a conference on universities in the Middle East held at the American University of Beirut. Sari, always a generous host, took me to visit Tyre, a beautiful, ancient city south of Beirut, from where part of his family hailed. Today, it has been devastated by Israeli bombing. On the way to Tyre, I remember Sari receiving a message on his cell phone that he had been denounced by a Lebanese lawyer in London for breaking the boycott of Israel. He had collaborated with Israeli philosophers in the writing of *The Power of Inclusive Exclusion* (2009), a critical assessment of Israeli rule in the Palestinian Occupied Territories. Knowing how precarious the position of Palestinians in Lebanon was, I panicked for Sari's security. But Sari is a survivor. He took this assault in his stride, insisting on holding a public debate at which he would distinguish between boycotting institutions and boycotting individuals. Working with Israeli universities was breaking the boycott but working with individual Israeli sociologists, critical of the Israeli regime, was not.

Sari wades into collaborations and debates others would not dare to enter. In this instance, he first collaborated with Israeli sociologists across national boundaries and, second, he undertook a vitriolic debate within the Palestinian diaspora about the political propriety of such a collaboration. This was a dialogue about a dialogue. He had the courage of his convictions, defending them openly in the public sphere, risking his job in the process. In the end, the American University of Beirut came to his defense on the grounds of academic freedom, supporting him against any potential legal action.

This story helps to understand the animus behind this book and the object of Hanafi's critique – symbolic liberals who enunciate principles they don't follow, or, as he puts it, "classically liberals but politically illiberal."

They are beneficiaries of the inequalities they condemn; they deploy the idea of intersectionality to divert attention from class inequality; they subscribe to clearly unviable market solutions to environmental justice; they confine questions of social justice to the national arena, missing the local and global arenas; they inflate the importance of an abstract and universal notion of human rights that proves to be ineffectual; they are caught between an excessive focus on identity politics and a singular conception of the good.

Hanafi gives this abstract indictment of symbolic liberals concrete illustration in four case studies which comprise the bulk of the book: (1) those who recognize academic freedom for themselves but not for others, such as those who use academic freedom to condemn peaceful protest against the Israeli state's genocide in Gaza; (2) those who treat secularism as a religion yet oppose religious expression in French schools; (3) those who impose the inclusion of gender fluidity in Western school curriculums without distinguishing between justice for LGBTQ+ students and a conception of the good; (4) Swedish social workers who remove children from families, whether on the basis of racial prejudice or state authority over the family. These are wide ranging and complex issues in which liberal principles of social justice clash with particular "common goods" as well as the plurality of the conception of the good. Examples can be extended upwards to states that pay lip service to notions of social justice (democracy, human rights, egalitarianism) and downwards to families which claim equality in the domestic division of labor while obscuring its gendered inequality. In short, there are few spheres of life where principle and practice coincide. Contemporary society is riddled with symbolic liberalism. It is the ideology of our age – a response to the pathologies of late modernity, namely the rise of authoritarianism, rampant inequality and environmental destruction.

Why do principle and practice diverge? Is it that external constraints, such as the ones Hanafi favors (neoliberalism and emotional capitalism), do not permit the realization of liberal ideals? Or is there something more sinister at work, namely a skin-deep commitment to ideals, designed to obscure and justify their violation? Do dominant classes have an interest in hiding their domination behind liberal ideals? And, if so, are the symbolic liberals unaware of the gap between principle and practice? The Israeli state, for example, claims to be a Western democracy in a sea of Eastern authoritarianism, but at the same time punishes political dissent and reduces Gaza to rubble. How do the agents of state power reconcile the two and bridge the divide between ideals and reality, especially when the separation becomes blatant? And from the dominated, what is the reaction to this glaring gap between democratic claims and despotic means. Is it to turn the expressed ideals against the symbolic liberals, demanding they fulfill their promise or substitute alternative principles and abandon social justice as a sham? Or do they simply shrug their shoulders in despair?

Does not every class society have a liberal ideology that mystifies or justifies domination and exploitation? Perhaps the most transparent gap between ideology and reality could be found in Soviet societies, where socialist ideals were asserted in all spheres of society. Under state socialism, the party state thrust an ideology of equality and efficiency down everyone's throats in the name of the universal interests of the working class. But the working class was disparaging of state support for its rights and interests. Accordingly, from time to time, the working class and allied classes responded with revolts that demanded the ruling class live up to its socialist ideals – Hungary in 1956, Czechoslovakia in 1968, and Poland in 1980. In the final analysis, however, the people largely abandoned the idea of socialism in favor of capitalism, which looked bright and beautiful from where they stood – a perspective many would later come to regret and reject. Symbolic socialism discredited the idea of socialism, bringing about its demise rather than turning it toward a democratic socialism. Could something similar happen to symbolic liberalism – the abandonment of liberalism for fascism? Is that what we are observing across the globe?

What is Hanafi's solution to the self-destruction of symbolic liberalism? Drawing on Rawls, Habermas and other philosophers, he proposes a Political Liberal Project in which a genuine commitment to liberal ideals becomes the basis for recognizing different principles of the common good. He proposes a public sphere where diverse cultural and political groups bring their "common goods" into conversation with each other. Presidential debates in the United States, as an example of such a dialogue, surface the obstacles to be overcome. What resources – social, political, economic and rhetorical – will be brought to bear on such a dialogue? Who will oversee and regulate the dialogue? Who will participate in this dialogue? Is it possible to have open access to the public sphere? Can we assume a shared commitment to a singular set of principles? Or would it be better to regard what we share as a hegemonic *system* of ideologies as Gramsci proposes? Different groups will pull and push on different strands of the system, trying to elevate their prominence. Will the dialogue look more like a law court in which each side appeals to different precedents in a shared body of law?

But is there a set of shared assumptions that includes different sales – local, national or global? Hanafi acknowledges that there might be global principles like the *Universal Declaration of Human Rights*, but its application will have to be tailored to the local community, if they are not to be imposed by fiat. What constitutes social justice in one country may not constitute social justice in another. How do we get people who revile each other into a common room? Israelis and Palestinians have had notoriously unsuccessful negotiations, not least because by entering the global arena vast inequalities appear. The Israelis have had the backing of the United States and Europe, in its flagrant violation of international law and UN declarations. But notice the very different outcome of negotiations within South Africa where the internal and international balance of forces were very different.

In the final analysis, Hanafi doesn't appeal to lawyers to settle the world's problems, but sociologists. As the subtitle of the book reads, this is a plea for Dialogical Sociology. But why not dialogical economics or dialogical philosophy? What is so special about sociology? In his famous *The Coming Crisis of Western Sociology* (1970), Alvin Gouldner drew attention to what he called "methodological dualism," in which sociologists constitute themselves as all-knowing, rational human beings whereas those they study are irrational and subject to forces they don't control. In his essay, "Sociologist as Partisan," Gouldner continues his critique, examining Howard Becker's claim that sociologists are on the side of the underdog. Gouldner shows how sociologists may appear to be on the side of the underdog, but they are as much on their own side, advancing their careers, subject to pressures from colleagues and building ties to the state. They are the prototype of symbolic liberals, but with a difference: they can grasp their predicament and exercise self-criticism.

Thus, Pierre Bourdieu insists that sociologists are distinctive in that they can and should be reflexive, which is reflected upon their practice of science. They are indeed compelled to be reflexive insofar as they engage the subjects of their studies. They, to cite C. Wright Mills, tie personal troubles to public issues. Conversation with others disposes sociologists to reflect upon who they are and what shapes their scientific practice. This reflexive trait is even more pronounced in feminism – the first theory to emerge from those whose interests it affirms (Catharine MacKinnon). Sociologists are unlike economists and philosophers who suffer from the " ," believing their removal from society guarantees truth. They are unable to conceive of their theories as also shaped by their participation in society, which includes the struggles within the academic field. In obscuring their own place in society, they produce abstract theories that are often unrelated to the behaviors of the human beings they supposedly describe. Like feminists, sociologists do have the capacity if not always the enthusiasm to apply sociology to themselves.

Reflexive sociology, therefore, can, minimally, understand the pitfalls of "symbolic liberalism" – the simple recognition that intellectuals are part of the world they study. Thus, Gouldner urges intellectuals to form a "community of critical discourse," through which they become conscious of their limitations and blind spots. They are, in short, a "flawed" universal class. Similarly, Bourdieu's proposal for an "international of intellectuals," explicitly committed to social justice, also recognizes the "corporate interest" behind their pursuit of the universal. Zygmund Bauman, a self-conscious product of his upbringing in Poland, has distinguished between two types of intellectuals – legislators who try to influence social policy and interpreters who mediate between contesting parties in the public sphere. Acting in the real world each type faces obstacles.

The most sociological of classical Marxists, Antonio Gramsci, makes an allied distinction between "traditional intellectuals" who by virtue of their autonomy are able to elaborate, legitimate and give universality to the ideas of the ruling class and "organic intellectuals" who by virtue of their intimate connection to the subordinate classes are able to develop the latter's common sense into a full-fledged ideology of social transformation. Erik Wright, a leading exponent of sociological Marxism, ran with Gramsci's ideas in search of organizations and institutions across the world – what he called "real utopias" – that concretized or strove to concretize ideals of democracy/freedom, equality/fairness and/or solidarity/community. His favorite real utopias were cooperatives, Wikipedia, basic income grants and participatory budgeting, which he explored with a view to demonstrating their internal contradictions, conditions of dissemination and potential challenges to capitalism. His last book, *How to be an Anticapitalist in the Twenty-First Century* (2019), was taken up as a manifesto and rallying cry by progressive social movements – an important antidote to the more abstract and normative constructions of Bourdieu, Gouldner and Bauman.

All these are moves from a reflexive sociology to a public sociology, or what Hanafi and others, such as Ramón Flecha, call a Dialogical Sociology. Yet again we must ask why sociology? Reflexive sociology self-consciously embeds itself in the world it studies, but it is also marked by a distinctive standpoint, namely that of civil society. This does not mean sociology is confined to the study of civil society; rather, it examines other spheres, specifically state and market, from the standpoint of how they shape and are shaped by civil society. The one normative claim, therefore, that sociologists share, is the commitment to the protection and expansion of civil society, the institutional basis of a vibrant public sphere, which in turn is the condition for divergent normative perspectives to fruitfully engage with each other. Without civil society there will be no independent public sphere, no meaningful dialogue and no recognizable sociology.

We live in an increasingly polarized world, not just economically, politically and culturally, but also generationally. Younger generations face bleak prospects about their futures, whether it be climate change, material well-being or wars. It is not surprising, therefore, that Sari Hanafi should be concerned to bring the advocates of disparate "common goods" into dialogue with each other to establish mutual understanding but also to solve the mounting problems of our earthly community.

First, Sari is a sociologist, believing, like his classic forebears, that humanity has to follow shared precepts of social justice, but refuse to use the precepts to obscure deepening crises or intensifying social inequality. On the contrary, Hanafi urges us to use those precepts to reveal social injustice – exclusion as well as exploitation, economic as well environmental, racial as well as gendered. Second, Sari has been actively engaged in the International Sociological Association, first as Vice-President for National Associations and then as President. He has, therefore, seen first-hand how sociology has failed to tackle the challenges we face every day, but also where it has succeeded, how it has brought about fruitful dialogue.

But third, Sari Hanafi is a Palestinian who grew up in Syrian Refugee Camp. He has not escaped to the West but circulated between Cairo, Ramallah, Damascus and Beirut, from where he has brokered sociological conversations between North and South, West and East as well as within the Middle East. Throughout his life he has experienced deadly wars that have killed and silenced his people, but has never let despair vanquish hope. No wonder he is skeptical of the exponents of decolonization in their citadels of privilege – a distraction from their complicity. No wonder he is outraged by symbolic liberals, pretending to be on the side of the colonized while enjoying the rewards of the coloniality. We should heed his indictment of symbolic liberals by examining our principles and acting on them. We should be inspired by Hanafi's life and work, recognizing that differences don't have to be resolved through violence, insisting that we try to make conflicts amenable to respectful dialogue. That is the mission of Dialogical Sociology.

Acknowledgments

This book project started three years ago while preparing my speeches for the events of the International Sociological Association and culminated with my Presidential address at the XX World Congress of the International Sociological Association in Melbourne (25 June–1 July 2023). In addition to this event, I had the occasion to make oral presentations of some chapters at many academic events, often as keynotes, but I need to mention at least five: my own department at the American University of Beirut (February 2023), the 5th ISA Council of National Association Conference (November 2022, Nova Gorica, Slovenia), the Third Annual Lecture of the *Contributions to Indian Sociology* (IEG-SAGE Lecture Series – December 2023, Delhi, India), The Conference of the East Asian Sociological Association (EASA) (August 2023, co-organized by Jilin University, China) and the Annual International Peace Lecture, University of Manchester (April 2024).

I must record my deepest appreciation and gratitude to all who have generously read parts of the book project, invited me to talk in their institutions or engaged in discussion with me, which helped in maturing my ideas: Michael Burawoy, Azmi Bishara, Abdie Kazemipur, Hossein Serajzadeh, Lutfi Sunar, Mohammed Bamyeh, Rigas Arvanitis, Frédéric Vandenberghe, Borut Roncevic, Filomin Gutierrez, Rita Brara, Bhrigupati Singh, Bandana Purkayastha, Blake Atwood, Geoffrey Pleyers, Peilin LI, Wonho Jang, Gennaro Iorio, Silvia Cataldi, Abdelfattah Ezzain, Mounir Saidani, Mabrouk Boutagouga, Juan Piovani, Gabriel Kessler, Marta Soler, Jasmin Ramovic, Tetsuo Mizukami, Pierre Lannoy and Abdellali Hajjat. Hats off to Bashar Haydar that I audited (and enjoyed) his class on John Rawls's Theory of Justice and benefited so much from his insights, and I thank Mounir Kchaou – our walks in Cornish of Tunis and Doha enriched this manuscript. At the beginning of each chapter, I acknowledge special thanks to those who have read the chapter. These scholars come from different intellectual inspirations and do not always agree with me, so the final version of the book is, of course, my own responsibility.

I am obliged to Ray Jureidini, who has, and not for the first time, labored to perfect my text through his valuable comments, and by eliminating infelicities and correcting my mistakes.

Contents

**Part II From Symbolic Liberalism to the Dialogical
Liberal Project: Some Themes**

List of Figures and Tables

Figures

Tables

Introduction

We live in a time of impossible reasonable debate – a demagogic time, animated by the vertiginous rise of populism, authoritarianism, environmental destruction and unbearable social inequalities. As I don't want to curse modernity, I will consider these as the present conditions of late modernity,[1] a situation that can be described as suffering from an entangled set of pathologies in the context of extreme polarization of elite formations. In our late modernity, and instead of a widening consensus about core democratic values, we witness a hierarchical polarization in various societies, manifested by the widening of the space between different elites. Many examples can be cited, such as the United States with the defeat of Trump in the 2020 election, to Israel after the last election in 2022 and in Turkey in its June 2023 election. The political (temporary) failure of the Arab Spring reflects this polarization as we see, for instance, in the mistrust between secular and religious elites.

I grew up and still live in the Middle East, a region afflicted with longstanding brutalizing authoritarian and colonial regimes, where torture, political kidnapping, assassination and dispossession are too common. My childhood and adolescence were spent in Syria, where this polarization of elite formations impacted me intellectually and politically. I felt the extent of the fractures of elite fighting, at best ignoring each other, without speaking to each other. I grew up in a religious and conservative family in the Yarmouk refugee camp near Damascus and was exposed to the leftist ideology of one of the Palestinian factions.

In that context and inspired by my old Maoism, which advocates for the constitution of a broad national front to face imminent threats

---

[1] Some would use post-modernity. Personally, I don't like "post"-isms: post-liberalism, post-modernity, post-capitalism, etc. Others, like Gilles Lipovetsky (2005), term this era as "hypermodernity."

(authoritarianism and colonialism), I felt the importance of alliance (or at least cross-fertilization) of different intellectual and political groups. Yet the reality has been a deep gap between leftist elites (and most likely academics in the social sciences and humanities), on the one hand, and the religious elite on the other. With the Arab Spring, these splits were manifested in the real world, which made some leftists take refuge in the army to salvage them from the popular rise of Islamic movements, making it a bloody break-up, like in Egypt, for instance. I am not denying the role of the counterrevolutions waged by external powers (whether among some Arab or Western countries) but the internal dynamic is really important as the gap between the two elites is genuine and often felt from both sides as incommensurable.

The sociological indicators of this chilling polarization are manifested in some of my previous studies (Hanafi 2024b). For example, there are no discussions between religious and leftist intellectuals in daily journals, and any discussion we do see between them on television usually only features heated spectacles and polemics, such as in the program *al-Itjihah al-Mu'akis* (The Opposing Side) on al-Jazeera TV. These polemics do not form a space for rational (not even reasonable) discourse, but rather a sort of "Pavlovian" reaction against each other. These sharp polarizations become rich material for the public to deepen their *takfiri* thought in all its binary religious or secular forms: national/traitor, resistance/infiltration, etc.

This sociology of rupture also manifests itself in the restricted nature of the participants in 23 seminars and lectures held at the American University of Beirut (AUB) in the years 2011 to 2015. Between the dozens of participants, only two invitees were of an Islamic leaning, compared to tens of leftist interlocutors. There were many papers on Islamic movements, but all with the same antagonistic shade that speaks of how these movements "stole the revolution" and the "insincerity of their demands for democracy."

Examples of this exclusion are repeated in several Arab countries. The religious have become used to defining women's religiosity by whether or not they wear the hijab, which they made the foremost symbol of chastity and purity; whereas for many non-religious people, it represents women's subjugation. This extreme polarization resulted in one side enforcing it with power in Iran, and the other banning it in France.[2] However, fortunately, the Islamic Ennahda party in Tunisia would break this reductive division between hijab-wearing and non-hijab-wearing, as it appointed women who did not wear hijab as candidates for parliament and to head the Tunis Municipality,

---

[2] Not only in France but also in Turkey (before Erdoğan Era) – and even in 1980s Syria in the time of Hafez al-Assad.

delivering the message that it is not only a party for hijab-wearing women, but rather for all women.

However, this self-confinement from other opinions is not limited to the secular versus religious, as some liberals are also self-confined in their concepts of liberty and pluralism. The Alwaleed Center for American Studies and Research (CASAR) at the American University of Beirut can also be critiqued. For a long period before 2014, a reductive representation of the United States was used for the Arab public that was closer to enforced demonization. It rarely presented the debates between different orientations that sweep across these states. It was therefore impossible for either the Center itself or American scholars to predict, for instance, Trump's electoral victory.

It was in this context of the weak spirit of liberalism in the region that I began to research the production of scientific knowledge in the Arab world, which culminated in my co-authored book *Knowledge Production in the Arab World: The Impossible Promise* (Hanafi and Arvanitis 2015), documenting how the authoritarian political elite – not to mention some of the religious authorities – were able to take advantage of the social sciences' problematic situation (born in the shadow of the colonial period and its foreign funding) as a means to de-legitimize and marginalize it. This is why it is rare to hear in the Arab world of a "white paper" written by academic researchers on the basis of a request from the public authorities to discuss it in the public sphere.

The landscape of contemporary polarization is marked by a profound complexity, rendering traditional frameworks like the Left/Right dichotomy increasingly inadequate. We find ourselves navigating a "zone of indistinction," where established categories are fluid and context-dependent, acting as "empty containers" whose contents shift according to historical and spatial circumstances (Mongiardo and Palmieri 2024). This fluidity is vividly illustrated by Ruth Braunstein's (2017) analysis of the United States, revealing that conservatism is no longer confined to religious demographics. She highlights the emergence of religious progressives and non-religious conservatives, ultimately characterizing the new religious divide as a clash between multiracial pluralist democracy and white Christian nationalism. Further evidence of this evolving dynamic comes from Rasheed al-Haj Saleh's (2023) research in the Arab world. Surveys indicate a growing ethical open-mindedness among ordinary people, who are moving beyond rigid ideological constraints in their political thinking. This trend also signifies a separation of ethics from identity, contradicting stereotypical perceptions held by both Arab and Orientalist intellectuals.

This book comes not only from my local and regional reflections on our late modernity and its pathologies but also from my research agenda in the last five years related to my involvement with the International Sociological Association (ISA) as its President (2018–23), during which I made three calls: the first in my candidacy speech for the ISA presidential election calling for a "global sociology," with specific qualifications;[3] the second in the middle of my mandate for connecting sociology (more broadly social sciences) to moral philosophy and third, my call in the Melbourne Congress of June 2023 for Dialogical Sociology.

Here, I argue that much of sociology's responses to pathologies of late modernity can be characterized as classically liberal but politically illiberal – in short, I call this "symbolic liberalism" or the "symbolic liberal project." This is an "ideal-type" in the Weberian sense and not a description of the characteristics of some sociologists; so, one may never find a pure "symbolic liberal," but each of us may carry some of its features. While I am discussing "symbolic liberalism" in the context of sociology and sociologists, it is important to bear in mind that symbolic liberalism is not the product of sociology alone; rather, it reflects changes in every sector of public life, including media, politics, law and education. These changes have occurred in the Global North and also in the Global South, reflecting some kind of global convergence, particularly in postcolonial settings.[4]

In the context of the current political landscape, characterized by a significant rightward drift and the ascendance of far-Right ideologies, this book intentionally shifts its focus away from analyzing the illiberal nature of these movements. Instead, it directs its attention to the liberal-Left discourse and praxis, with the goal of identifying potential conceptual and practical limitations and exploring the ways in which internal contradictions within liberalism have contributed to its own challenges.

Why should I write about liberalism when liberal democracy is in retreat in many parts of the world and under significant strain even in the oldest democracies, such as the United States and Europe? My answer is twofold. First, despite its shortcomings and failures in many places, I see no serious alternative to liberalism. Second, I come from the Arab region, where we have

[3]   To further the development of global sociology, and, in my capacity as President, I worked alongside the publication committee to provide training to sociologists from the Global South. This training was to provide the skills needed to perform original research, and to publish that research in international journals.

[4]   Let me clarify what I mean by "postcolonial settings," echoing Gurminder Bhambra (2014) – that it is neither a reproduction of colonial relations nor a return to a pre-colonial order but rather refers to the ways in which colonizers and colonized handle the consequences of colonization, decolonization and the forms taken by the global entanglement of social power relations.

yet to experience true liberalism – at least since our independence. Chibli Mallat (2015) rightly reminds us that life in the region was better during the period roughly between the two world wars, a time Albert Hourani (1983) famously described as the "Liberal Age." This perspective highlights an important distinction: critiques of liberalism differ depending on whether they come from a pre-liberal context or a post-liberal one.

My critiques in this book align closely with liberal values, understood in a specific way, as they shape my reflections on mitigating symbolic liberalism. I propose a liberal society with a stronger emphasis on dialogue – a vision I call the Dialogical Liberal Project, which echoes what I term Dialogical Sociology. Both frameworks seek a balance between collective and individual political liberal ideals, actively addressing social inequality and advocating for justice while preserving the plurality of conceptions of the good.

In this introduction, I first make the case for three pressing pathologies of our time: (1) authoritarianism, populism and the rise of the Right; (2) rampant inequality, precarity and exclusion; and (3) environmental destruction – all unfolding within an intensely polarized political climate. I then examine the two driving forces behind these crises: neoliberalism and emotional capitalism. I argue that this polarization is deeply intertwined with the pathologies of late modernity, which manifest across different yet interconnected spheres, affecting all societies – just as modernity itself brought a sweeping conceptual transformation that reshaped every region.

Pathologies of Late Modernity

Authoritarianism, Populism and the Rise of the Right

In the political sphere, there is a simultaneous emergence of authoritarianism in the South which is increasingly brutal (al-Haj Saleh 2021), and Right populism in the North that has been gaining momentum for at least the past two decades. In the Global South, this trend takes many shapes. In the North, conservative parties have become more socially liberal; social-democratic parties have become more market-friendly; and the parties to the Right and Left are growing while the electoral bases of the established parties on the Left–Right political spectrum are shrinking (Grindheim 2019). Despite these developments, right-leaning populist parties warrant particular attention. As Jan Erik Grindheim (2019) demonstrates, in a comparative study, support for these parties grew between 2003 and 2018 across eight well-established European democracies, with Norway being the only exception. However, with updated data in 2024, even Norway no longer stands apart, as the surge of populist right-wing movements was evident in nearly every European election that year.

While concerns about immigration have sometimes fueled right-leaning populism, they alone cannot account for such a profound ideological shift. In some countries, demographic decline has resulted in aging populations, who tend to be more conservative and inclined toward stability. According to Lorenzo Marsili (2024), disorientation, fear, and anxiety have fueled a resurgence of nationalism and "my-country-first" attitudes, offering false yet compelling explanations for the complexities of our time. This shift is also evident in the transformation of political allegiances – such as former left-wing voters turning to the Right (Democrats to Republicans in the United States) or former Marxists embracing Islamist movements (Larzillière 2013). However, these shifts extend beyond electoral politics. The growing demand for more participatory decision-making could be interpreted as a positive development, yet it also signals the erosion of trust in representative democracy (Flecha 2022). People are increasingly resisting the ideological influence of dominant institutions – governments, political parties, trade unions, and associations – without necessarily abandoning ideology altogether. Ideological struggles remain significant but now unfold through dual dynamics: not only from above, led by intellectuals and political elites as "ideology-enablers," but also from below, driven by grassroots movements. The emergence of hybrid or tactical parties, rather than traditional Left–Right structures, reflects this shift, acting as mediators between these opposing forces.[5] In non-democratic regimes, particularly in some Arab countries where free elections have been permitted, the majority of popular votes have gone not to "leftist" political groups but to religious parties, further underscoring this evolving political landscape.

To further complicate the picture, authoritarianism – understood as a practice rather than merely a political regime – is not confined to the Global South. It also manifests in the Global North, where citizenship is increasingly eroding, and the coercive state, through heavy-handed police intervention, has grown more aggressive toward social movements. This is especially evident when protesters belong to ethnic minorities or challenge

---

[5] Mongiardo and Palmieri (2024, 664) conceptualize hybrid–tactical parties as: "born outside of the system of traditional politics...and characterised by their blurred edges that are hybridised with doctrinal elements and ideas that pertain to different ideological traditions. ...Due to their ideological patchwork, they allow a tactical positioning in the field of the political offer that is functional to keeping electoral consent."

mainstream political narratives, as seen in the recent crackdowns on Palestinian encampments in various parts of the world.

Rampant Inequality, Precarity and Exclusion

Rising levels of inequality, precarity, and exclusion in the socioeconomic sphere are not only deepening social divisions but also undermining political systems, fostering a growing sense of vulnerability even in industrialized nations. Globally, absolute income disparities have widened over the past 30 years, with the income gap between the "core" and the impoverished "periphery" remaining stark – if China is excluded. In 2018, the ratio between median income in these regions exceeded 8 to 1 in purchasing power parity terms and 22 to 1 in nominal dollars (Milanovic 2024). Even purchasing power parity fails to capture the vast discrepancies in the cost of non-tradable services and their contribution to GDP, particularly when comparing Western countries to economies like China, complicating international comparisons. Fadi Lama (2023, 69–72) highlights how living costs have surged dramatically. In the United States, while median household income rose by only 27 percent between 1968 and 2020, healthcare expenditures skyrocketed by 787 percent – equivalent to 2,900 percent of wage increases and 400 percent of GDP growth. The cost of college education between 1980 and 2020 increased by an astonishing 1,200 percent. These figures illustrate the predatory nature of neoliberal economic policies, particularly in the healthcare and education sectors.

At the end of 2023, an estimated 117.3 million people remained forcibly displaced, including internally displaced persons (IDPs). They were driven from their homes by persecution, conflict, violence, human rights violations and events that severely disrupted public order.[6] There are other important indicators of such trends.[7]

---

[6] See UN Refugee Agency, "Global Trends: Forced Displacement in 2023." www.unhcr.org/sites/default/files/2024-06/global-trends-report-2023.pdf.

[7] In 2023, approximately 345.2 million people were classified as "food insecure," more than twice the number recorded in 2020. Famine conditions now affect nearly 1 million people worldwide – a tenfold increase since 2018. Around 828 million people are uncertain about their next meal, while over 800 million suffer from malnutrition, even as 20 percent of the world's food production goes to waste (Food Waste Index Report 2021). Despite these alarming statistics, the issue remains insufficiently addressed in human rights discussions. That said, there are also positive trends over time, reflected in global awareness efforts such as the UN Millennium Development Goals. According to Johan Norberg (2023), the percentage of the world's population living in extreme poverty declined from 29.1 percent in 2000 to 8.4 percent in 2022.

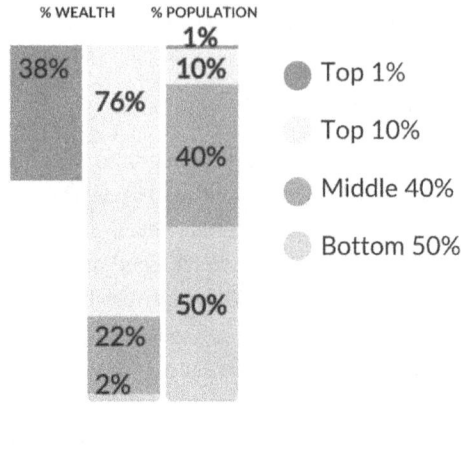

% WEALTH   % POPULATION

38%   1%
76%   10%
      40%
22%   50%
2%

● Top 1%
○ Top 10%
◍ Middle 40%
○ Bottom 50%

WID.WORLD

Figure 0.1 Inequality in the United States
Source: World Inequality Report 2023. https://wid.world/news-article/
whats-new-about-wealth-inequality-in-the-world/.

According to the *World Inequality Report 2022* (Chancel et al. 2022), the top 10 percent owns nearly three-quarters of the world's wealth, while half the world's population is almost entirely deprived of wealth.[8] Inequality is highest in North America and Europe and has grown considerably in recent years. In the United States, the richest 1 percent accounted for 30 percent of the nation's wealth in 2024, up from 22 percent in 1980,[9] while the top 10 percent accounted for 67 percent of all wealth (see Figure 0.1).

What is noteworthy about these recent trends of rising inequality is that they have largely affected segments of populations who were previously part of the growing middle class. These groups increasingly feel left behind and that they are leaving less for their children than their parents left for them. The idea that earning a salary and abiding by the law no longer guarantees stability or survival fuels a deep sense of resentment and anger – one that can easily escalate into violence. Numerous examples illustrate this trend in France, such as the "Yellow Vests" movement in November 2018, the protests

[8] See "What's New about Wealth Inequality in the World?" https://wid.world/
     news-article/whats-new-about-wealth-inequality-in-the-world/.
[9] See "The Wealth of the 1% Just Hit a Record $44 trillion." www.cnbc.
     com/2024/03/28/wealth-of-the-1percent-hits-a-record-44-trillion.html.

against pension reforms in March–April 2023 and the demonstrations against police violence in July 2023.

Is capitalism, in itself, solely responsible for the sweeping social inequalities we see today? My answer is a qualified no – at most, only partially. I differentiate between capitalism as a historical economic system, in which private property and market competition play a central role, and the way capitalism has evolved under colonial, imperialist and technological transformations. These shifts have led to its neoliberal and emotional forms – permeating all aspects of life – thereby exacerbating inequality, precarity, vulnerability and climate change in late modernity. Swedish historian Johan Norberg (2023) rightly challenges those who argue for discarding capitalism entirely rather than reforming it. In my view, the solution lies in integrating socialist and cooperative principles into the system (see Chapter 3).

Environmental Destruction

In the age of the Anthropocene, the global ecological crisis has reached an unprecedented and alarming level, with rising global temperatures, climate change, biodiversity loss, deforestation, carbon pollution and plastic waste. This crisis is not merely environmental – it is a meta-crisis, deeply intertwined with humanity's relationship to nature, animals, the economy, social structures, and consumption patterns. As Dipesh Chakrabarty (2019) argues, it is a "crisis of civilization," in which the climate emergency has revealed a fundamental rupture between natural history and human history. In response, he calls for a reinvention of historical scholarship to better reflect the realities of our time.

Global warming has created an intricate interdependence between the Global South and the Global North. In our "carbon society" (Wagner 2024), both regions contribute to global carbon emissions, even though, historically, the Global North has been the primary driver. By 2022, the global average carbon emissions per capita reached 6.5 tons. While countries like the United States, Australia and Canada continue to emit at significantly higher rates – around 15 tons per person – China has surpassed the global average, with emissions reaching 8 tons per person.[10]

The COVID-19 pandemic has aggravated this meta-crisis. The surreal atmosphere of this pandemic exposed fault lines in trust among human beings, among countries, between citizens and governments, and it is

---

[10] See "Distribution of Fossil Carbon Dioxide Emissions Worldwide in 2023, by Select Country." www.statista.com/statistics/271748/the-largest-emitters-of-co2-in-the-world/.

making us raise big questions about ourselves, our social relationships and life generally.

In the "terrestrial community" (Mbembe 2023), where all species coexist, humans betray other species through their irrational exploitation of the earth's resources. As a result, the ontology and epistemology that underpin the rational worldview have come under scrutiny. Australian philosopher Val Plumwood (2002), for example, argues that the ecological crisis represents not only an environmental failure but a crisis of reason and culture, which has led humanity to ignore the earth's limits and the needs of other life forms. Plumwood critiques modern rationality, particularly the hyper-separation between self and other, and between humanity and nature. She contends that Enlightenment rationality has fostered a fragmented self, enabling a ruthless exploitation of the "Other," reducing it to mere "resource." This rationality also prioritizes "efficiency," "competition," and the corporate bottom line, where, for example, the battery chicken is denied even an extra inch of cage space, or fish-catching technology is designed to maximize catch size, regardless of the harm to non-target species (2002, 34).

Are we sufficiently aware of the ecological crisis? Peter Wagner examines the ecological crisis through the lens of a "Great Acceleration" politics, in which climate change is driving a triple displacement of problems:

> In material terms, as already argued, problems are displaced onto nature and the planet by exploiting the very ground on which human life is only possible; in spatial terms, problems are solved in Western societies by displacing them to other world-regions; in temporal terms, problems are solved today by displacing them into the future. These displacements were to become problematic at different times and in different combinations, generating the political historicity of the Great Acceleration. (Wagner 2023, 33)

While historically the "Great Acceleration" is mainly in the West, Wagner considers that Asia, particularly China and India, is responsible for the second or Asian "Great Acceleration" (roughly 1990–present) that "can be seen as a regional political response to Western problem displacement given the absence of any globally negotiated solution" (Wagner 2023, 37).

Forces Behind these Pathologies

There have been many forces behind the above pathologies but let me here highlight two major factors: neoliberalism and emotional capitalism.

Neoliberalism

The collapse of the Keynesian consensus, triggered by the economic crisis of the 1970s, paved the way for a new set of ideas and practices that came to be known as "neoliberalism." By neoliberalism, I refer to the retreat of the state from its role in guiding and regulating the economic sphere, alongside the expanding influence of the financial sector, a phenomenon often referred to as "financialization." On a global scale, barriers to the free movement of capital, goods and services (though not people) have been increasingly dismantled. Since the early 1980s, the marketization (or "privatization") of public services like health and education has not only commodified these services globally but also intruded into the private lives of citizens. Neoliberalism, which promised the benefits of a "trickle-down effect" – the economic theory that suggests that benefits provided to the wealthy or businesses will eventually "trickle down" to the broader population, cannot be understood as rising tides lifting all boats in society. Instead, financialization has come to dominate all other economic activities, functioning simultaneously as a system of exploitation: "The president of the United States [Donald Trump] is not a tax avoider because he is an especially fraudulent financier; he's a tax avoider because he is a wealthy man in a system premised on such deceit" (Nesvetailova and Palan 2020, 3). Fraud concerns not only individuals but also states. According to Fadi Lama,

> For the US, EU, and UK whose currencies are reserve currencies, ballooning deficits do not pose a major problem. They can continue printing money out of thin air and maintain the value of their currencies for as long as the instruments of virtual reality are able to project an image of healthy and leading economies, enjoying high ratings from [credit rating agencies] Moody's, S&P and Fitch, whose ratings are accepted as valid. (Lama 2023, 77)

The impact of neoliberalism is truly global. François Gauthier (2021) rightly observes that the political-embedded, National-Statist regime has been replaced by a global-market system, where economics now plays a central, structuring role. This global market is dominated by powerful tech platforms, major banks and large commercial corporations. However, the state's withdrawal is far from absolute – it is highly selective. As Ruchir Sharma (2024) points out, the state has transformed into an expensive entity that guarantees different levels of support: bailouts for the rich, entitlements for the middle class and welfare for the poor – though not equally so. This shift overlooks the substantial costs of funding wars, such as the European and American support for the war in Ukraine and the Israeli war on Gaza. While neoliberalism has fueled the rise of monopolies, "zombie" firms and billionaires, the redistributive policies – adopted not only by the Left but also by the populist Right – have proven ineffective in alleviating poverty. This inefficacy has sparked a significant shift in public sentiment, leading to growing disillusionment with neoliberalism and even a nostalgic longing for a more socialist economic system.[11]

Neoliberalism is not merely a political and economic doctrine; it exerts profound effects on society, resulting in deeply contradictory outcomes and the fragmentation of political, cultural, familial and private spheres. The pursuit of immediate gratification through consumption and neoliberal individualism (Todorov 2011) has come to define the only measures of socioeconomic success and cultural achievement, while shifting the responsibility for failure from the state to the individual citizen.

The fragmentation caused by neoliberal marketization has deeply impacted social and political forms of collective action. Trade unions and political parties, for example, have increasingly been seen as relics of the past in many countries and sectors, especially under the influence of the platform economy – except for a few notable instances, such as strikes at Amazon. Socialization no longer occurs within large, collective bodies; instead, it happens through opinion-making and position-taking, rather than in-depth debates. Interactions now primarily occur between individuals who are not representing any collective groups. Given the individualistic nature of the Internet, virtual social networks have further amplified this fragmentation (Bernstein 2023). This "New Spirit of Capitalism" (Boltanski and Chiapello 2018) deepens the fragmentation of individuals and networks, which can only be understood within the context of project-oriented work structures. This dynamic fosters inequality, exploitation and a growing erosion of trust in society and its institutions. According to Milbank and Pabst (2016), the

---

[11] According to the latest Pew polls, support for capitalism has fallen among all Americans, particularly Democrats and the young. In fact, among Democrats under 30, 58 percent now have a "positive impression" of socialism; only 29 percent say the same thing of capitalism. www.ft.com/content/7650d057-be19-45ce-9a4e-b5ac0418d5c4.

2008 economic crash marked a key moment in the transition from wealth models rooted in land and labor to more abstract notions of capital, detached from real communities and people.

Emotional Capitalism

Martijn Konings (2015), in *The Emotional Logic of Capitalism*, presents a compelling argument that contemporary capitalism and its subjects are mutually constitutive of everyday life. He emphasizes that the emotional and meaning-producing dimensions of capitalism must be considered – an aspect that progressives have largely overlooked. As a social regime, neoliberalism is reinforced by the commodification of emotions and the deep intrusion of capitalism into the private sphere. This phenomenon, which Eva Illouz refers to as "emotional capitalism," is characterized by:

> emotional uncertainty in the realm of love, romance, and sex [which] is the direct sociological effect of the ways in which the consumer market, therapeutic industry, and the technology of the Internet have been assembled and embedded by the ideology of individual choice that has become the main cultural frame organizing personal freedom. Sociology has an immense contribution to make in its insistence that psychological experiences – needs, compulsions, inner conflicts, desires, or anxiety – play and replay the dramas of collective life, and that our subjective experience reflects and prolongs social structures, *are*, in fact, concrete, embodied, lived structures. (Illouz 2019, 15)

Some have attempted to theorize the cultural legitimation of sexual choice by claiming it is based purely on subjective emotional and hedonic grounds. But is it truly subjective? British socialist writer, academic and novelist Raymond Williams developed the concept of "the structure of feeling" to refer to a historical understanding of "affective elements of consciousness and relationships" (O'Connor 1989). This concept underscores the need to interpret emotions, moods and atmospheres as historically and socially constructed phenomena. This dynamic has only intensified in an era dominated by social networking, artificial intelligence and ubiquitous media, all deeply embedded within a culture of commodities and advertising. The politics of the body reflects not only personal subjectivity but also the influence of the market. Who today is not "on a diet" – aside from the very poor? Is this truly a personal choice, or one shaped by an industry of cookbooks, television cooking programs and supermarket shelves filled with specialized diet products? Similarly, sexuality is no longer confined to the private sphere in many countries; instead, it has become highly public and commercialized. Social media, once hailed as a tool for citizen journalism – "Davids exposing the propaganda machine of the Goliaths" (DiResta 2023) – has evolved into a battleground of influencers competing for profitable niche audiences. Platforms like YouTube, Instagram, and TikTok enable sponsorship and ad-revenue sharing, shifting the media landscape from centralized propaganda to highly targeted niche media propaganda. This shift serves not only globalized culture but also regional and local interests, including religious and ideological outlets. As a result, social media has played a major role in deepening cultural and political polarization. Instead of fostering open debate, it has reinforced ideological "echo chambers," where users are "exposed to information and opinions that align with their own, leading to the reinforcement of their existing beliefs and the exclusion of diverse perspectives" (Al Azmeh and Baert 2025, 7). In authoritarian states, however, social media has sometimes created informal, parallel public spheres, as seen during the Arab Spring. Yet, in *A New Structural Transformation of the Public Sphere and Deliberative Politics* (2023), Jürgen Habermas revisits his earlier theories with a more pessimistic outlook, highlighting the corrosive impact of digital technologies, micro-targeted algorithms and social media. Long wary of the media's colonization by market forces and capitalism, Habermas warns that these factors now confine online discussions to homogeneous groups with narrow perspectives, limiting rational debate and ultimately undermining meaningful deliberation.

Everyday life, a kaleidoscope of emotions, will be pushed to be mediated by psychologization/psychiatrization – the growing influence of psychology and psychiatry in understanding and addressing various aspects of human experience and behavior. The number of those who visit counselors (in person and online) has risen exponentially in the last decade. According to the World Health Organization, nearly 10 percent of the world's population is affected by common mental disorders at any given time (Beeker et al. 2021). One out of every two people in the world will develop a mental health disorder (such as, schizophrenia, depression, bipolar disorder, anxiety disorder, eating disorder, autism spectrum disorder or conduct disorder) in their lifetime, according to a large-scale study conducted in 29 countries by researchers from Harvard Medical School and the University of Queensland (McGrath et al. 2023). When I started teaching at AUB in 2005, I used to receive from the university psychological counselor a letter of "accommodation" for a student (often requesting more time for exams or explaining recurrent absences) once every two years. I now receive two or three such letters per semester.

In the emotional turn of late modernity, numerous studies highlight the highly ambivalent effects of psychologization and psychiatrization. As Beeker et al. argue, their significance stems largely from the risks they pose:

> While individuals with minor disturbances of well-being might be subjected to overdiagnosis and overtreatment, psychiatrization could also result in undermining mental healthcare provision for the most severely ill by promoting the adaption of services to the needs and desires of the rather mild cases. On a societal level, psychiatrization might boost medical interventions which incite individual coping with social problems, instead of encouraging long-term political solutions. (Beeker et al. 2021, 1)

The overuse of therapy not only increases the risk of over-diagnosing mental disorders and over-prescribing psychiatric medications but also prioritizes individualized solutions over community-based approaches. For instance, Devin Atallah (2017), in a systematic review of 203 peer-reviewed journal articles on youth and family health in the Middle East, found that nearly 73 percent of the studies focused on Palestine and Palestinian refugees, with 58 percent reporting elevated rates of PTSD, depression and aggression among participants. Such studies not only stigmatize Palestinians as inherently pathological but also obscure the potential for life-affirming outcomes, overlooking the resilience, kinship networks and grassroots strategies of strength and solidarity that sustain these communities.

At least in part, the effects of emotional capitalism can be seen in the ways gender identity is increasingly constructed as separate from biological sex, as well as in the hyper-individualization of society and the erosion of family authority.

Methodology

My sociological approach does not compartmentalize different spheres – politics, economy, society, secularism, religion and so on. Following Borut Rončević (2024), I adopt the cultural political economy framework, which seeks to understand the dynamic interplay between culture, politics and the economy. This approach encourages us to take seriously not only political economy but also the role of discourse and imaginaries – how social sciences influence society, and how culture, media and knowledge economy actors shape these sciences. As Rončević (2024) states, "discourse and imaginaries can be analyzed as sets of mechanisms playing a vital role in the continual and unstable process of societal reproduction and transformation," emphasizing the need to consider reason, emotion and imagination together. In essence, cultural political economy acknowledges both the "relative autonomy" of culture and the "analytical independence" of culture, society, politics and the economy, drawing from Jeffrey Alexander's (1990) theory of culture. While John Rawls remains an important influence in this book, I do not adhere rigidly to any single theorist. Instead, I engage in theoretical bricolage, a methodological approach that will become evident throughout the chapters.

In this book, I adopt what might be called a "meta-empirical" approach, drawing on the works of various social scientists to identify a shared core of descriptions, analyses, concerns and issues. These insights are interwoven with my own intellectual trajectory, which itself becomes an object of analysis. This work is also the product of years of intense fieldwork, shaped by numerous interviews and interactions with sociologists worldwide during my 13 years of leadership in the International Sociological Association – first as a member of the Executive Committee, then as Vice President for National Associations and later as President. These roles involved active engagement with national sociological communities, extensive travel and participation in conferences, all of which provided me with a rich body of material to reflect upon in this book

At the same time, my knowledge is inherently situated, shaped by my multiple positionalities: born in a Palestinian refugee camp, raised in Syria, intellectually formed within the French academic tradition and currently working at an American institution in Lebanon. As the American feminist scholar Donna Haraway (1988) famously argued, all knowledge is a "partial perspective." It is through this lens that my global sociology is produced. The term "global" only holds meaning when geographical space is recognized as central to knowledge production, and when sociology is reoriented from below (Hanafi 2019). This perspective underscores that a truly global sociology cannot exist without acknowledging national sociologies (Burawoy 2008) and the diverse intellectual traditions that inform them (Patel 2009).

In advancing my critique of symbolic liberalism and advocating for a Dialogical Sociology, I acknowledge that the theoretical, historical and political implications of my arguments do not apply universally. Critiquing aspects of liberalism takes on different meanings depending on context – such critiques may resonate in liberal democratic societies while being less applicable in regions where liberalism, both as an intellectual tradition and as a political institution, has not deeply permeated social structures. I hope one day to follow this book with another that explores symbolic liberalism in greater depth within the Arab world – my own region, where I have conducted research for over three decades. I also hope that scholars from other regions will undertake similar inquiries within their own contexts.

Finally, rather than presenting a consolidated literature review, I engage with relevant scholarly discussions organically throughout the chapters, allowing themes to emerge naturally alongside my analysis.

The Organization of the Book

Combining reflection, statistical analysis and ethnographic vignettes, this book is structured in two parts. The first part offers a theoretical exploration of liberalism and its various manifestations, tracing its evolution from the foundational ideas of classical liberalism to the political liberalism of John Rawls. I argue in favor of liberalism as a "thin" theory – one grounded in core principles – while critically examining where it has gone astray when interpreted as a "thick" theory, shaped and implemented by self-identified liberals (Chapter 1). Building on this, Chapter 2 focuses on symbolic liberals, unpacking how they distort the concept of justice by diminishing the significance of social justice while overemphasizing the universality of human rights, ultimately imposing a singular conception of the good. In response to the symbolic liberal project, Chapter 3 introduces my call for a Dialogical Political Liberal Project, a framework that aligns with and extends the principles of Dialogical Sociology.

In the second part of the book, I explore four key themes of polarization, examining how they have been addressed by symbolic liberals and how the Dialogical Political Liberal Project can help mitigate their effects. The first theme is societal intolerance, particularly in relation to academic freedom, with a special focus on Palestine, which I discuss in Chapter 4. Chapter 5 addresses the tensions between secularism and religion, explored through case studies in France, Iran and other contexts. In Chapter 6, I examine debates over sex and gender diversity, comparing perspectives from the West and the Middle East. Finally, Chapter 7 explores conflicts over family authority, highlighting how the Swedish state and its symbolic liberals violate their own ideals by forcibly removing children from allegedly abusive parents. Through these discussions, I argue that the Dialogical Political Liberal Project offers a more constructive framework for addressing these deeply contested issues.

All the examples I use to illustrate my four themes not only highlight how sociologists and social scientists become symbolically liberal but also reveal the broader involvement of all knowledge economy producers – academics, media professionals, politicians, lawyers and others. By adopting the cultural political economy approach (as outlined in the methodology section, above), my aim is to explore the dynamic interplay between culture, politics and the economy, demonstrating how sociologists shape other knowledge economy producers just as much as they, in turn, shape sociological knowledge production. For example, Alain Touraine wrote an article in *Libération* in 2003 defending girls' freedom to wear headscarves at school. However, just weeks later, he voted in favor of banning headscarves as a member of the Stasi Commission[12] When a journalist questioned him about this apparent contradiction, he responded that it wasn't he who had changed his opinion, but rather, that French society had changed.

The chapters in this section aim to challenge some of our liberals and progressives, urging them to reconsider the assumption that their ideas are self-evident truths or should be unquestioningly aligned with cultural trends. They should be aware of their perspective as minority liberals.[13] Some readers may find the ideas presented in this book controversial or even provocative. While I have been reluctant to take sides in the debates I examine, I do not position myself as an enlightened observer above the complexities of collective dispute. Rather, if this book sparks debate (and dialogue), I see that as a meaningful contribution to the advancement of research.

[12] The Stasi Commission, established in 2003 by President Jacques Chirac, was tasked with examining the application of the principle of secularism. Chaired by Bernard Stasi, the French Republic's ombudsman, the commission comprised 20 members. In its findings, the commission's report characterized "Islamism" as fundamentally at odds with prevailing interpretations of French culture.

[13] The "minority" does not refer necessarily to its number but rather to access to power.

PART I

Liberalism and its Avatars

CHAPTER 1

From Classical Liberalism to
Political Liberalism

Today, the majority of [Arab] regimes justify their existence
with arguments based on the principle of sovereignty, national
interests, matters of security and stability, people's alleged cultural
incompatibility with democracy, and, increasingly, what they term
the failure of liberalism in the West.

Azmi Bishara, "On Comprehensive Liberalism,
Political Liberalism, and Ideology" (2023)

Friday at noon, while I was writing this chapter, I heard the Friday sermon
from the mosque in my quarter in the Hamra district of Beirut. The Imam
denounced liberalism, deeming it responsible for bringing immorality to
Lebanon and to the world. For him, liberalism is synonymous with atheism.
One day earlier, while presenting an early draft of the thesis of this book at
my university, a leftist colleague challenged me, asserting that some of my
ideas were liberal, which, in their view, equated to being anti-Left, against
social justice, and pro-capitalism. For students, this meant aligning with
Western thought.

In France, I cannot use the word liberalism without making a long qualification of the term.[1] In some countries, including the United States and the
United Kingdom, liberalism stands in direct opposition to conservatism. The
outstanding American political scientist Pippa Norris (2023) separates social/
moral liberalism–conservatism from economic positioning (Left/Right). To
gauge social values, survey participants – including political scientists – are

---

[1] Liberalism, particularly John Rawls's version, has had a tumultuous journey in
gaining traction in France. In his book on the reception of Rawls in France,
Mathieu Hauchecorne (2019) demonstrates how Rawls's thought was reshaped
within the French national context, which was marked by the fight against Marxist
paradigms and the struggle for intellectual hegemony within the left. This process
gave Rawls's ideas a much more political identity than a philosophical one.

asked to self-identify using prompts such as: "People differ in their social values. Liberals prioritize expanded personal freedoms (e.g., abortion rights, same-sex marriage, democratic participation), while conservatives emphasize order, tradition and stability, viewing government as a moral authority on cultural issues." Based on responses, individuals are categorized as "Social Conservatives," "Moderates" or "Social Liberals." For economic positioning, respondents (political scientists) were given a 10-point scale prompted by the statement: "People hold varying views on economic issues like privatization, taxes, regulation and the welfare state." Here, the "economic *Left*" advocates for active government intervention in the economy, whereas the "economic *Right*" supports minimal state involvement.[2]

With all this polysemy, what the hell is liberalism? This is the object of the current chapter.

As I mentioned in the introduction to this book, I argue that much of sociology's responses can be characterized as classically liberal but politically illiberal. This is symbolic liberalism. The symbolic liberalism project is not only carried out by sociologists but also by actors from the knowledge economy, including academia, media, politics, law and education and in the Global North and the Global South. Before discussing symbolic liberalism in the next chapter, I will spell out what I mean by classical liberalism and political liberalism in a Rawlsian variation and how the latter has been amended and improved by many subsequent scholars.

In this book, although liberalism is presented as a normative theory for governance and society, I advocate for it as a "thin" theory – one that is built upon a set of core values but is otherwise minimal in scope. Beyond this, I will critically examine the points at which liberalism faltered as a "thick" theory – an approach that was adopted, theorized and implemented by various liberals. This analysis will set the stage for the next chapter, where I will situate symbolic liberals within the broader social and ideological spectrum. For now, however, I will make a clear analytical distinction between classical liberalism and political liberalism.

---

[2]   In most countries, political scientists' economic and social values align, with some exceptions that exhibit two distinct patterns. In certain countries – such as Austria, the Netherlands, Spain, Australia, Turkey and Colombia – political scientists tend to hold more left-leaning economic views than socially liberal values. In contrast, in countries like Japan, Denmark, Chile and Mexico, the opposite trend is observed (Norris 2023, fig. 4).

Classical Liberalism

The primary architects of classical liberalism are Thomas Hobbes (the state), John Locke (individualism, private property and self-ownership), David Hume and Adam Smith (economic exchange governed by the law of price), Jean-Jacques Rousseau (social contract, republicanism), John Stuart Mill (liberty), among others.

Classical liberalism refers to values such as individual freedom and substantive economic rights, but also an acknowledgment of government's legitimate economic regulatory authority. It considers human rights as fundamental and universal, emphasizing civil and individual liberties, freedom of religion, speech, press and assembly, as well as the value of individual autonomy. Subsequently, liberals defended group and minority rights.

Classical liberalism is primarily grounded in natural law philosophy, evident in concepts such as "inherent dignity" and "inalienable rights," which emphasize civil and individual liberties. However, it was also influenced by various other ideologies, including religion, positivism (the authority of the state) and even Marxism.[3] Liberalism took a significant turn with John Rawls's *A Theory of Justice* (1971), in which he redefined the foundation of rights by grounding them in justice – the first virtue of social institutions. Rejecting the notion of rights as derived from natural law, he argues in favor of the objectivity of practical reason and the centrality of fairness to justice. By balancing basic liberties (freedom to hold private property, freedom of thought, speech and assembly; liberty of conscience) and equality, he argues that social contractors who are in the original position of choosing their own status and prospects under the "veil of ignorance" will choose two fundamental principles of justice: "The Principle of Basic Liberties" (Strict Egalitarian Principle): "Each person is to have an equal right to the most extensive total system of equal basic liberties compatible with a similar system of liberty for all" (Rawls 1971, 46); or "The Difference Principle": "Social and economic inequalities are to be arranged so that they are both: (a) to the greatest benefit of the least advantaged, consistent with the just savings principle, and (b) attached to offices and positions open to all under conditions of fair equality of opportunity" (Rawls 1971, 48). For Rawls, the protection of basic liberties takes precedence, and any restrictions on these liberties are justified only when necessary to preserve liberty itself.

This Rawlsian conception of justice has important features. First,

[3] For more discussion about the philosophical foundations of human rights and liberalism, see Shestack (1998).

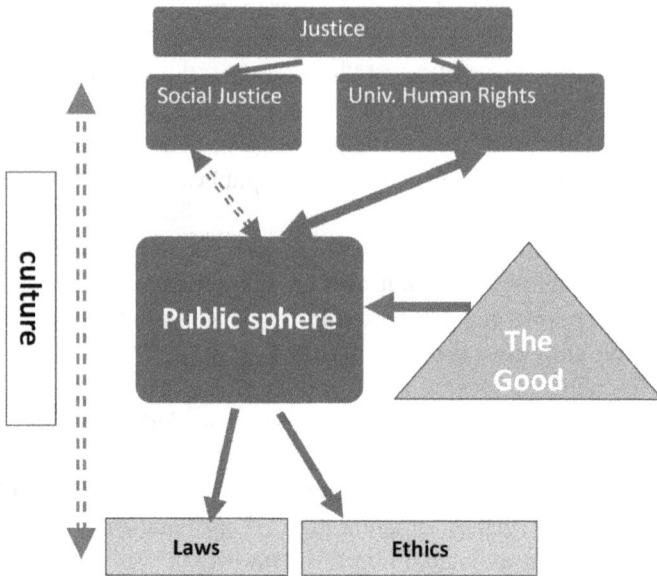

Figure 1.1 Classical liberalism

the insistence on "fair equality of opportunities," which enriches the literature on inequality; second, the need for special attention to those worst off (distributive justice and welfare state); and, finally, the way in which primary goods are conceived, which gives people the opportunity to do what they would like with their own lives (conception of goods) (Maffettone 2011).

Liberalism is based on the distinction between the conception of justice from that of the good. The conception of "the good" is a set of "final ends and aims which specifies a person's conception of what is of value in human life or, alternatively, of what is regarded as a fully worthwhile life" (Rawls 2001, 91). It includes all social bases of self-esteem, one's preferences and desires (and second-order desires)[4] regarding dress, food, using spare time, ideals of personal character, friendship and family, etc.

---

[4] Harry Frankfurt (1971) argues that "the good" is not merely a matter of desires and preferences but is instead shaped by "second-order desires." To be good is to aspire to become a person with certain desires. For example, desiring drugs or wealth does not necessarily make them good. One may also wish not to desire certain things, and it is this reflective capacity that shapes our understanding of the good.

One should notice that in this classical liberalism the emphasis is more on individual human rights (conceived more as universal and with little input from culture) and less on social justice. As we see in Figure 1.1, culture plays a minor role in the thinking of classical liberals.

Political Liberalism

Among the many who reshaped classical liberalism, the most influential was John Rawls, who developed what he called *Political Liberalism* (Rawls 1993), revising his preliminary thoughts on justice. He was haunted by this cardinal question:

> How is it possible that there may exist over time a stable and just society of free and equal citizens profoundly divided by reasonable though incompatible religious, philosophical, and moral doctrines? (Rawls 1993, xx)

Writing from the mid-1980s, Rawls argued that while primary goods – such as health, education and human rights – are essential, they represent only one part of overall well-being. A just society must balance the preservation of diversity and the coexistence of reasonably pluralistic conceptions of the good while maintaining social cohesion. These conceptions are often rooted in comprehensive doctrines – frameworks that organize and give meaning to all recognized values and virtues, whether religious, philosophical or moral in nature.

He underlines that while many comprehensive doctrines exist in society, people still cooperate fairly because they agree on political principles grounded in constitutional rules. For example, people with differing beliefs may still agree on the necessity of aiding those in need, even if their moral justifications differ: some may see it as an act of solidarity or fraternity (a republican perspective), others as a religious duty, and some as a pragmatic measure to prevent crime and social unrest (a utilitarian view). To go beyond the individual act, citizens need to formulate moral reasoning – at least for "constitutional essentials" and questions of "basic justice," concepts that are accessible to all, regardless of religion or culture, and open to debate in the public sphere. Reasonable citizens, Rawls contends, must also acknowledge the "burdens of judgment" (1993, 54) – the challenges of interpreting complex and conflicting evidence, weighing competing values and understanding moral and political concepts differently based on varied experiences. These deliberations require justifications that extend beyond localized or temporary notions of rightness. Rawls refers to this form of justification as "public reason" – a mode of reasoning that enables diverse citizens to engage in democratic discourse on fair and equal terms.

Rawls is aware that clashes may occur between liberty and other interests, such as security and public order, or efficient measures to ensure safety and public health. He proposes the "Principle of Reconciliation" under which basic liberties may be restricted only when moral reasoning acceptable to all makes it clear that unrestricted liberties will lead to consequences generally agreed to be harmful for all.

An "overlapping consensus" can be created when people endorse the political concept from their own point of view. Like many liberals, Rawls admits that public debate is a collection of competing arguments that encourage "reasonable" outcomes, rather than "rational" outcomes, as they seek a common basis for reciprocal cooperation with the other. Still, the debate itself reconstructs the moral powers of persons as related to their capacity for a "sense of justice" and a "conception of the good." The liberal state, as well as the decent state (but to a lesser degree), will ensure that society reaches one unified conception of justice that would be neutral concerning people's conceptions of the good, or at least when a certain conception of the good becomes controversial.

For Rawls, citizens will engage in civil society through open and free deliberation, relying on nonpublic reasons or comprehensive doctrines. Yet, I think that when tensions emerge from conflicting conceptions of the good, we need public reason – understood as non-authoritarian practical reasoning (as will be explained in the next section) – to resolve it. In fact, Rawls conceived public reason for "constitutional essentials" and questions of "basic justice," as he wanted no involvement of comprehensive doctrines. However, other liberal scholars allow for the conditional use of religious and philosophical arguments in public discourse. They also advocate for extending the scope of public reason beyond basic justice to include debates on conflicting conceptions of the good. Perfectionist liberals took this further, asserting that certain conceptions of the good should be actively promoted – particularly in states that are historically rooted in a specific comprehensive doctrine. We will explore the perfectionist critique of Rawls in greater depth later.

In brief, Rawls develops a political and moral philosophy that integrates elements of both deontological ethics – focused primarily on moral duties without reliance on a transcendental foundation – and virtue ethics, which considers the character of social actors (Kchaou 2024a). His deontological

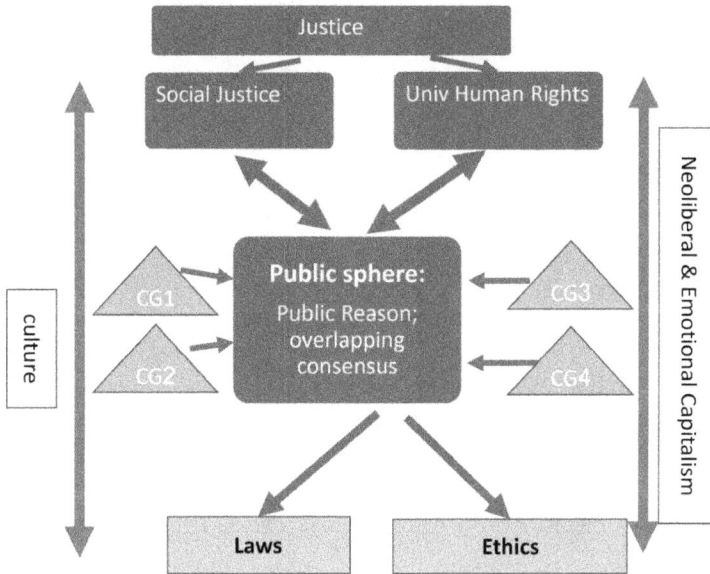

Figure 1.2 Political Liberal Project
CG = Conception of the good

framework is rooted in a social contract that upholds two key principles of justice, prioritizes rights and justice over conceptions of the good, and distinguishes between public reason (for matters of basic justice) and nonpublic reason (for other aspects of life). Rawls also draws on elements of Kantian ethics, viewing virtue not as a comprehensive ethical system but as a foundational principle in which moral duty compels individuals to act ethically without seeking personal gain or pleasure. This is why his model of deliberation presupposes the "veil of ignorance" – a mechanism that discourages self-interest in moral and political reasoning, similar to how religious ethics often emphasize impartiality.

Within this framework, cultural and subcultural contexts play a crucial role in shaping conceptions of justice. However, the forces of neoliberalism and emotional capitalism threaten to undermine key aspects of political liberalism, potentially distorting its principles and implementation (see Figure 1.2).

Political Liberal Project: Enhancing Rawls's Political Liberalism

Rawls's views on many critical issues, such as religion in the public domain, have changed over time. Yet, Rawlsian liberalism has its own problems. Since the publication of Political Liberalism in 1993, his political liberal project has been enhanced and amended by numerous scholars. But before addressing these changes and noteworthy criticisms, Rawlsian political liberalism has been used and abused from different directions. I agree with François Gauthier (2023) that for some this liberalism is a champion of radical egoism, while for others it is close to utilitarianism, and appears as the herald of altruism. For Andrew Stephen Sartori (2014), it can be seen as a normative framework for both a triumphant colonial capitalism and a critique of capitalism from the standpoint of peasant property.

The amendments and objections are not to be seen as equivalent to a refutation of Rawls's political liberalism and theory of justice; rather, they provide complementarity. I organize this enhancement into seven themes.

Liberalism and Colonialism

The international human rights regime has been established through two key acts: the developing of an *International Bill of Human Rights*, and, second, deciding who is a human. For the first, we can refer to the *Universal Declaration of Human Rights* (1948), the French *Declaration of the Rights of Man and of the Citizen* (1789) and to the US *Declaration of Independence* (1776). However, those who contributed to these declarations comprised a narrow definition of humanity. We should wait until Karl Marx tells us that humans are even those who do not own property, moving the conception in the last two declarations from simply abolishing all aristocratic and feudal distinctions in law and introducing class analysis and that a worker's life matters. The same for national liberation movements in Algeria and India (among others), which extended the notion of humans from colonizers to the colonized. Feminist movements further broadened this scope, advocating for women's rights, including suffrage, wage equality and bodily autonomy. Liberalism thus only has meaning when these actors play a role in extending the concept of humans beyond the confines of nation-states and elite social classes.

Liberalism, much like the Enlightenment, exists in a paradoxical tension with its conceptual and ideological "Others." The evolution of human rights as a framework to combat racism reflects decades of grassroots struggle, both within nations and across international platforms. Drawing on the work of

Indian legal scholar Upendra Baxi, Bandana Purkayastha (2024) contends that the prevailing human rights–humanitarianism nexus represents a politics of human rights – distinct from the politics for human rights, historically championed by marginalized groups during the drafting of the *Universal Declaration of Human Rights* and the *International Bill of Human Rights*. For Purkayastha, the problem persists today, with the current politics of human rights continuing to "remain state-friendly, that is, friendly towards already powerful states, accommodating of the missions of powerful NGOs, celebrities and other actors that fit current neoliberal political economies" (2024, 96). This critique finds resonance in Lori Allen's (2020) analysis of Palestine, where liberal democracies and international legal institutions have perpetuated a cycle of unfulfilled promises. Allen examines 20 international commissions conducted in the twentieth century investigating violence and rights abuses in Palestine (and later Palestine/Israel), revealing their consistent failure to enact meaningful change. Instead, these efforts shifted responsibility onto Palestinians, demanding moderation and urging empathy toward the perspectives of their occupiers.

More broadly, liberal democracy is designed to regulate politics and governance within a nation, not international relations. As a result, democratic nations can – and often have – pursued deeply problematic or even harmful foreign policies. John Mearsheimer (2018) has already argued that liberal hegemony, the foreign policy pursued by the United States since the Cold War ended, is doomed to fail in helping other countries to alleviate their economic problems or to transit to democracy. This could be seen as a limitation of liberal democracy or something that democracy was not meant to address in the first place. A similar critique can be made of the conflation of democracy and the notions of national and international justice. In reality, the Rawlsian distributive justice paradigm falls short when confronted with diverse populations and global neoliberalism.

We must acknowledge that liberalism functions differently within an empire than it does in the colonizer's metropole. Andrew Sartori (2014) traces an alternative history of liberalism and refers to Partha Chatterjee's famous dictum about "the rule of colonial difference" to highlight how Bengali Muslim peasants in the late nineteenth century were subjected to what he terms "plebeian liberalism." This form of liberalism not only shaped their political and social realities but also served to justify the imperial expropriation of New World lands under the doctrine of terra nullius.

However, I should note that the double discourse and the different treatment of nations are not only related to liberal democracy and liberal hegemonic multiplexity (rather than multipolarity). China, India and Russia currently complicate our understanding of international relations (Acharya, Estevadeordal and Goodman 2023).

Public Reason: More Open to Different Types of Arguments

Many scholars highlight the tension between dogmatism and open-mindedness and the danger of excluding the public sphere from debate while also advocating for a diversity of reasonable and accessible opinions, including religious arguments. Raja Bahlul (2003) critically examines the concept of public reason, arguing that it is, in reality, liberal reason presenting itself as "public" and therefore neutral. The moral justification of political and social convictions can no longer be removed from religious (or non-religious) beliefs, given the central role religion plays in shaping individual, group and societal moral frameworks. Religion can no longer be ignored, and distinguishing between purely moral and religious decisions is often challenging, as these choices are also shaped by sociological, psychological and pragmatic considerations – whether for individuals or political parties. This is because we sit at the intersections of various intellectual traditions, and religions and their various institutional carriers have produced many forms of religiosity in late modernity. The place of religion in democracy in general, and in the public sphere, in particular, has changed. It is intriguing to think that one is supposed to remove one's religious beliefs in order to formulate political concepts from moral reasoning – an act that, paradoxically, is required to conform to the ideal of public reason.

Jürgen Habermas (2006) acknowledges the place of religion in the public sphere, but he limits it to informal deliberations outside the framework of the state and excludes it from public institutionalization. Habermas traces back how deeply philosophy has been associated with religion from the Axial Age up to the present time, arguing that a public sphere can be opened to both philosophical and religious experience. In this way, he reconstructs the common basis of reflexive learning through communication which is of universal significance, crossing the boundaries of philosophy and religion, on the one hand, and the territorial and cultural boundaries of the East and West, on the other. He holds that religious groups must engage in hermeneutical deliberations in order to develop epistemological attitudes toward the claims of other religions and worldviews, which in turn allows the formation of secular knowledge, which employs scientific expertise. But is it indeed possible to disentangle "religious" justifications from "secular" ones?

Darren Walhof, who studied the same-sex marriage debate in the United States, rightly posits that "theology, politics and the identity of a religious community are all tied up with each other, as religious leaders and citizens apply and reformulate their theologies in new political contexts" (2013, 229). In the same vein, The Irish philosopher Maeve Cooke (2005) states that the problem of religious positions is not that they appeal to a single non-shared framework, as Habermas would contend, but that they tend to be authoritarian and dogmatic in their formulations. However, if non-authoritarian arguments are formulated by religious actors, in which positions are not taken as absolutes but are subject to argumentation, then those arguments can be translated into the public sphere without jeopardizing the freedoms and democracies necessary for its existence. Following her conception of "authoritarian versus non-authoritarian practical reasoning," Cooke defines "context" and "history" as the key factors that distinguish authoritarian claims from non-authoritarian ones. She offers a more precise characterization of authoritarian practical reasoning by identifying two interrelated components: knowledge and justification. First, authoritarianism restricts knowledge access to a privileged group, detaching its perspective from history and context. Second, it justifies propositions and norms by separating their validity from the reasoning of the very human subjects to whom they apply (Cooke 2007). While these two components are crucial in deconstructing authoritarian arguments, the (liberal) assumptions that underpin the public sphere must still be maintained.

A different measure for non-authoritarianism could be the integration of secular and religious knowledge into a single framework, in which both sets of knowledge are understood in relation to one another. The attempt of religious individuals to reconcile their worldview with the findings of science, and/or justify them using science, is an example of this. This approach allows religious individuals to retain the certainty they derive from faith – an issue closely tied to ijtihad (hermeneutical innovation) and the application of Maṣlaḥa (human interest and well-being). At the same time, it fosters a public dialogue in which secular and religious languages are not in opposition but integrated into a shared worldview (Sadek 2014).

A few years ago, I applied Cooke's conception of authoritarian versus non-authoritarian practical reasoning to Tunisia's 2018 public debate on gender equality in inheritance (Hanafi and Tomeh 2020). We found that the debate transcended the familiar antagonistic dichotomies of religious parties opposing equality and liberals supporting it. In Tunisia, these dualistic divisions no longer hold in the same way, as many social and media actors exhibit a heightened self-awareness. However, such polarizing discourses persist among certain leaders within the leftist and Islamist elites.

Cécile Laborde takes a similar approach in her outstanding book,

Liberalism's Religion (2017), which challenges the traditional binary of religion versus secularism – where religion is often linked to backwardness and irrationality, while secularism is seen as embodying rationality and liberation, particularly in the context of gender issues. For example, there is Islam and liberalism, Islam within liberalism, Islamic post-liberalism and so on. In this context, Rawls's limitation of public reason to questions of basic justice becomes debatable. It suggests that public reason could also encompass discussions of competing conceptions of the good.[5] We will explore this issue in greater depth when we discuss secularism in Chapter 5.

The more radical critique of Rawls's conception of public reason comes from some liberals known as perfectionists. For them, the state may promote valuable conceptions of the good life while discouraging those deemed worthless or harmful (Mang 2023). This version of perfectionist liberalism might work in a society that is homogeneous in its adherence to a single comprehensive doctrine. However, can such a homogeneous society truly exist? And if not, does this approach risk opening a backdoor that allows comprehensive doctrines to infiltrate the domain of public reason?

Great care must be taken to avoid the assumption that because the vast majority of Iranians are Muslim, the state can justify using Shiite Islam as a comprehensive doctrine to impose the veil on women in the public sphere. A relevant example can be found in the work of Chinese historian Jiang Qing (2012), who advocates for a Confucian constitution – one that seeks to link China's past to its future by positioning Confucianism as an official religion guiding state governance and reform. However, this position has been challenged by Sungmoon Kim (2015). For Kim,

> Public reason Confucianism has two core premises: (1) there is a valuable Confucian way of life that is distinct from (if not starkly opposed to) a liberal way of life and (2) it is permissible for a state to promote or discourage some activities, ideas, or ways of life on the grounds of key Confucian values such as filial piety, respect for elders, ancestor worship, ritual propriety, and social harmony. (Kim 2015, 190)

These premises are further supported by six propositions that collectively shape public reason Confucianism into a form of democratic perfectionism. The most significant of these propositions are:

---

[5]   See the excellent article by Mounir Kchaou (2019) on how liberal philosophers, particularly Rawls, have changed their position regarding the role of religion in the public sphere.

> The Confucian (democratic) state respects constitutional rights held by its citizens, among others, the rights to religious freedom, freedom of conscience, freedom of expression, and freedom of association; thus the state has no desire either to suppress value plurality in civil society or to elevate Confucianism as the state religion...Confucian public reason... delineates the legitimate boundary of state action and provides moral content (which is open for public contestation) for basic rights, duties, and liberties...While Confucian public reason must be justifiable to all citizens in a Confucian society, including immigrants, immigrated citizens must strive to negotiate their religious or nonreligious comprehensive doctrines with Confucian public reason in order to fully exercise their constitutional rights and liberties. (Kim 2015, 192)

Even if Kim in his last book used the term "Confucian Constitutionalism," he means the Confucian-inflected design of political institutions, including the public sphere of deliberation (allowing value and societal pluralism and moral disagreement), the legislature and the judiciary, and not a state religion. This specific Confucian democratic constitutionalism is facilitated by the "syncretism" characteristic of East Asia in which Buddhism, Taoism and Confucianism could be espoused simultaneously and serve the people's moral and material well-being. It is rather a civic Confucianism that Kim (2023) characterized by "benevolence, valuable relationships, trust, filial piety, ritual propriety, respect for elders and harmony."

This accommodating vision of public reason appears reasonable in acknowledging China's Confucian heritage while maintaining a principled distance between state and religion – drawing on Rajeev Bhargava's (2019) framework – and upholding a form of restricted state neutrality, as echoed by Laborde (see Chapter 5). However, this approach has not gone without criticism. Scholars of Confucianism, such as Loubna El Amine, challenge this perspective by arguing that Confucian heritage should not be viewed primarily through the lens of morality and virtue but rather as being driven by political concerns (El Amine 2015a). From her perspective, this emphasis on Confucianism as a guiding framework ultimately undermines pluralism.[6]

Kim pursues the importance of this exercise

> in a society where 'I' is understood in relational terms, family values and ritual propriety are publicly promoted, the society as a whole is deemed (or idealized) as a nationally extended family, and therefore

---

[6] See her review (El Amine 2015b) of Sungmoon Kim's *Confucian Democracy in East Asia: Theory and Practice.*

social harmony and familial citizenship are valued, the value of freedom of expression is appreciated and exercised differently than it is in a liberal society. (Kim 2015, 196)

For Kim,

> while liberal people embrace the "costs" accompanying their expressive liberty such as reputational injury and emotional distress and make it a virtue to tolerate someone's free expression, though the expressed values may not be agreeable, Confucian people make every effort to avoid incurring even such mild harms to others...by constraining the way they exercise this freedom by means of ritual propriety and making the expression agreeable to communal norms and moral sentiments. The practical consequence of this difference is rather dramatic: whereas liberal people, by bearing certain costs of the freedom of expression and thus putting up with the "vicissitudes of pluralism," try to keep the state at bay from civil and private conflicts, Confucian people are more worried about uneasy social relationships than what liberals would consider "intervention" of the state, which they conceive of in terms of the image of the family. Thus understood, in a Confucian democratic society, freedom of expression is still valued as a citizen's constitutional right but its moral content and social scope is always balanced with Confucian mores, values, and moral sentiments. Confucian public reasoning involves this complex balancing process." (Kim 2015, 196–97)

I increasingly observe Muslim scholars striving to accommodate liberalism while infusing it with a distinct cultural and religious tone. The 2024 Ummatics Institute conference, organized by eminent political scientist and Imam Ovamir Anjum, reflects this trend. Held in Kuala Lumpur, the conference aimed to explore innovative strategies of public reasoning that enable meaningful participation and debate on pressing public issues – while preserving the foundational cultural and religious unity of an Ummatic (Islamic) society. I look forward to reading further insights on these emerging approaches. Indeed, significant scholarly reflections on this matter have already emerged. Louay Safi (2021; 2023) has developed the concept of "rational idealism," which seeks to bridge liberalism with Islam's role as a comprehensive doctrine in many countries in the Muslim world. Mohammed Hashas (2023) expanded the scope of public reasoning beyond the strictly public sphere by introducing "spiritual self-criticism," which integrates both private and public dimensions of moral deliberation. Khaled

Abou El Fadl (2014) offers a critical examination of contemporary interpretations of Islam that have diminished its potential for peace and love. His advocacy for a "universal overlapping consensus"– as a means to combat global atrocities and advance social justice – resonates with the earlier ideas of John Rawls. Finally, Hossameldeen Mohammed and Ray Jureidini (2022) highlight instances where the Muslim Ummah has demonstrated transnational solidarity, particularly in hosting refugees, both Muslim and non-Muslim. They also examine the successful adaptation of the Islamic charitable obligation of Zakat within the UNHCR framework, which has attracted significant Muslim donor contributions. As we will see in Chapter 6, there are also serious efforts by religious scholars, such as Yasir Qadhi, to reconcile a liberal – yet socially conservative – stance on LGBTQ movements, further illustrating the complex engagement between Islamic thought and contemporary liberal discourses.

Balancing Between Individual and Communitarian Liberalism

Rawls and contractualist theorists offer compelling reasons for defining human society as a system of cooperation. This framework prevents society from being reduced either to a mere collection of individuals, as seen in methodological individualism, or to an assembly of constraining rules, as in methodological holism. However, as Paul Ricœur poses, one might ask: How can a historical pact, such as the one formed in the original position under the veil of ignorance, bind a concrete historical society? This question lies at the heart of the concerns raised by liberal communitarians, including Michael Sandel, Nassif Nassar, Charles Taylor, Amitai Etzioni, Michael Walzer and Abdie Kazemipur, who critique Rawls for not adequately considering the role of communities within society. These theorists address this gap by seeking to reconcile (individual) autonomy with the sense of dependency on community and others, striking a balance between freedom and collective responsibility. As Nassar (2003) notes, responsibility toward community/society is before (individual) freedom. Bruno Latour further extends this notion of dependency and freedom with his statement, "I depend on others, so I exercise my freedom."[7]

Sociology offers compelling critiques of the rational choice approach inherent in rights-based liberalism, particularly through recent writings. For Peter Wagner, this form of liberalism frames the individual as the only

7   See "Bruno Latour, 'Le philosophe doit travailler à redonner des puissances d'agir.'" 9 October. www.lemonde.fr/disparitions/article/2022/10/09/bruno-latour-le-philosophe-doit-travailler-a-redonner-des-puissances-d-agir_6145059_3382.html.

category that is both exempt from contestation and, in many cases, incapable of being questioned:

> The individual is simply there, whereas everything else – for instance, what criteria of justification are to be applied when determining the collective good – is subject to argument. Substantive aspects of human interaction are dependent upon communication and consensus. And it is even uncertain...with whom should one enter into communication because the boundaries of the community are not themselves given, but subject to agreement. (Wagner 2021, 170)

Another notable sociologist, Anne Warfield Rawls, daughter of John Rawls, challenges her father's philosophy by drawing on a new interpretation of Durkheim. For Durkheim, what was striking was the extent to which modern societies achieve order, meaning and morality without requiring consensus. He argued that not only are the practical and moral demands of these societies compatible with the principles of individual freedom, equality and justice, but that the new, differentiated forms of sociality in the modern era actually produced these ideas about individualism and morality, rather than the reverse. Rather than beginning with institutional arrangements to frame political liberalism and the moral philosophy they embody, Durkheim urged a focus on the new constitutive forms of social practices – such as mechanical and organic solidarities – and the requirements they impose, shifting away from traditional moral philosophy. By adopting this approach, Ann Rawls situates the study of moral duties and obligations within the social practices that give rise to them, and she does so empirically (Warfield Rawls 2021). In doing so, this political liberalism strikes a balance between the importance of the individual and the community, understanding the latter as a source of morality, solidarity and social structure, and reflecting the critical forms of social order that shape modern societies.

I will not expand this section further, as I plan to explore liberal communitarian perspectives in the upcoming chapters. In those, I will present my own vision for balancing the individual and the community, while also examining the various forms that community can take, including the role of the neighbor.

Feminist Critiques

Despite its origin in the liberal tradition, some feminists are critical of how liberalism has been conceptualized – both as a philosophical theory and as a framework for political institutions and arrangements. I will not start from the classical predecessors of liberalism – who were blind to or at best indifferent toward women's rights in areas such as voting, invisible domestic work, unequal remuneration and other feminist concerns. I focus instead on the limitations of contemporary liberal thinkers. Even within modern social justice discourse, figures like John Rawls have not adequately addressed group-based social inequalities, particularly the deeply gendered structures of family and public life, which impose significant constraints on women's freedom (Hartley and Watson 2022).

To elaborate further, feminists argue that liberalism treats the existing gendered division of labor within the family as voluntary, thereby implying that the family is inherently just. But to what extent is this true? Does this notion of voluntariness obscure the power dynamics that uphold gender inequality in domestic labor? Feminist scholars, such as Italian philosopher of care Elena Pulcini, emphasize the need for a dual approach: both critiquing and deconstructing how care is framed as altruism while simultaneously reinforcing the gendered nature of the family as a social structure:

> On the one hand, we need to examine the figure of the sovereign subject, from the Cartesian subject to the Homo economicus of liberal tradition, and reveal the unilateral nature of what has been referred to, appropriately, as the "disengaged self"...a masculine and patriarchal Self separated from any relationship; on the other hand, we need to restore dignity to the notions of dependency and relationship by freeing them from the self-sacrifice and abnegation which have always been associated with the feminine. (Pulcini 2021, 84)

For Pulcini and other feminists, rehabilitating care requires rethinking the subject beyond the dichotomy of prioritizing either the Self or the Other. Instead, it entails an approach that integrates autonomy with dependency and freedom with the capacity to relate. Women can move beyond their historical condition of being "enslaved to caring" (and to giving) by actively and voluntarily embracing their role as "subjects who give care" (and gifts) on their own terms (Pulcini 2021).

The most compelling feminist critique of liberalism targets its rigid separation between the public and private spheres. Feminists challenge this distinction by questioning how these spheres are defined and insisting, for example, on the necessity of state intervention in private matters such as domestic violence. Another key feminist critique is directed at the concept of the "atomistic man" – liberalism's masculinist ideal of an isolated, self-sufficient individual. In this vein, Rawls's depiction of the "original position" in A Theory of Justice – framed by the "veil of ignorance" as an "ideal of impartiality" that strips individuals of their particular social attributes, including sex – has been criticized for embodying an atomistic view of the person, one that disregards the fundamental reality of human connection (Zerilli 2015). In the context of the Global South, some feminists have sought to engage in dialogue with conservative social groups, including religious elites, who often hold a more expansive understanding of public reason. These feminists aim to foster discussions on justice and historical gender inequalities while navigating culturally specific frameworks that can accommodate both feminist principles and local traditions.

Sungmoon Kim offers us the example of the work of Hee-Kang Kim, who powerfully shows that

> the feminists were finally able to garner overwhelming public support by the time of the abolition of the family-head system by the Korean Constitutional Court in 2005, when they abandoned the "liberal versus Confucian" framework and began to argue that "gender equality in the family would not deny other Confucian family values and that the family rearrangement achieved by the abolition of the family-head system would, indeed, help to preserve the family, a core institution of Confucianism". (Kim 2015, 196, quoting Hee-Kang Kim 2007)

In the same vein, Line Nyhagen (2017) argues that feminists who seek to reform religious traditions from within reject the notion that religions are inherently patriarchal. Islamic feminists such as Fatema Mernissi, Amina Wadud, and Asmaa Lamrabet have made significant contributions to advancing gender equality, despite facing considerable challenges and resistance (Abboud 2019). For them, reducing Islamic thought solely to its opposition to liberalism is an oversimplification.

In short, different strands of feminism have not only criticized aspects of liberalism but have also reshaped it, making it more attuned to the implications of structural gender inequality in both the private and public spheres.

Problematizing Institutionalism and Agency

In The Idea of Justice, Amartya Sen (2011) respectfully distances himself from Rawls in criticizing Rawls's "transcendental institutionalism" when discussing what a perfectly just society should look like. Instead, Sen argues that the most important problems are comparative – concerned with how societies can become less unjust. Moreover, Sen and Rawls consider institutions very differently. For Rawls, justice is essentially about institutions – just institutions lead to a just distribution of goods. In contrast, Sen sees justice as primarily concerned with individuals' actual well-being, emphasizing real-life conditions over institutional design (Maffettone 2011).

Sen does not want to pit the individual against the institution but instead emphasizes the importance of capabilities (the "doings and beings" that people can achieve if they so choose). Unlike Rawls's focus on primary goods, Sen introduces intermediary categories, such as family and group, which can enhance an individual's capabilities. The primary goods approach, while valuable in some respects, offers an economic framework that overlooks human differences, failing to account for the distinct needs and capabilities of individuals. Sen's "capability" approach critiques this "transcendental institutionalism," advocating for a more context-sensitive approach to justice – one that prioritizes human development and capabilities over the abstract notion of primary goods.

Even though Rawls's *The Law of Peoples* (1999) tempers his institutionalism by extending a form of "mini" political liberalism to decent states, he relegates these states to the ahistorical realm of values (El Amine 2021). In doing so, Rawls makes unjustified concessions to these states, such as exempting them from the responsibility to guarantee fundamental rights like freedom of expression for their citizens (see Kchaou 2023).

The Problem of the Democracy of Opinion

Political liberalism is fundamentally a constitutional arrangement grounded in democratic principles and procedures. According to Danielle Allen (2023), justice can be realized solely through democracy, which entails equal political participation in the public sphere. This ideal, however, is increasingly threatened in many liberal democratic nations as power becomes concentrated among the wealthy. Additionally, this form of democracy has been transformed into what Karl Van Meter and Jean-Pierre Pagès (2023) term the "democracy of opinion," a model advanced by both power and counter-power:

> All the recent work on public opinion demonstrates that public reason is animated not only by reason but by values and emotions and there are a multiplicity of actors of power (established through classical political mediums such as political parties) and counter-power exercising politics outside these mediums. Social, economic and political public

controversies are always there during elections but beyond carry out not only debate in the public sphere but also violence. (Meter and Pagès 2023, 25)

Many scholars provide compelling criticism of how democracy has been distorted from the inside. One of them is the Chinese philosopher Tingyang Zhao who thoroughly diagnosed the crisis of the liberal democracy system and how powerful forces that control capital and the media are subverting democracy – a sort of "Trojan horse" that has destroyed democracy in such a way that the threat to democracy comes from within itself. For Zhao, democracy becomes a "publicracy," and while the former is unintelligent, the powers underlying the latter are much smarter. Democracy is a way to decide on the distribution of rights and power, but not the definition of goodness, truth or justice. Therefore, democracy needs its own mind. The smart democracy he proposed is better to ensure the exercise of public reason for resolving social problems (Zhao 2012).

Whose Justice?

It is debatable whether any society can achieve a single conception of justice. Following the ideas of Alasdair MacIntyre and Luc Boltanski, the question arises: "Whose Justice?" "Justice as fairness" involves a collective decision procedure and a constructive interpretation of certain social practices and those who participate in them. This approach results from fair terms of the contract and agreed principles recognized as fair by the parties involved. According to both authors, this differs from common sense of justice or ethical principles, which may relate to the desire for a good life "for and with others," as expressed by Ricœur.

The contextual approach to justice is not addressed in the Rawlsian conceptualization of justice, as it does not incorporate empirical research findings. The work of Luc Boltanski and Laurent Thévenot (1991) on different justification orders "cites," and various conceptions of justice complements, the mainstream liberal view of justice.

In the same vein, Paul Ricœur also contests certain conceptualizations of justice and calls for a dialectical approach to justice. According to Ricœur, the idea of justice is not the same when it is considered from an ethical or from a moral point of view. From an ethical point of view, the idea of the just is linked to the good, while from a moral point of view, it is linked to the legal (rules and principles of distributive justice) (Kandil 2020).

We will explore further the complexity of these different conceptual-izations of justice in the following chapters.

Conclusion

Identifying various strands of liberalism reveals how political liberalism has evolved without being disproven. I will emphasize key conclusions from these changes.

First, public reason should tolerate religious arguments insofar as they are presented as non-authoritarian practical reasoning, according to Cook's definition.

Second, certain reflections from perfectionism present an intriguing perspective by proposing that comprehensive doctrines could potentially be integrated into both the concepts of justice and the good, subject to stringent conditional scrutiny. For me, Confucian public reasoning is particularly persuasive. Nonetheless, while I maintain a distinction between the concepts of justice and the good, I take issue with Rawls's approach of privatizing the latter and reducing it to that conceived by an individual. I will introduce in Chapter 3 a third category, namely the "common good" or shared culture, and I will employ both terms interchangeably.

Third, liberal communitarians contribute to balancing political liberalism by mediating between the individual and the community. However, I propose introducing a third element: "the neighbor." A neighbor is not necessarily part of one's community but serves as a measure of one's humanistic regard for the other. A neighbor can be a fellow citizen or a refugee in one's neighborhood, but they can also be in a neighboring country, where one's well-being is intrinsically linked to theirs.

Fourth, the current distortion of democracy as a guiding philosophy is deeply concerning. It not only undermines the very conception of justice – as fairness – but also distorts the core principles of liberalism itself.

CHAPTER 2

Symbolic Liberalism

The incessant issuance of new rights, like the wholesale printing
of currency, causes a massive inflation of rights that devalues
their moral claims.

Amitai Etzioni, The Spirit of Community (1993)

In early 2015, I gave a talk in Rabat on knowledge production in the Arab
world following the Arab uprisings. The discussion quickly turned around
to the reasons for the failure of these uprisings. A leftist sociologist argued:
"Islam is the worst enemy of democracy." Another participant opposed this
view, arguing that "the bad implementation of Islam is responsible for the
failure of these uprisings." In fact, in any discussion about the problematic
behavior of a group in my region, the question of religion appears as a major
source of morality. The debate then takes a familiar turn: non-religious voices
often argue that Islam itself shapes this behavior, while religious perspectives
frame the issue as a misapplication of Islamic principles.

I encountered the same dichotomy when discussing the War on Gaza and
Western support for Israel with my students. Some argued that the situation
reflects the inherent nature of liberalism, while others insisted it results from
a distorted implementation of liberal principles. In this chapter, I tackle
the central question of the book: Does sociology (and related disciplines)
respond to the pathologies of late modernity in a way that aligns with revised
versions of political liberalism? Or, to frame it differently: Are these so-called
"symbolic liberals" (liberals who are classically liberal but politically illiberal)
simply unaware of these revised versions of political liberalism, or does
political liberalism itself inevitably produce such responses to these crises?
Have they merely *talked the talk* without *walking the walk*? Have they, in
the end, reproduced the very injustices they claim to oppose?

To address these questions, I examine how the Symbolic Liberal project
distorts the very notion of justice. It does so by deflating the concept of

social justice while inflating the universality of human rights – ultimately endorsing only a single, hegemonic conception of the good, often presented as an inherent component of justice itself. However, before going further, I would like to qualify the term "hegemony." I don't mean the power of a state, but, drawing on a more Gramsci-inspired definition, "a form of intellectual and political leadership which educates and transforms" (Schwarzmantel 2014, 38).

Deflating the Concept of Social Justice

If I were to summarize the mission of the social sciences – particularly sociology – in one sentence, it would be this: they are meant to defend social justice. Whether rooted in Marxism or liberalism, social justice remains a central theme, albeit interpreted in different ways. But if social justice is the answer to inequality, the crucial question remains: which version of social justice should prevail? Kiran Odhav and Jayanathan Govender (2023) distinguish between three dimensions of inequality:

> Historical inequality is determined by inheritance, wealth transfers and family prestige. Normative inequality is related to race, class and gender. Structural inequality is framed by access to freedom, agency and distribution of rights, political power, public goods and services, financial services and public participation. (Odhav and Govender 2023, 350)

While some adopt Max Weber's comprehensive view of class and stratification, considering multiple inequalities among individuals and social groups with different social statuses, others focus on a specific dimension. Among the latter are the symbolic liberals.

The following analysis addresses unresolved issues and tensions associated with symbolic liberals in relation to certain aspects of social justice in four key areas: first, being primary recipients of the inequalities they critique; second, discursive interpretation of intersectionality; third, the neoliberal approach to environmental and climate justice; and, finally, the consideration of social justice beyond and below the nation-state.

Being Primary Beneficiaries of the Very Inequalities They Condemn

Symbolic Liberals hold influence as they are part of "symbolic capitalism" and participate actively in a polarized society. The African American sociologist

Musa Al-Gharbi (2024) defines symbolic capitalism as "a new class of social elites who have not attained their social position by owning material assets, nor by developing or trading material goods or services. Instead, they traffic in symbols and rhetoric, images and narratives, data and analysis, ideas and abstractions." He offers some thoughts on the American context by saying:

> symbolic capitalists are, themselves, among the primary beneficiaries of contemporary inequalities. And we don't just passively benefit. We actively exploit, exacerbate, and reinforce the very stratification that we are pledged to abolish. Indeed, for almost any action we condemn by superelites, multinational corporations, and corrupt politicians, it's people like us who actually make it happen. Yet our sincere commitments to social justice often blind us to the role we play in contributing to social problems. (Al-Gharbi 2024, 304)

Thus, it is difficult for those symbolic capitalists to preach for social justice. These knowledge economy producers use symbolic politics, conceptualized as driven primarily by emotions and intuitions. Ideological beliefs, normative values, and prejudice are the actors' predispositions that shape emotions. In war, belligerents use emotional rhetoric very strongly, not to appeal rationally to followers' interests but to appeal emotionally to predispositions (Kaufman 2017), and the war on Gaza clearly demonstrates this. In the framework of symbolic politics, in the time of peace, emotions provoke agreement among followers. Moreover, in both contexts, those symbolic capitalists play a significant role in increasing the polarization of society.

The broader issues of economic inequality and social justice are lost. Symbolic liberals can be found among the Left (but not exclusively), particularly when the Left overstates identity politics based on cultural differences. This cultural Left cannot create a unified vision that can appeal to a broad range of people. In *The Death of the Left: Why We Must Begin from the Beginning Again* (2022), Simon Winlow and Steve Hall identify the root causes of the Left's maladies in how new cultural obsessions displaced core unifying principles such as social class struggles. The Left, more than the Right, formulates policies "strictly as a means of gaining votes," rather than seeking to gain votes "in order to carry out certain preconceived policies." As a result, voters start looking for alternatives among competing groups that use the same tactics, and the electorate becomes polarized (Downs 1957). Elections become arenas of competing groups disconnected from the issues related to social structures, reflecting individual choices. A good example of the effects of such political change is the transformation of the Socialist

Party in France, which changed from a strongly ideological party to a "party of elected people" and not a party of militants (Lefebvre and Sawicki 2006).

In authoritarian countries, where people fight for democracy, social justice, and dignity, the cultural Left does not prioritize democracy (Achcar 2022). This view is shared by some postcolonial Left in the West. However, Elizabeth Suzanne Kassab (2019) presents a nuanced perspective, showing how another Left has balanced cultural and political challenges. They often achieve more political than intellectual enlightenment. By advocating for human dignity and moral guidance amidst tyranny, they embrace enlightenment as a humanist ideal.[1]

While culture influences politics and the economy, another dynamic exists where politics influence ethics. Milbank and Pabst (2016) highlight the separation between politics and ethics in their critique of contemporary liberalism. They describe a division within liberalism: a "liberal Right" that emphasizes economic and political negative liberty, and a "liberal Left" that focuses on cultural and sexual negative liberty.

Discursive Distortion of Intersectionality

Socio-economic inequalities are often considered the primary negations of social justice, at least in one of the three entangled dimensions – historical, normative and structural. In fact, symbolic liberals are less interested in historical inequality than in defending normative inequality, where the question of identity politics or group rights prevails.

In the Arab world, symbolic liberals tend to map and locate social justice issues geographically for quick interventions, often using flawed data (Hanafi 2020). Gilbert Achcar gives a compelling account of what he calls the "Arab Inequality Puzzle":

> The debate about the reality of social inequality in the region has developed since 2011 – particularly in regard to Egypt, where income and consumption data are periodically collected by means of household surveys. Inequality measures based on this method alone, while income taxation data are inaccessible, are highly questionable and conflict

---

[1] I cannot extend this argument more here for lack of space, but one can refer to an excellent debate in the pages of *Aljumhuriya* about the crisis of the Arab Left and its position vis-à-vis the Arab uprising. Among those who wrote about this issue are Yasine al-Haj Saleh, Samer Frangieh, Hazem Saghieh and Farah Qobeisi. See https://aljumhuriya.net/ar/article_types/english/. Azmi Bishara and Yassin al-Haj Saleh also wrote extensively about the Arab uprisings.

with various observations and calculations based on other indicators such as national accounts, executive income or house prices. Yet, the World Bank upholds official inequality findings in portraying the Arab upheaval as the revolt of a "middle class" that aspires to greater business freedom, in consonance with the neoliberal worldview. (Achcar 2020, 746)

Some criticize the downplaying of class analysis at both national and global levels (Heilinger 2019; Hamouchene and Sandwell 2023: 12). Of course, I understand the definition of social class according to the cultural political economy approach, so that the working class will be defined not in a classical Marxist sense but as restricted by limited amounts of economic, cultural and social capital forms. Workers have undergone tremendous changes to become less numerous and better educated, dovetailed with robotics, automation and AI leading to a more diverse array of categories seeking social justice.

A stronger commitment to social class analysis – particularly to the historical economic causes of social exclusion – is essential for any meaningful conceptualization of social justice. At the very least, class analysis should hold a dominant position within any intersectional framework. Let me elaborate. Any historical analysis inherently requires an intersectional perspective, a debt we owe to feminist scholars since Kimberlé Crenshaw (1989) first coined the term. Since then – and even before – Kathy Davis and Helma Lutz (2023) have traced the genealogy of intersectionality, exploring the complexities of the debates surrounding it and its mainstreaming within feminism. This evolution led Flavia Dzodan to declare, emphatically: "My feminism will be intersectional or it will be bullshit!"[2]

However, intersectionality as a discourse (in the Foucauldian sense, rather than as a theory) has at times essentialized race, overlooking its relational nature (Phoenix 2023) and its integral connection to social class analysis. Ann Phoenix provides a critical assessment of how intersectionality has been adopted in Europe, highlighting both its limitations and potential future directions. She advocates for expanding intersectional analyses to encompass historical social relations and trauma, recognizing that both shape contemporary social dynamics and manifest psychosocially in unexpected ways. Similarly, Nira Yuval-Davis (2023) calls for a "situated intersectionality," cautioning that "focusing only on the racialised 'other' can add to the surveillance culture that social scientists contribute to, of the weak and vulnerable in society." She, along with Fawwaz Traboulsi

---

[2]   See https://tigerbeatdown.com/2011/10/10/my-feminism-will-be-intersectional-or-it-will-be-bullshit/.

(2014), argues for redirecting the intersectional lens toward the rich and powerful, ensuring that privilege and structural advantage are equally interrogated. This perspective resonates with Nancy Fraser (2016), who foregrounds social class and contends that wealth redistribution stands in direct tension with the meritocratic ideals embraced by certain mainstream feminist movements.

All of this must remain context-sensitive, but it is crucial not to lose sight of the fact that race, ethnicity, gender, religion, age and sexuality serve to complement an analysis of social class – not the other way around. For example, while fair intersectional wealth redistribution is a pressing issue across all societies, the challenge of wealth production is particularly urgent in the Global South. Issues such as soaring unemployment and economic productivity are far more critical in the Global South today than in the Global North.

Neoliberal Recipe for Environmental and Climate Justice

Today's unprecedented global ecological crisis is closely related to the irrational use of the earth's resources. Symbolic liberals remain too passive concerning these issues.

In all countries, discussions, plans and policies increasingly focus on the transition to green energy. However, numerous studies highlight how symbolic liberals, while advocating for sustainability, often align with a neoliberal agenda driven by states, international financial institutions, multinational corporations and banks. This alignment has ultimately failed to achieve climate justice. What is presented as the "green economy" and "sustainable development" often serves as an extension of existing systems of capital accumulation, commodification and financialization – including the exploitation of the natural world (Hamouchene and Sandwell 2023). Under directives from international financial institutions, state-owned energy enterprises are dismantled, and the energy sector is privatized, frequently falling under the control of foreign transnational corporations – in Morocco, "a local ruling elite that is free to plunder the state and generate as much profit as it wishes, within a culture of authoritarianism and nepotism" (Moustakbal 2023, 223).

Symbolic liberals often promote a one-size-fits-all approach to development, advocating for energy policies that prioritize public–private partnerships or, in the worst cases, full privatization. However, these policies frequently overlook how societies and social movements engage in debates and negotiations over their own conceptions of sustainable development.

As a result, economic growth continues to disproportionately benefit ruling elites and oligarchic classes, particularly in authoritarian states.

Absence of Social Justice Beyond and Below the Nation-State

Symbolic liberals, much like symbolic capitalists, have shown little interest in addressing global issues such as world poverty and the structural injustices embedded in the global economy. Their conception of social justice is often confined within the boundaries of the nation-state, revealing a critical limitation: many liberal scholars rarely engage with the idea of global solidarity. Historically, even classical liberals failed to denounce colonialism – and in some cases they openly praised it. As a result, the distributive justice paradigm seldom accounts for its impact on diverse populations and transnational economies.

Over the past two decades, several countries in the Global South have demonstrated a stronger commitment to global solidarity than their counterparts in the Global North – whether in hosting refugees, providing international aid, or fostering South–South economic cooperation. Today, this contrast is particularly evident in the Global South's solidarity with the Palestinian people, compared to the Global North, where many liberal democracies continue to supply arms to Israel's genocidal war on Gaza.

The lack of solidarity from the Global North toward the Global South became starkly evident during the COVID-19 pandemic – a moment when the world's interconnectedness was no longer just a metaphor but a lived reality. Yet, despite this unprecedented global crisis, it did not lead to greater solidarity or a more humanistic form of globalization.

Symbolic liberals tend to perceive the world through a framework of relationships that move from the most distant inward. Some acknowledge social inequality as a global phenomenon rooted in histories of imperialism and colonialism, while others limit their focus to the big cities where they live. In both cases, their engagement with the suffering of the marginalized often remains abstract, detached from the lived realities of those most affected.

In contrast, many grassroots social movements – including religious and conservative ones – approach relationships from the inside out, starting with close-knit communities before extending outward. They emphasize the importance of community work, family bonds, and neighborhood solidarity. For instance, in Lebanon, faith-based organizations emerged as the most proactive NGOs in supporting families who lost their livelihoods during COVID-19 and the 2019 economic crisis, stepping in where state institutions and international organizations often fell short.

Symbolic liberals have failed to reinvent their traditional approach – whether from the outward-in or the inward-out – and to develop methods that embrace multi-scale perspectives. This requires rethinking the significance of family, community and the ethics of love, hospitality and care (affective politics) before scaling up to the nation-state and humanity as a whole. Eric Macé (2020) conceptualizes such a multi-scale approach, moving beyond Durkheim's notion of society as *sui generis*. Instead, he shifts the focus to the different levels of social relationships and the actors within them – how they establish networks, classify their modes of organization and practice solidarity at various scales. These relationships, whether ephemeral or stable, are shaped by the specific logic of the actors and their social groups. His "augmented sociology" seeks to move beyond the paradigm of dominance,[3] replacing it with an understanding of power as either robust or vulnerable.

Inflate the Conception of the Universality of Human Rights

While social justice is often downplayed, symbolic liberals tend to inflate human rights in a specific manner. How do they do this? A rights-based approach to social issues can yield positive outcomes, particularly in resolving conflicts over resource allocation that enable freedom, as well as in mitigating the effects of relative powerlessness and deprivation. It also serves as a safeguard against colonialism, torture and tyranny. However, symbolic liberals focus on "identities" as the core of rights or champion individualistic choices, both of which are treated as universally applicable. Despite the fragmentation of identities within subculture politics, symbolic liberals assert their conception of the good as superior to all others, attempting to impose it on society by extending norms and deculturizing them. Yet, their views are often too insular and self-referential to resonate with the broader shared culture or the common good. Rather than engaging in open debate, they prefer these views be imposed, as they hesitate to address certain sensitive issues. Their underlying concerns often revolve around hypothetical scenarios – What if the enemy of liberty benefits from liberty and rejects it? What if Islamists gain power? What if...

---

[3] Domination can stem from various sources: the idea of society as a necessary and functional dominant structure, the ideology of ruling classes (as in Marxism), the notion of modernity as a form of domination (as argued by Max Weber and, to some extent, Michel Foucault), or even from the subalterns themselves, who may perceive their resistance as merely marginal, creating only limited spaces of autonomy (Macé 2020).

Let me now address two key issues: the universality of human rights and the excessive emphasis on identity politics.

The Universality of Human Rights: Abstract vs. Concrete

The most widely recognized universal values, documented with the greatest global consensus, are those outlined in the *Universal Declaration of Human Rights* (1948). However, symbolic liberals have often interpreted this Declaration not as a constellation of abstract principles open to cultural interpretation, but as a rigid set of legal axioms – a "one size fits all" framework. In this view, specific cultures were not considered participants in defining these concepts, nor was there room for adaptation to local conditions. Late modernity has further reinforced this tendency by prioritizing formal legality over more nuanced, context-sensitive moral judgments.

By detaching legal norms from historical and lived realities, human rights become increasingly formalized, and in this legalistic approach, they serve as instruments wielded by both the powerful and the weak. As Clifford Bob (2019) compellingly argues in *Rights as Weapons*, rights are often used strategically, even as camouflage for ulterior motives that can further marginalize vulnerable groups. For instance, Palestinian national liberation movements are sometimes framed as antisemitic, while veiled students in France and Quebec are denied access to public education under the guise of secularism.[4]

Similarly, Azmi Bishara (2023a) critiques the way Western societies have positioned personal liberties as universal imperatives, leading to their imposition on societies still under authoritarian rule. This approach, seen as a form of paternalism, can easily slide into cultural imperialism. Today, we witness the increasing politicization and ideologization of human rights discourse. Abdelwahab El-Affendi (2024) highlights how the field of Genocide Studies has become deeply polarized, with democratic nations simultaneously participating in genocidal acts while denying their existence, particularly in the context of the war on Gaza. For El-Affendi, this represents a profound crisis – one that threatens the very endeavors of genocide prevention.

Finally, symbolic liberals' discourse on human rights often evades the issue of socio-economic inequality. Upendra Baxi (2002) critiques a fundamental shift in the human rights paradigm – away from its original focus on human dignity and well-being and toward the interests of global capital and corporate welfare. This shift, he argues, has led to the erosion

---

[4] I know I am simplifying the debate here. For a deeper analysis of the question of the full-face veil in France, see Kchaou (2023).

of the state's redistributive role and the commodification of human rights themselves. Human rights movements, once driven by principles of justice and equity, risk becoming mere "human rights markets." Drawing from his extensive experience in India, Baxi underscores the growing dissociation between humanitarian actors and the lived realities of the poor and oppressed. As human rights advocacy becomes increasingly institution-alized and market-driven, it loses touch with the very people it was meant to serve – the marginalized, the dispossessed and those suffering under systemic inequality.

Excessive Identity Politics

Regarding identity politics, changes take place at a dizzying speed. In the past, identity relied on social class, national or religious allegiances, and was associated with broad and diverse populations. Nowadays, identities rely on subcultures, defined by a limited and external set of traits (race, sexual orientation, or even lifestyle choices like dietary habits), often against the internal "other." For Kenneth Gergen,

> identity politics stands often for a mode of political activism, typically initiated by groups excluded from traditional main-stream politics. These marginalized groups generate a self-designated identity (group consciousness) that is instantiated by the individual identities of its constituents...Politics and personal being are virtually inseparable. (Gergen 2000, 34)

This dynamic differs significantly from traditional social movements, where collective action is directed against oppressors, and individual experiences are secondary to the broader struggle. In principle, there is nothing wrong with this shift, but it can become problematic when identity-based groups cultivate a rhetoric of victimhood – what Jonathan Haidt (2013) describes as the rise of "sacralized victims" – fueled by deep resentment. The issue often arises at the intersection of identity politics and what Kenneth Gergen (2000) calls the "saturated self" – an isolated, individuated and bounded self. Bounded by what? By technological innovation, which, in our late modern age and the era of social media, has enabled an unprecedented proliferation of relationships, leading to social saturation. Zygmunt Bauman (2003) echoes Gergen's concern but emphasizes that these relationships tend to be superficial and transient, offering little stability. For these saturated individuals, social life often feels like a battlefield, a war of all against all, where identity politics become a tool to assert one's oppression through the oppression of others. As excessive identity politics rely more on moral intuitions than on rational moral deliberation, I find Moral Foundations Theory (MFT) particularly compelling in explaining the underlying tensions within these movements.

Let me first summarize MFT as it was developed by Jonathan Haidt and Craig Joseph (2004). For them, morality is both innate and learned. An intuitive ethics is an innate preparedness that human beings

> feel flashes of approval or disapproval toward certain patterns of events involving other human beings. Much of mature moral functioning is intuitive rather than deliberative and...among our moral intuitions four are innate. These four patterns are those surrounding suffering, hierarchy, reciprocity, and purity. These intuitions undergird the moral systems that cultures develop, including their understanding of virtues and character. By recognizing that, cultures build incommensurable moralities on top of a foundation of shared intuitions. (Haidt and Joseph 2004, 57)

These moral "modules" may trigger a full-fledged emotion: suffering triggers compassion; arrogant behavior by subordinates triggers contempt; cheating triggers anger; purity triggers disgust. To these four modules, they later added an ingroup module that triggers loyalty and trust toward the group's members. MTF then connects John Dewey's (1922) virtue theory which construes virtues as dynamic patterning of perception, emotion, judgment and action. Virtues in this meaning are social skills that one should develop through discipline. This virtue theory is thus a departure from theories of morality that see deliberation as the basic moral psychological activity. MFT emphasizes that a flash of intuition is not a virtue. But it is an essential tool in the construction of a virtue.

In reference to their fieldwork, Haidt and Joseph (2004) found that

> American Muslims and American political conservatives value virtues of kindness, respect for authority, fairness, and spiritual purity. American liberals, however, rely more heavily on virtues rooted in the suffering module (liberals have a much keener ability to detect victimization) and the reciprocity module (virtues of equality, rights, and fairness). For liberals, the conservative virtues of hierarchy and order seem too closely related to oppression, and the conservative virtues of purity seem to have too often been used to exclude or morally taint whole

groups (e.g., blacks, homosexuals, sexually active women). (Haidt and Joseph 2004, 58)

Beyond this outcome, whether it is generalizable or not to other countries, I found MFT very compelling in explaining how we can all get along in a morally diverse society. For Haidt and Joseph, there are two steps: the first step is simply to

> recognize that all sides in the debate are morally motivated. We tend to assume the worst about our opponents, to regard them as evils who are motivated by hatred and bigotry. [The second step is to] try to frame appeals in language that may trigger new intuitions on the other side. For example, conservatives tend to value social order and stability; a concerted effort to show that gay marriage is about order and stability, that it's about helping people to form life-long commitments that will often create stability for children, may be more effective in changing hearts and minds than the familiar arguments about rights and fairness. (Haidt and Joseph 2004, 58)

What I find particularly compelling about MFT is its insight that people with a liberal outlook tend to rely on a narrower moral template – primarily emphasizing care and fairness – whereas those on the Right incorporate all five moral foundations, including authority, group loyalty and purity. This broader moral spectrum helps explain the differences in moral reasoning between political orientations. MFT also provides a useful lens for understanding excessive identity politics and, by extension, symbolic liberalism, which operates within this narrower moral framework. This limitation tends to reinforce rigid identity categories, defining certain groups – such as refugees, migrants and LGBTQ+ individuals – as inherently vulnerable, rather than recognizing their context-specific vulnerabilities. For instance, Palestinian refugees in Lebanon face discrimination under Lebanese labor laws, but they are not inherently vulnerable in all contexts – such as when interacting with Syrian refugees. Identity politics often thrives on absolute or historical victimhood, making it less adaptable to nuanced social realities. A compelling study by Horowitz, Yaworsky and Kickham (2019) surveyed anthropologists in US graduate programs, examining their views on science, advocacy, moral and epistemic relativism and evolutionary biological explanations. Their findings reveal that political orientation, along with gender and disciplinary specialization, significantly influences anthropologists' perspectives. For example, MFT helps explain why radical-left anthropologists are particularly inclined toward advocacy for marginalized groups, often prioritizing activism over detached analysis.

In short, from a moral philosophy perspective, those who engage in excessive identity politics tend to frame pleasure and happiness – primarily at the level of the individual within an identity group – as the ultimate ethical goal, aligning them with utilitarianism and, more broadly, consequentialism. However, they also request rights based on social contract theory and deontological ethics. Their advocacy diverges from Rawlsian political liberalism, which integrates the deontological foundations of the social contract with Kantian notions of virtue.

Ann Phoenix (2023) reminds us of the critical position of the black feminist, Jennifer Nash, who advocates a move away from "the identity politics of intersectionality to a post-intersectionality *affective politics* where love...is transformative. Nash...takes an intersectional perspective on this, examining how emotions serve to produce alliances between some people, and against others."

Olivier Roy's seminal book, *L'Aplatissement du monde* [The Flattening of the World] (2022), confirms the increasing reference to "identity" in the political discourse, on both the Left and the Right. The current crisis is not a crisis of cultural change, but a crisis of the very notion of culture (or, in my vocabulary, the common good – see the next chapter on the features of the Dialogical Liberal Project). Identities are now fragmented and don't create a society but a collection of subcultures that are looking for safe spaces, either on the Left (campuses) or on the Right (from gated communities to national borders) (Roy 2022). These new identity groups seek protection by law and international conventions without taking into account how some of their rights might enter into tension with other groups.

A Hegemonic Conception of the Good

Because of their symbolic capital, some symbolic liberals – leveraging their dominance in this sphere and their ability to use legal mechanisms to shape societal norms – can impose their conception of the good onto the (republican) public sphere. In doing so, they make two errors. First, certain symbolic liberal groups present their conception of the good as a universal conception of justice, failing to distinguish between pluralistic values and normative principles. Second, their individualism is ontological – they perceive society as composed solely of individuals and their attributes, reducing it to nothing more than a sum of discrete individuals. This ontological individualism blinds them to structural and societal properties, preventing meaningful engagement with social structures that shape individual well-being. For example, family and community are often dismissed as secondary concerns, even when they play a crucial role in shaping individual flourishing. In contrast, Amartya Sen challenges this ontological individualism by advocating for ethical individualism – a perspective in which the individual remains the ultimate moral unit, but one whose capabilities and opportunities are deeply embedded in and constrained by social structures.

A prime example of this issue is the debate over Muslim headscarves in France. For many pious Muslim women, wearing a headscarf is an essential part of their conception of the good. However, banning the headscarf – whether in the name of gender equality or to uphold the principle of state neutrality in public schools – constitutes a restriction on the personal freedoms of many French Muslims, disregarding their autonomous moral and religious choices. A parallel argument applies to conservative Iranian authorities, who enforce the compulsory wearing of the headscarf as part of their state-mandated vision of the good. In both cases, the state imposes a singular conception of morality on its population, denying individuals the right to self-determination in matters that do not harm others. The headscarf is a deeply embedded religious and cultural practice – one that falls within a comprehensive doctrine of belief. As such, banning it not only violates personal liberty but also infringes upon the strong conception of freedom of religion.

While a hegemonic conception of the good can be debated in the formal public sphere, symbolic liberals – and to a lesser extent, their conservative counterparts – have increasingly shifted these debates toward legal regulations and state-imposed mandates, neglecting the informal moral accommodations that people naturally develop to navigate social tensions. A Parisian friend once shared how, in the past, when hosting a party, he would inform his neighbors in advance, acknowledging the possibility of noise beyond 10 p.m., and sometimes even invited them to join him. Today, however, the first visitors after 10 p.m. are not friendly neighbors but the police, responding to a noise complaint from someone invoking the letter of the law. This shift illustrates how tolerance, once a beautiful concept rooted in mutual understanding and social negotiation, has increasingly become a matter of dislike, disapproval, regulation and punishment. In her influential book, *Regulating Aversion: Tolerance in the Age of Identity and Empire* (2008), Wendy Brown meticulously analyzes how tolerance, rather than fostering mutual respect, often serves as a mechanism of power. It enforces norms that consolidate the dominance of the powerful, sustain the abjection of the tolerated and cast the intolerant as barbaric.[5] The erection of cultural silos, far from breaking down social divisions, may reinforce them. This identity-driven politics, where the rights of disadvantaged groups are frequently pitted against one another, risks becoming, as Brown suggests, regressive, obscuring deeper social class dynamics and perpetuating the very injustices it claims to challenge.

While ethics and law must serve as daily instruments for restraining negative emotions, some symbolic liberals – like their conservative counterparts – grant legitimacy to disgust as a basis for lawmaking, as Martha Nussbaum (2009) has critically examined. Consider the case of the "burkini" ban on French beaches. Are cultural majoritarian French citizens genuinely disgusted by the sight of the burkini? Is this why they banned it? A strikingly similar dynamic unfolded in the Muslim-majority Lebanese city of Saida, where the municipality attempted to ban bikinis on the public beach. Conservative WhatsApp groups labeled bikinis as "disgusting," while others argued that wearing them failed to respect the culture of Saida's residents. Ali Kassem (2024) examines negative reactions to the Muslim veil in Lebanon, showing how anti-Muslim racism in the country intersects with – and even mimics – European anti-Muslim racism. As Bhrigupati Singh (2024) put it: if in the Kantian dictum morality takes the form of law, in the contemporary world, majoritarian prejudice or disgust has begun to take the form of law.

Extension of the Deculturized Norms but Lack of the Common Good

Olivier Roy (2022) highlights a paradox: while individual freedoms – both political and sexual – have expanded since the 1960s, so too has an inflation of laws and regulations governing social and intimate life. These range from workplace policies and garbage sorting to rules on forms of address and health regulations. According to Roy, the very nature of the emancipation project has shifted. Initially rooted in reason, it has increasingly become driven by desire. This shift has undeniably enhanced individual liberties, particularly in advancing gender equality and bodily autonomy, encapsulated in the popular slogan: "My body is my business!" However, for Roy, this emancipatory project went too far in the direction of establishing norms while undermining what culture it used to regulate.

For Roy, the term "culture" has a variety of meanings, but all are rooted

---

[5] See her analysis of the content of the Simon Wiesenthal Center, the Los Angeles Museum of Tolerance, and how this museum manipulates the concept of tolerance by conveying the idea that the Palestinian resistance to Israeli occupation is inherently antisemitic.

in two key poles. The first is culture in the anthropological sense, referring to the shared horizon of meaning and representation specific to a society or community. The second is culture as corpus, that is, haute couture and a body of intellectual or artistic production selected and considered good to know or to practice. The former is implicit and must therefore be decoded by society itself or by the anthropologist who studies it. The latter is explicit and therefore requires selection and transmission. However, Roy argues that today, we face more than a mere crisis of culture. There is an erasure of anthropological culture – the crisis of the "implicit," or what was once a shared and unspoken culture.

For Thorsten Botz-Bornstein (2019), when creative ambiguity no longer exists, everything must be turned into an explicit code of how to speak and how to act. We end up either promoting globalized culture (international university ranking, with the standardized criteria of "academic excellence") or a very privatized culture ("be yourself!"). In the domain of aesthetics, kitsch is decultured art: "Kitsch is aesthetic excellence, and it occurs when art is not achieved through lengthy processes of cultural mediation, but when the value of an aesthetic expression (its beauty) is produced and enjoyed instantaneously." For Botz-Bornstein, Dubai represents a city of deculturation: "The city never attempted to be more than a computer-generated image and *immediately* engaged in self-abstraction, which is the most radical act of deculturation." I would nuance this because this city has developed its own sense of culture in some areas. Then, he argues, cultural values have been linked by symbolic liberals "to old authoritarian structures and need to be abandoned. Ethical scruples derived from concrete cultures are declared arbitrary because they are 'merely' historically determined. True ethics must be decultured" (Botz-Bornstein 2019, 10).

Identity politics, victimhood and trauma have become highly significant, alongside attempts to judicialize them. For Roy, this normativity lacks the axiological purpose of the good. A norm without value but with a price to pay – this is the paradox of neoliberalism. Classic examples include suing a transportation company for a minor delay, despite no major disruption, or using medical language to describe criticism as injury, then seeking reparation. Litigation has replaced what was once a negotiation between social actors, aimed at achieving fluid, reasonable accommodations that account for the culture of human relationships. The concept of "diversity, equity and inclusion" (DEI) has evolved into a multi-billion-dollar industry involving bureaucrats, trainers and lawyers. Historically, individuals with specific food allergies would inform staff directly. However, in the UK, the responsibility has shifted by law to staff, who are now required to ask every customer about allergies. Litigation has become part of a broader process of control, discipline and surveillance, where accountability extends not only to the state but also across a plethora of bureaucratic entities.

The work of Béatrice Hibou (2012) is particularly insightful, with her notion of neoliberal bureaucracy, which is a vector of discipline and control – of continuously filling forms, producing social and political indifference. Under the pretext of depoliticization, this bureaucracy cannot hide the exercise of normalizing power. Operating as it does through individuals, bureaucratization does not come "from above." It is a much wider process of "bureaucratic participation," a response to the need to voice material and vested interests and give answers to legitimate demands, as well as expressing the quest for efficiency; but it also reflects day-to-day conflicts and negotiations between actors.[6]

Tension between Morality and Codified Norms

The salient problem with symbolic liberalism is that it prioritizes rights and law over the moral deliberations people once used in their daily lives. Carole Smith (2002) rightly criticizes British sociologist Anthony Giddens, who views late modernity as a time of moral renewal. For Smith, it is actually a time of invoking rights in the governance of human affairs – what she calls "rights talk" – which has come to dominate moral thinking and leads to the sequestration of morality in late modernity. Smith contrasts this with what Giddens terms the "sequestration of experience," meaning the removal of experiences and events from social life that require our *moral* attention.

While moral thinking and action require direct engagement – empathy, commitment and a concern for the well-being of others – the rhetoric of rights "polarizes debate; it tends to suppress moral discussion and consensus building. Once an agenda is introduced as 'Right,' sensible discussion and moderate positions tend to disappear" (Mary Ann Glendon, cited by Gergen 1997, 4), or worse, it uses medicalized language to call for reparation. For Zygmunt Bauman (1993), as morality is *ungovernable*, society transforms it into an ordered assembly of codified norms, laws and contractual exchanges. Although the identification of legal rights may stem from the importance of moral rights, legal codes cease to require moral justification. As the antipathy to moral thinking, this process relinquishes responsibility to the state and replaces moral struggle with

[6] In the same vein, one should take notice of the work of David Graeber (2016) about endless bureaucracy and frustrating administrative tasks in relation to finance, healthcare or almost everything else.

the seductive certainty of ethical codes (subject to surveillance and compliance), encouraging moral indifference. Some Islamic theologians (e.g., Khan 2019) advocate for the Ethics of *Ihsan* – doing good for others without being obligated to do so. Similar ethics can likely be found in other religions and local communities.

Conclusion

As a result of the dynamics described above, the formal public sphere, colonized by symbolic liberalism, will be contested wherever it exists, forcing societal groups that feel marginalized and lack access to it to create an alternative public sphere. This alternative sphere takes the form of a collective or communitarian project in liberal states (such as communities of ecological colonies, migrants, religious groups, far-Right factions, etc.) and a virtual community in authoritarian states. During the Arab Spring, for instance, young people engaged in their own debates on social, cultural and political issues. This new sphere will prioritize cooperation between communitarian actors through moral accommodation rather than through formal laws (Figure 2.1).

All of this reinforces the polarization between symbolic liberals and their opponents. It is interesting to note that France, which champions an assimilative policy for migrants, has ended up creating a communitarian life for those who resist symbolic liberalism's cultural majoritarianism, a point that will be discussed in detail regarding French exclusionary secularism in Chapter 5. In the climate of victimized identity politics, with each identity group seeking a safe space, this generates a society with multiple separated silos. Now, any minor conflict between two individuals with a hierarchy between them may result in one refusing to meet without the presence of a third party. Last year, a male graduate student in my department complained to the Department Chair about the criticism he received from his supervisor, a newly recruited female faculty member. When she kindly asked him to meet, he refused to come to her office and requested a "safe space" for the meeting.

As symbolic liberals have deflated the concept of social justice, becoming the primary beneficiaries of the very inequalities they condemn, they also distort the discourse of intersectionality, disconnecting individuals and society from the underlying nature of these issues, even when aware of current climate change and environmental catastrophe. Their neoliberal approach has failed to seriously address ecological emergencies. All of this is closely tied to how symbolic liberals approach social justice beyond and below

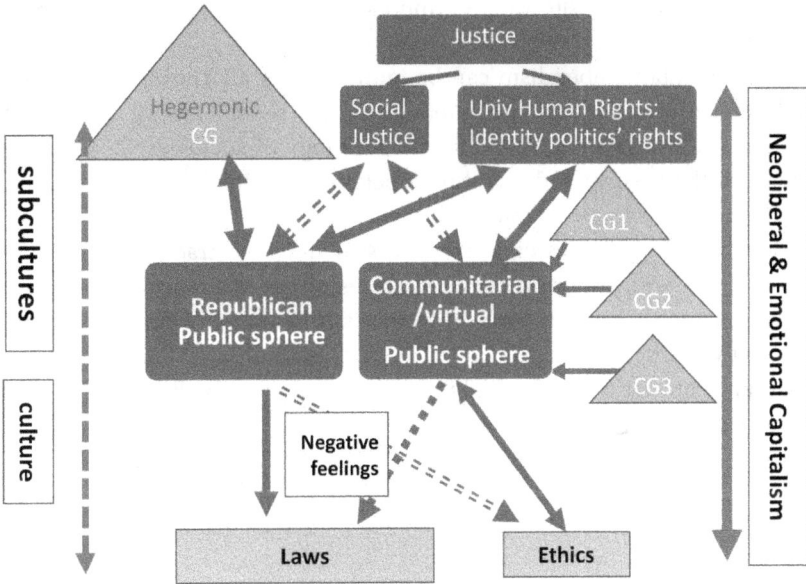

Figure 2.1 Symbolic liberalism
CG = Conception of the good

the nation-state, particularly at the communitarian level or in addressing global social inequalities.

Symbolic liberals also inflate the concept of the universality of human rights, viewing them not as abstract but as concrete, for example, insisting on the same laws across all countries, with little regard for local cultures where these laws are implemented. "Rights talk" becomes the hegemonic paradigm for victim-oriented, excessive identity politics. Using the Moral Foundation Theory approach, I argue that symbolic liberals, by privileging a narrow moral template (fairness and care), fail to understand the moral deliberations of people who often prioritize purity and loyalty alongside these two intuitions.

Finally, and more gravely, as a consequence of the above, symbolic liberals impose a hegemonic conception of the good on others, clearly violating the principle of pluralism in political liberalism. By doing so, symbolic liberals not only extend deculturized norms (which are culturally specific to the hegemonic group) but also marginalize shared culture or the common good. This has created incommensurable tensions between morality (how people resolve conflicts when different conceptions of the good clash) and codified norms (the privileged site where symbolic liberals impose their conception of the good).

While symbolic liberalism can be found among all knowledge economy producers, my critique of the symbolic liberal strand among sociologists is twofold: it serves as both a political sociology of sociology (how politics influences their work) and a cultural sociology of sociology (how changing cultural contexts impact their work).

How all these processes operate is still quite abstract. The following four chapters will explore the consequences of the symbolic liberal agenda in four areas: societal intolerance, secularism, sexual and gender identities and family authority (Chapters 4–7). In contrast to this symbolic liberalism, I will advocate for a Dialogical Liberal Project, which will be the focus of the next chapter.

CHAPTER 3

Dialogical Liberal Project

Introduction

As I have unpacked before, the symbolic liberal project itself contributes to the pathologies of late modernity. These pathologies are not only about authoritarianism and populism, increased inequality, precarity, and exclusion, or climate change and ecological crisis. If modernity was once defined by taming our violence (Elias 2000), it has lately become a form of violent *control over passions*, ultimately leading to the creation of the "individual without passions" (Spini 2021). But can we have care without passion? In fact, instrumental rationality, rules, laws and rights-based identity politics have induced multiple crises, which we are witnessing now. This requires rethinking our normativity to establish what I call a Dialogical Political Liberal Project, which echoes Dialogical Sociology.

The first step in the Dialogical Political Liberal Project is recognizing that our liberal democracy, influenced by neoliberalism, emotional capitalism and the threat of populism, is in crisis. What Francis Fukuyama (1989) described as "the end of history," with the triumph of liberalism in the form of Western political democracy, has been upended – not by populists, conservatives or dictators, but from within its own ranks: liberalism has become its own worst enemy.

Being dialogical means engaging all sectors, from urban planners who will reorganize cities to enable different socio-economic classes and cultural groups to coexist, to social scientists, journalists and artists who will foster spaces where these groups can meet. While the agenda is broad, I focus on sociology – my mother's discipline – and my conversations with sociologists around the globe through my various roles in the International Sociological Association. After outlining what I mean by Dialogical Sociology, I will define key features of the Dialogical Liberal Project, highlighting some implications for addressing intolerable social inequalities. Further implications regarding the plurality of conceptions of the good will be explored in the following chapters in Part II.

Dialogical Sociology

Dialogical Sociology draws upon a wide variety of works carried out by many sociologists and social theorists, but I will highlight some works that are particularly important.

First, Michael Burawoy's "Public Sociology" (2005) defines the role of sociology as standing with civil society against the domination of both the state and the market. Later, in *Public Sociology: Between Utopia and Anti-Utopia* (2021), Burawoy aligns Erik Olin Wright's project with his own public sociology, framing it as a moral or normative science that advocates for certain values to be realized (the utopian side) and examines how these realizations are obstructed (the anti-utopian side). This concept of public sociology was further enriched by South Africa's idea of "critical engagement" (Bezuidenhout, Mnwana and Holdt 2022).

Second, *The Dialogic Society* (2022) by Ramón Flecha and *Achieving Social Impact* (2017) by Marta Soler Gallart, present compelling concepts developed with their research team within the Community of Research on Excellence for All (CREA) at the University of Barcelona. They view the social impact of scientific research as essential for the realization of a vibrant liberal democracy. By linking three realms – ethics, truth and aesthetics – they integrate sociology with moral philosophy and establish a communicative methodology for research. According to Flecha, the dialogic society should unite the beauty of the arts, the truth of science and the goodness of human rights, recognizing how these elements are intertwined:

> Without science there are no human rights; the rights to health, to education, and all the others can only be real with the contribution of scientific discoveries. Without human rights, science has strict limitations. The benefits of the discoveries do not reach everybody, they do not reach those excluded from human rights. (Flecha 2022, 79)

Along with Flecha, Soler Gallart (2017) develops insightful ideas on how to address Habermasian rationalistic public sphere deliberation regarding validity claims. She identifies

> three limitations that are overcome by using the concept of dialogic relationships, which includes (a) placing claims in social structure, (b)

considering the ethics of responsibility and (c) accounting for both feelings and desires in the analyses. (Soler Gallart 2017, 34)

Third, Dialogical Sociology is grounded in the work of the convivialist movement, developed by scholars such as Alain Caillé, Frédéric Vandenberghe, François Gauthier, and others, in opposition to individualistic political liberalism and the politics of ressentiment. It rehabilitates care and the Maussian logic of the Gift (Caillé 2015).[1] Dialogical Sociology also connects to Gennaro Iorio's and Silvia Cataldi's conceptions of social love (Iorio 2016; Cataldi 2020), Hartmut Rosa's (2019) notion of resonance and relational well-being, and Eva Illouz's (2007) critique of emotional capitalism.

Beyond the Euro-American sphere, Dialogical Sociology is also inspired by the work of some Chinese scholars. The Chinese philosopher and leading intellectual, Tingyang Zhao, wrote *All Under Heaven: The Tianxia System for a Possible World Order* (2021), based on Confucian thought that could improve the global liberal order and its democratic system. For Zhao, the conceptual Tianxia system of "all under heaven," which was practiced during the Han Dynasty (220–202 BCE), should envision an all-inclusive world of "no outside" with a "great harmony" of all peoples, or the "compatibility" of all civilizations. Echoing Fadi Lama's comparison of Chinese expeditions between 1405 and 1433, which visited Arabia, Brunei, East Africa, India, the Malay Archipelago and Thailand, with the Portuguese occupation of some of these areas, we see the effect of Tianxia: "Chinese expeditions brought back to the imperial court ambassadors and dignitaries in lieu of slaves. Chinese expeditions gifted gold and silver to foreign rulers instead of killing them to steal their gold and silver" (Lama 2023, 146). For Zhao, it is an open question why China began its politics with a concept of a systematic world like Tianxia, while Greece had a state as polis – two of the most significant starting points of politics. More than a world system, Tianxia suggests an alternative concept of the political, as a methodology or the art of changing hostility into hospitality, as opposed to Carl Schmitt's recognition of the enemy, Marxist class struggle, Hans Morgenthau's struggle for power or Huntington's clash of civilizations. Zhao's renewed conception of Tianxia claims three *constitutional* concepts: (1) *internalization of the world*, a shared universal system inclusive of all nations, eliminating negative externalities;

[1] Refer to the Second Manifesto of the Convivialist International (2020), co-signed by nearly 300 intellectuals from 33 countries and various disciplines. The manifesto outlines five key principles: common naturalness, common humanity, common sociality, legitimate individuation and creative opposition – the idea of opposing one another without resorting to violence.

(2) *relational rationality*, which prioritizes *mutual minimization of hostility* over maximization of exclusive interests;[2] and (3) *Confucian improvement*, which is a non-exclusive improvement for everyone, better than Pareto's improvement, and defined by the principle that *one improves if and only if all others improve*. Confucian improvement means *everyone* receives Pareto's improvement if anyone does.[3]

Finally, Dialogical Sociology builds on work from the Arab world, particularly over the last 15 years following the Arab uprisings, on how liberal values can be accommodated in non-liberal states. There have been attempts to rethink liberalism in the Arab context, such as those by Mounir Kchaou, an Arab philosopher whose Ph.D. thesis focused on John Rawls and who has written extensively on liberalism (Kchaou 2007; 2016; 2023; 2024a). The Palestinian philosopher Azmi Bishara, particularly in his reflections on the state and public morality, examines how the Arab Spring conflates state institutions with political regimes as part of his broader project on civil society, democracy, secularism, sectarianism and the Arab uprisings – all approached from a critical liberal perspective (Bishara 2021; 2023a–c; 2024). Abdelwahab El-Affendi (2003) questions the prioritization of religious reformation over political reformation. Elizabeth Suzanne Kassab (2009) analyzes transformations in Arab cultural and political debates concerning cultural malaise, identity and authenticity, linking them to postcolonial issues in Latin America and Africa. She highlights the shared struggles of these regions and argues that Arab uprising activists pursued political enlightenment without intellectual enlightenment (Kassab 2019). Notably, these four scholars are affiliated with the Arab Center for Research and Policy Studies and its Doha Institute for Graduate Studies. Both institutions serve as research hubs for outstanding Arab scholars with diverse political, ideological and religious perspectives – unlike many other research centers in the Arab world, which often promote a single political or ideological stance.

Where does the Dialogical Political Liberal Project sit in relation to this literature? My intention for sociology to be dialogical is to disentangle its commitment to civil society into two levels: the level of mediation or soft normativity and the level of strong normativity.

---

[2]   In *The Ontology of Coexistence: From Cogito to Facio*, Zhao (2012) challenges Descartes' *Cogito* and instead proposes *Facio* ("to be is to do"). He emphasizes "relational rationality" as a key theoretical framework for transforming human coexistence, arguing that coexistence takes precedence over individual existence. This foundation allows him to assert that coexistence precedes existence and that human obligations should take priority over human rights.
[3]   See my interview with Zhao Tingyan (Hanafi and Zhao 2024).

Level of Mediation

On the level of *mediation,* sociology provides scientific research that is important for public deliberation and for social movements which are carried out mainly by different groups in civil society, whether progressives or conservatives. It entails the possibility of providing knowledge to governments or organizations that we don't agree with, at least all the time. Thus, I would like to extend the sociological mission beyond civil society, to the civil *sphere* in Jeffrey Alexander's sense (2008). Alexander reminds us that civil society is only one sphere among others within a broader social system, into which the family, religious groups, scientific and corporate associations, and geographically bounded regional communities should be incorporated, as they all produce goods and organize their social relations according to different ideals and constraints. This extension of our mission is very important if we are to keep seeing ourselves as guardians of this civil sphere and liberal democratic ideals.

This scientific knowledge informs the majority by the reasoning of the minority and, to a lesser extent, the reverse. However, this should not be understood as sociologists acting like Plato's philosopher, who emerges from the cave to reveal a deeper reality beyond the shadows perceived by the captives. Instead, in the communicative methodology of Flecha and Soler, research should involve an *egalitarian dialogue* between researchers and participants from the outset, aiming to mitigate potential power dynamics.[4]

In order to mediate, Dialogical Sociology needs to be close to the public, not only in understanding how they establish their rational arguments, but also their emotions that often impact moral reasoning. It is therefore important to understand the emotions of the other, which can take the form of moral sensitivity – that is, positive social feelings such as compassion, care, friendship and benevolence, all feelings that play a decisive role in the ethical process of mutual recognition. Or the moral enervation of the other, sometimes making them blind to social suffering. Having worked for a long time on Palestinian and Syrian refugee issues, I have observed how some people are committed to donating to refugees yet refuse to accept them into their country, region or community when they arrive at the

---

[4] In the Community of Research on Excellence for All (CREA), where this methodology was developed, power dynamics are being replaced by dialogic interactions to foster consensus. For example, in a case study on the Roma people in Spain, researchers not only incorporate Roma voices into the study but also actively engage with them in reflecting on and interpreting the knowledge provided by the scientific community.

border – a dilemma Luc Boltanski (1999) terms "suffering at a distance." Emotions, like morality, both bind and blind. Sociological knowledge offers mediation resources to complement others, such as Paul Ricœur's supra-ethical approach, like Christian charity, or infra-ethical approach, like love (Kandil 2020).

Mediation must respect what is understood as universal social justice, including the *Universal Declaration of Human Rights* and social welfare rights. Here, universality is conceived abstractly, while universal social justice is instantiated concretely through culture and history within a given society. This aligns with Habermas's communicative theory, which holds that universalist normative ethics cannot be justified by an appeal to purposive or means–end rationality. Thus, this level entails *soft* normativity. It is akin to Nathalie Heinich's (2004) call to move from a normative to a descriptive theory (in critique of Bourdieu's "critical sociology"), although she does not uphold this stance in her more recent public interventions (e.g., as a co-founder of the Observatory of Decolonialism) (see Chapter 4).

Level of Strong Normativity

The second level is *strong normativity* where sociology not only engages with civil society but also takes a position in favor of marginalized groups against hegemonic powers and defends certain values dear to sociology. Sociology, as an emancipatory science, believes in social change and wants to advocate for a more just world in each nation-state and globally. This entails the possibility of actively participating in social movements and even revolutions when the system cannot be changed from the inside. This level, where critique is privileged, requires what Jana Bacevic (2024) formulated as "establishing distance from our object of knowledge, which enables us to perceive the world as something other than natural or 'given.'"

The current ISA president Geoffrey Pleyers clearly articulated this connection to make "a collective project that combines researchers' and actors' reflexivities in a common quest to a better understanding of social movements, our world and how to transform it" (Pleyers 2024). It is co-constructions of the observer and the observed. Yet the division of labor is more complex than researchers who co-provide theory while activists provide the political dimension. In our research, there is a political sense, but not in the technical meaning of policy. For example, Gennaro Iorio and Silvia Cataldi and their team set a social love index in order to understand how and to what extent people are generous with others, conceptualized as social love, agape, gift and how and when they are not. This is the first level:

the level of providing descriptive knowledge important to mediation. But then they engage in cases where social love is expressed, like paying for a cup of coffee for someone who cannot afford it. Their "politics" is to show researchers that the world has plenty of instances where social relationships are not commodified and to tell people that happiness and well-being are not individual but collective. This is sometimes where I get bored when we miss this "social theory" moment in sociological research, or when the social sciences here describe and criticize social life, but do not aim to intellectually construct a more meaningful framework for society (Dubet 2020).

Having said that, this strong normativity always requires justifications. Tariq Modood is right in his definition of what he labels "Normative Sociology" as a sociology that not only deploys normative ideas but also justifies them. In the process of justification, again, sociology should be a good listener (and debater) of how social actors form justifications about issues in debates (Modood 2022a).

I worry when sociology analytically conflates the two levels, or, worse, neglects the first level and becomes incapable of engaging with all strata of society. For instance, forms of anti-clerical or symbolic liberal sociology have become incapable of engaging with religious communities in the Arab world and, I am sure, elsewhere also. Conflating the two levels means no distinction between scientific knowledge/critical thinking and position-taking or policy formulation – or, in the vocabulary of Ghassan Hage (2013), between the critical (academic) and radical (political). Wendy Brown (2002) reminds us of Foucault's response to an interviewer who asked whether he wrote *The Use of Pleasure* and *Techniques of the Self* for the liberation movement. "Not for," replied Foucault steadily, "but *in terms of*, a contemporary situation." For Brown,

> The difference between "for" and "in terms of" is critical: it indicates whether intellectual life will be submitted to existing political discourses and the formulation of immediate political needs [that those discourses pronounce, or whether it] will be allowed the air of independence that it must have in order to be of value *as* intellectual work for political life. (Brown 2002, 389)

Dialogical Sociology should play a salient role in guiding the Dialogical Political Liberal Project, which I will share in the following section to develop some features of this project.

Features of the Dialogical Liberal Project

The Dialogical Political Liberal Project is defined by five key features that outline its framework and the transition from the dominance of symbolic liberals to a more inclusive model: 1. the primacy of justice over the good; 2. a serious commitment to addressing the ecological crisis; 3. the enhancement of spaces for dialogue; 4. factoring in the power from above and below; 5. abstract versus concrete universality.

The Primacy of the Just Over the Good

There is an issue of how to reinforce a unified conception of justice while still allowing space for pluralistic conceptions of the good, and, at times, how to reconcile competing visions of the good with the interests of the common good.

By positing the primacy of the just over the good, the Dialogical Political Liberal Project revitalizes social justice through a stronger commitment to social class analysis – or at least to the economic foundations of social exclusion – and places it at the center of any intersectional analysis. Naturally, this approach will be context-sensitive, but it can begin with a focus on social class (i.e., class as the starting point, followed by race, ethnicity or gender). A prime example of such an analysis can be found in the work of Jeffrey Karam and Rima Majed (2022), who examine Lebanon's October 2019 revolution (*thawra*), where hundreds of thousands took to the streets to protest austerity measures. Rima Majed's (2022) work is particularly insightful in exploring the intersectionality of social class and sectarianism within the consociational regimes of Lebanon and Iraq, while introducing the concept of "sectarian neoliberalism."

Symbolic liberals tend to conceive social justice in terms of a disconnection between the social and the economic spheres. However, in line with the cultural political economy approach, social justice can only be fully understood through the social embeddedness of the economy. Karl Polanyi (1983 [1944]) outlined three forms of integrating society into the economy: *exchange, redistribution,* and *reciprocity.* The market, as a space of exchange, must be subject to state control and moral oversight from civil society to curb speculation and excess. Redistribution, in turn, cannot be effectively achieved without substantial measures to prevent the concentration of wealth in the hands of a few corporations in each sector,[5] as well

---

[5] According to Geoffrey Pleyers (2020), "the level of global inequalities is such that the 'top 1%' and global corporations have major political power [on a] national and global scale."

as the implementation of heavy taxation on high levels of capital and wealth, while also fostering a slow-growth economy. In this context, it's fascinating to observe similar issues, albeit in varying degrees, across both the Global South and the Global North. For instance, Louis Chauvel's (2023) sociology of social stratification highlights that "occupational classes" in the West cannot be fully understood without considering the context of wealth-based domination. This is echoed in Chunling Li's (2023) analysis of "wealtherization," driven by housing wealth inequality in China, despite the relatively higher importance of the rural population in China compared to Western nations.[6] Yet, significant differences persist. China, for example, stands out, with home-ownership rates above 90 percent in many cities (Dreyer 2024). Regarding *reciprocity*, society integrates into the economy because not all relationships can or should be commodified. The Maussian gift relationship and the moral obligation of reciprocity are crucial for fostering social cohesion and ensuring that resources are preserved for future generations. There's much to unpack here.

Rawls provided us with a framework for working with his two principles of justice – the Principle of Basic Liberties (or Strict Egalitarian Principle) and the Difference Principle – with a stronger emphasis on the former, given his focus on individual liberties. While the task of applying these principles is left to social scientists, it is clear that social inequalities have reached intolerable levels across the globe, both in the Global North and the Global South. In this context, I will highlight some "real utopias," as Erik Olin Wright (2010) would call them, that offer practical visions for addressing these inequalities.

The Universal/Unconditional Basic Income (UBI) is gaining increasing support, not only among social scientists (e.g., Piketty 2014; Chandler 2023; Caillé 2015), but also among some politicians.[7] But how should it be conceived – as an entitlement or as charity? Catarina Neves (2023) emphasizes that "different framings of a *UBI* yield different moral and political justifications, with important implications for the debate on *UBI* in terms of democratic–economic expectations of reciprocity." She echoes Alain Caillé's concept of UBI as a form of "conditional unconditionality,"

---

[6] I found it refreshing that this comparativist approach gained new momentum with the rise of numerous works by post-Western sociologies, particularly on the sociology of BRICS (Brazil, Russia, India, China and South Africa) and its newly joined members – Egypt, Ethiopia, Iran, Saudi Arabia and the United Arab Emirates. These studies have highlighted the formation of new East–South assemblages that transcend the traditional North–South dichotomy (see, for instance, Li, Gorshkov, and Scalon 2013).

[7] See, for instance, many political and business personalities who endorse basic income. www.ubi.org.

where unconditional cash transfers can provoke feelings of indebtedness and gratitude, which in turn foster a moral obligation to reciprocate the UBI received. A similar psychological tension arises with refugees who receive financial and other forms of assistance. By framing UBI in this way, we could reassert the socio-democratic welfare system and challenge the stigma that often associates welfare with degradation (as seen in some studies where middle-class people have used such terms). Interestingly, those who benefit from UBI often include individuals performing difficult manual labor and those with higher fertility rates, both of whom contribute to society's labor force – particularly in Western countries and China. In this sense, the reciprocity is already there.

How can we fund UBI, as well as affordable education and healthcare for marginalized populations? I believe this is unlikely to be achievable with the current concentration of wealth and power in the hands of a few (as discussed in the Introduction). The central challenge lies in how neoliberalism has elevated private property to an absolute, unconditional right. While I believe in the right to private property, we must address its excesses by taxing inherited assets (Piketty 2014) and promoting a solidarity economy, such as cooperatives, or what Milbank and Pabst (2016) refer to as the "civil economy." One compelling example is the Mondragon cooperative, which employed over 81,000 people in 2019 and is considered by some studies to be "the most dialogic group of successful companies worldwide" (Flecha 2022, 37). Other examples include the participatory budget in Porto Alegre, Brazil (which has served as a model for many municipalities), and, of course, Wikipedia.

This does not go far enough, but I will leave it to my colleagues to pursue these ideas further. These are simply examples and each country gives priority to specific areas of intervention in order to mitigate social inequalities.

A Serious Commitment to Addressing the Ecological Crisis

The struggle for the environment is deeply intertwined with our conception of justice, particularly in its relation to political economy, and the type of economic system we aspire to create – and these connections between human beings and nature have never been more intimate than they are today. In recent decades, rapid growth was based on the assumption that the costs of raw materials and energy would remain stable in the long term. However, this assumption is no longer valid. Financial speculation has intensified, profits have dwindled and distributional conflicts have arisen between workers, management, owners and tax authorities. Despite these challenges, we cannot conceive of a society independent of its relationship with nature – what Vandana Shiva (1993) calls "Eco-Apartheid": society is indeed society–nature.

As part of a broader conception of justice, we must transition to a slow-growth economy, along with its necessary corollaries: the development of affordable, low-carbon public transportation, viewing public services as investments rather than liabilities and enhancing labor market security. Many scholars point to Japan as an example, where a slow-down phase is underway, and people are no less happy than before (Dreyer 2024).

Yet, part of the concept of the good is allowing people to envision their *buen vivir* ("good living" or "living well"), as conceptualized by Uruguayan scholar Eduardo Gudynas (2011). This concept emphasizes harmony, among human beings and between humans and nature. A related idea is the sense of the "common good." Gudynas has long inspired social movements across South America. What is crucial here is how we can rehabilitate the idea of common space and address what impedes the sustainability of our development, such as excessive carbon footprints and consumerism. These issues should not be part of the conception of the good but they should be moved up to be part of Environmental Justice. This requires societal agreement and heightened awareness of the ethics of sustainability, which pertains to human beliefs and behaviors regarding environmental conser-vation and the health of Earth's ecosystems.

In this context, Frank Adloff (2023) raises a critical question: Can sociology continue to focus solely on human relations? His comprehensive review of scholars challenging the division between humans and other living beings – referred to as "non-humans" – suggests that this epistemological division is no longer sustainable. A multi-species theory, drawing from Marcel Mauss's concept of the gift relationship, is now needed.

The Enhancement of Spaces for Dialogue

The dialogue in the Dialogical Political Liberal Project is not about discussion forums where we bring opposing views in order to mitigate differences and enhance commonality. This definitely will be with limited efficiency. Dialogue starts from the re-organization of the cities and habitats to overcome current urban segregation. We need a city that is not composed of gated communities and slums but a habitat that accommodates different socio-economic social classes and cultural groups to live together. It is interesting to note that the first speech of Labour leader Keir Starmer when he became UK Prime

Minister in July 2024 was to talk about the crisis of housing and the necessity to improve social housing. Traveling to different cities in Algeria, I noticed the importance of social housing, and maybe this is the best reminder of its socialist era. Dialogue is not only of the head but also of the heart, and everyday encounters are best conducted through common spaces, including public schools and affordable entertainment spaces for all social classes.

Cultural productions may be uniquely suited to creating spaces for dialogue. At the outset of the Syrian revolution against the tyrannical regime, social media was flooded with short documentary films on YouTube and TikTok, portraying scenes in support either of the revolution or the regime. However, in 2013, Abounaddara, a collective of anonymous filmmakers, began producing films depicting the everyday lives of Syrians without reference to the political struggle.[8] Watching their films was initially shocking to me due to their reluctance to engage with the Syrian political revolutionary project. Yet, upon reflection, I realized that in the highly polarized Syrian media landscape, Abounaddara's films serve as a dialogical space *par excellence*, allowing Syrians to reflect on their shared experiences despite their differing political commitments

As I mentioned in the previous chapter, symbolic liberals disregard the common good and completely privatize the good, reducing it to the individual level. In fact, the Dialogical Political Liberal Project rehabilitates the common good and considers common spaces where people live as part of it. In addition to Oliver Roy's reflection on the shared culture (see Chapter 2), I would consider the common good as an ethical dimension of the good. Here I will use Paul Ricœur's distinction between ethics and morals. For Ricœur, the ethical prescriptions are teleological (the desire for a good life with and for others), while moral prescriptions are deontological (related to the rules and principles at the basis of just institutions).

The concept of the common good should not be used to justify the invocation of the "values of the republic," which are often framed in opposition to migrants' lifestyles. This idea is similar to how Jean-Claude Michéa (2018) and George Orwell (2020 [1938]) conceptualize "common decency" – a notion often adopted by the lower strata of society – which is understood as loyalty to a society/community, provided that this loyalty does not undermine a shared conception of justice and allows for the possibility of a plurality of conceptions of the good.

---

[8] This collective produced around 300 short films between 2010 to 2017, broadcast online. The shorts (plus two feature films) are available to view on Abounaddara's Vimeo pages. http://vimeo.com/user6924378.

Factoring in the Power from Above and Below

Critiquing symbolic liberals for their hegemonic conception of the good and their role as symbolic capitalists – uninterested in taking social justice seriously – cannot be done without addressing power structures. The Dialogical Liberal Project is attentive not only to culture but also to power. In this regard, Marta Soler Gallart (2017) strengthens Habermas's communicative action theory by explicitly incorporating the dimension of power and a feminist perspective. She distinguishes between dialogical communicative acts and power communicative acts, emphasizing that dialogue extends beyond words to include body language, such as gestures, looks, and caresses.

Deliberations in the public sphere aimed at overcoming cultural hegemony and rampant social inequalities are meaningless without a certain balance of power between opponents and the inclusion of all voices in the conversation. In most cases, this balance is unattainable without the formation of social movements. This underscores the significance of movements such as the protests in France against the new retirement law, the Tunisian movement opposing President Qais Saeed's authoritarianism, and the US Black Lives Matter movement. In some cases, revolution – defined as an attempt to change the political system from outside its norms (Bishara 2021) – becomes necessary, particularly in the face of prolonged, brutalizing despotic regimes, as seen in Syria and Myanmar.[9]

In order to factor in the power from above and below, there is much to unpack. I will address this through five key points.

First, before discussing revolutions, the Dialogical Liberal Project should focus on improving political representation, with an emphasis on political equality. I would also incorporate, drawing from Black American philosopher Danielle Allen's *Justice by Means of Democracy* (2023), the shift from meritocratic liberalism to *power-sharing* liberalism. As I write, a few billionaires are influencing the US electoral campaign, with mainstream media largely controlled by them.

The Democracy Voucher Program in Seattle offers a new way to encourage residents to participate in local government politics by supporting campaigns and/or running for office themselves. Since 2015, the Seattle Ethics and Elections Commission (SEEC) has distributed "democracy vouchers" to

---

[9]   Revolutions can be either violent or nonviolent. Notably, many uprisings during the Arab Spring were largely nonviolent. In *Philosophy of Nonviolence* (2015), Chibli Mallat highlights this aspect, emphasizing the crucial role of both nonviolence and constitutionalism in the pursuit and establishment of justice.

eligible Seattle residents. Other campaign reforms include campaign contribution limits for lobbyists and contractors.[10] Evaluating this program and the result of the Seatle election of 2021, Heerwig and McCabe (2022) show that six of the eight general election candidates funded their campaigns with democracy vouchers. Participation in the program increased across all demographic groups. Relative to 2017, some of the largest percentage gains in participation were concentrated among people of color, and younger and lower-income residents. The experience of Seattle deserves to become more the norm.

In many countries today, one of the fears expressed by the population concerns migrants and refugees, represented in the mainstream media as the real threat to the welfare of their citizens and to their national identity. There is no way to get out of this fear without addressing the question of who owns these media.

Other ideas for addressing the current concentration of power include ensuring gender parity among candidates and setting stricter criteria for eligibility. For example, candidates should present an electoral program endorsed by a group that includes members with relevant scientific expertise. The aim is to introduce mechanisms for controlling the populist rhetoric of political parties. For instance, during this year's legislative election in France, Marine Le Pen, leader of the National Rally, repeatedly claimed that migrants were responsible for drug trafficking, a statement contradicted by official drug crime statistics. This doesn't propose legal action against Le Pen but rather the creation of a mechanism that would force her to correct factual errors in her program and speeches. Further discussion on this will follow in the next point.

Second, Foucault reminds us of the nexus between knowledge and power. Criticism generates conflicting opinions, often driven by intuitions (particularly loyalty and purity), emotions and social media. To address this, the Dialogical Liberal Project must enhance knowledge-based opinion by introducing, among other measures, more public assemblies and forums where different stakeholders and scientists can engage. I support mixed forums that include scientists alongside representatives of unions and civil society organizations. While such forums exist in democratic countries, their composition is often politically homogeneous. As a former sociologist of migration, I offer a pressing example from Europe and the Middle

---

[10] Seattle voters approved a property tax of $3 million per year in 2015 to fund the Democracy Voucher Program for ten years. The Democracy Voucher Program costs the average homeowner about $8 per year. See www.seattle.gov/democracyvoucher/about-the-program.

East, regions I have observed closely. Rarely do forums present both the benefits and challenges of hosting refugees and migrants while linking these discussions to labor market dynamics. Symbolic liberals frequently impose their ethical choices (which, as a humanist and former refugee, I often appreciate) and their policy implications without facilitating serious mixed forums. Even on university campuses, critical issues remain undebated, and key stakeholders are absent. A well-structured commission would encourage consideration of public policy consequences not only in the short term but also in the long term. Some committee members should be historians to provide insights from a *longue durée* perspective.

The Left/Right divide is evident among social actors and the public. However, committee composition should also consider other factors, such as profession, age, income, gender, religion and media consumption habits. In short, the ways individuals interpret and respond to stimuli from the media-political system appear to be socially structured. While these factors help distinguish differences between groups of citizens, they are insufficient to fully explain individual expressions in conversation. To move beyond classical social determinism, participants must also be understood through their emotional lives and values (Meter and Pagès 2023).

Third, another crucial area of power to address is workplace democracy. According to Elisabeth Anderson (2019), one in four American workers describes their workplace as a "dictatorship." Employers tightly control workers' speech, clothing and behavior, leaving them with little privacy and few rights. This authority often extends beyond the workplace, as workers can be fired for their political speech, recreational activities or even dietary choices. Even the European Human Rights Court has permitted employers to dismiss veiled employees without justification.

In the 1930s, corporations transitioned from shareholder ownership to managerial control, shifting from being managed by their owners to being run by a managerial class (Berle and Means 1932). However, despite discussions and advocacy – particularly by trade, industry and enterprise unions – worker representatives were still excluded from decision-making. Should we seek an intermediary position between managerial control and the more radical option proposed by anarcho-syndicalists and worker control movements, who advocate for workers to take over enterprises and form cooperatives? Mondragon is just one example, alongside the worker cooperative movement in England led by the late MP Tony Benn, as well as cooperatives in former Yugoslavia and the early Israeli kibbutzim. Even today, the French government continues to fund a significant cooperative sector. Notably, there is a distinction between consumer cooperatives and producer cooperatives, the latter of which have been severely weakened and prevented from becoming significant under the pressures of hyper-individualism (Jureidini 1979).

Fourth, power is not solely a top-down project dependent on liberal institutional arrangements, as Rawls heavily emphasizes, nor is it a zero-sum game. It also involves how bottom-up initiatives can counterbalance and reshape power dynamics. This includes revitalizing the fluidity of moral argumentation in society, as well as the ways individuals and communities practice Montesquieu's *doux commerce* in their daily interactions and cultivate strong, supportive neighborhoods. Loving one's neighbor and caring for their needs with sympathy (more than empathy) is a central tenet of Christian, Islamic and Buddhist ethics – and probably of other religions as well. All forms of love – filial, neighborly and universal – are crucial aspects of power from below, provided they are understood "as a synthesis of these three dimensions [*agape, eros* and *philia*]: namely love as that special form of interaction which relates two subjects who are ready to expose themselves to the risk of a relationship with the other, without falling into the trap of forgetting themselves or cancelling the other" (Pulcini 2017, 66).

Along the same lines, I would argue that power is not only external to the individual but also internal. Alasdair MacIntyre (1988) and Taha Abderrahmane (*Trusteeship Paradigm*) would both agree that "freedom does not come about through an absence of exterior obstacles, but through the absence of interior obstacles. Freedom must include a juncture where a conception of good is instituted, allowing one to withdraw these obstacles" (Brahimi 2020, 224). Self-empowerment is crucial, provided that legal freedom (negative freedom) is guaranteed. Saba Mahmood (2011) illustrates how women's religious practices in Cairo played a significant role in cultivating piety in their daily lives.

Symbolic liberals have focused so intensely on liberty and equality – seeing the other as an obstacle to one's freedom – that they overlook how Rawls (1971) emphasizes *civic friendship* as a virtue and moral duty essential for grounding public reason. More importantly, since the French Revolution, *fraternity* has been one of the three core values. I agree with Eva Illouz (2022) that this term is less economistic than *solidarity* and mobilizes not only individuals but also communities to care for one another, making it a crucial safeguard for liberal democracy against populism. Thus, these ideas are not naive about power structures; rather, one should consider power from below, not only from above.

Fifth, the Dialogical Liberal Project must never abandon its critical stance toward authority and power, even temporarily. As suggested by the sociology of criticism, social actors must be understood as possessing the ability to distinguish between legitimate and illegitimate forms of criticism and justification. Rather than labeling social groups (laborers, religious, secular, liberal, conservative, leftist, woke, etc.) and confining them to specific types of arguments, priority should be given to analyzing social situations. How can we replace fear of the other with the underlying question, "What if?" through empirical observations of how people justify their moral actions? This is precisely what Boltanski and Thévenot (1991) undertook in their seminal book *On Justification: Economies of Worth*, examining how individuals articulate their indignation and justifications before addressing conflict resolution. A key objective of "pragmatic critique" – as well as the Dialogical Political Liberal Project – is to help the oppressed transition from fragmented opposition to collective action. In this way, a normative model of justice can be constructed based on the actors' own sense of justice.

Abstract vs. Concrete Universality

When it comes to the question of human rights, the Dialogical Liberal Project distinguishes, as Mohamad Fadel (2022) and Abdullah An-Naʿim (1992) point out, between the universality of the *Universal Declaration of Human Rights* and the cultural particularity of each *system of human rights*. The right to culture is an inherent part of this declaration and should be balanced with the promotion and protection of all human rights and fundamental freedoms. The 1993 Vienna Declaration (World Conference on Human Rights) stated clearly that:

> While the significance of national and regional particularities and various historical, cultural and religious backgrounds must be borne in mind, it is the duty of states, regardless of their political, economic and cultural systems, to promote and protect all human rights and fundamental freedoms.[11]

In other words, we always need processes of cultural mediation of human rights, which involves the risk of having to accept a prioritization, or a re-prioritization, of social values that one believes to be contrary to universal human rights values (An-Naʿim 2013).

---

[11] Vienna Declaration and Programme of Action, World Conference on Human Rights, Vienna, 14–25 June 1993, U.N. Doc. A/CONF.157/24 (Part I) at 20 (1993), 5. Cited in Schaumburg-Müller 2011.

Yet, this cultural particularity, which forms the basis of diversity, was often regarded as an essence. What is needed is to transform this particularity from a barricade we hide behind into an inexhaustible specificity, not confined to us, but rather a dangling fruit ready to quench the thirst of anyone seeking this sweet resource. Neither tradition nor cultural particularity is a domain that is neutrally valid; both are imbued with ideology. Regardless of how difficult public debate may be on what are perceived as incommensurable values (e.g., same-sex marriage, migration), engaging in dialogue is crucial between those who identify as traditionalists or modernists.

A Balance Between Individual and Communitarian Life

Dialogical Sociology is built on an amended version of Rawlsian political liberalism that accommodates culture and communities and not only autonomous individuals. It starts not from metaphysical assumptions or abstract ideals but from the world as it operates, namely, as cultures in motion rather than cultures as fixed, homogeneous, eternal entities. Social statistics reveal that people in all societies express significant support for religion, family and community, as well as individual liberty and equality. However, there are tradeoffs between these values. In some contexts, greater support for liberty and equality comes at a cost to religion, family and community, while in other contexts it is the opposite. That being said, such tradeoffs are not all or nothing affairs. Rather, they are matters of degree. Different societies strike different balances between values, and these balances shift over time (Nakissa 2021). Any excessive individualistic approach often comes at the expense of others (e.g., the marginalized, minorities, migrants). In his *Freedom, Culture, and the Right to Exclude: On the Permissibility and Necessity of Immigration Restrictions* (2022), Uwe Steinhoff considers that large-scale immigration from "illiberal cultures" tends to "severely compromise the way of life, the values, and the institutions of liberal democracies." This is an example of reducing the way of life and values in one possible "civilized" set. The counter-example of this book is *Migrations in the Mediterranean: IMISCOE Regional Reader* (2023), by Ricard Zapata-Barrero and Ibrahim Awad, where both positive and negative impacts of migration are studied, demonstrating how European cities become vibrant and cosmopolitan and at the same time capable of overcoming many of the challenges of diversity.

For a long time, the World Happiness Index has overlooked the concepts of balance and harmony, whose importance became especially evident

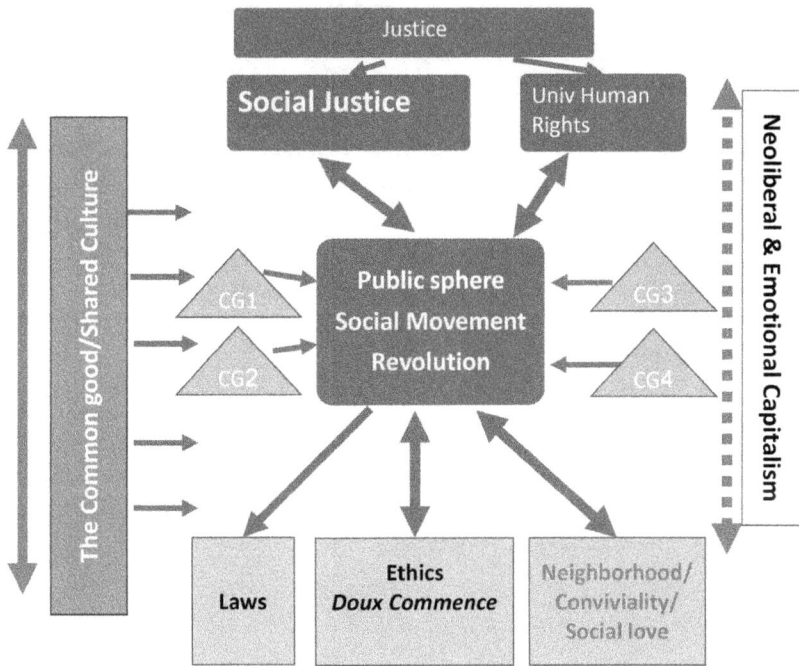

Figure 3.1 Dialogical Political Liberal Project

through studies from the Global South. The 10th edition of this Index (Helliwell et al. 2022) shows that these concepts matter to people's happiness worldwide. Balance and harmony variables are strongly linked to life evaluations.[12] Further results indicate that balance and harmony are significant for everyone, and play a central role in the dynamics of well-being.

Conclusion

As I have argued so far, the Dialogical Political Liberal Project seeks to address how (power-sharing) liberal egalitarianism has been distorted by symbolic liberals. It is not merely a utopia; it already exists through ongoing ideas that have taken root in parts of academia and have led to concrete policy initiatives that must be pursued (Figure 3.1). The Dialogical Political

[12] Regression analysis indicated that, apart from experiencing calmness, balance/harmony items all had a significant association with life evaluation ($p < 0.001$), including especially balance (0.37) and peace (0.46) (Helliwell et al. 2022, chap. 6).

Liberal Project requires a long process, as dialogue is not only verbal (conversations aimed at achieving better mutual recognition) but also physical (living together, which necessitates reorganizing cities and habitats and enhancing common spaces) and involves thinking about justice not just as rationality, but also as passion, love and generosity, which are essential for care.

In the second part of this book, I will explore four themes to show how they have been addressed by symbolic liberals and how the Dialogical Political Liberal Project can mitigate their effects. These four themes are societal intolerance in general and in relation to academic freedom (Chapter 4); secularism (Chapter 5); gender diversity (Chapter 6); and, finally, family authority (Chapter 7).

PART II

From Symbolic Liberalism
to the Dialogical Liberal Project:
Some Themes

CHAPTER 4

Societal Polarization and Academic Freedom

We're fine with people who don't look like us, as long as they think like us.

Nicholas Kristof, "A Confession of Liberal Intolerance" (2016)

[In the time of war,] the notions of Right and Wrong, Justice and Injustice have there no place. Where there is no common Power, there is no Law: where no Law, no justice. Force, and Fraud, are in war the two Cardinal virtues.

Thomas Hobbes, *Leviathan* (1651)

Introduction

In October 1992, a student strike took place in France. The National Union of French Students (UNEF) organized an event with all student bodies to support the movement. At that time, I was the President of the General Union of Palestinian Students (GUPS) in France. As soon as I was called to the podium by the Chair, a group of students shouted me down. At the end of the event, I asked them why they had done this before I had spoken. They told me that they didn't like Palestinians.

This incident is not isolated. Society is increasingly polarized between groups that label each other and refuse to listen to one another. While this polarization does not have the same intensity everywhere, it has prompted numerous writings under various labels (e.g., war of cultures, cultural backlash, politics of outrage) (see Ben-Porath 2023; Norris 2023), particularly

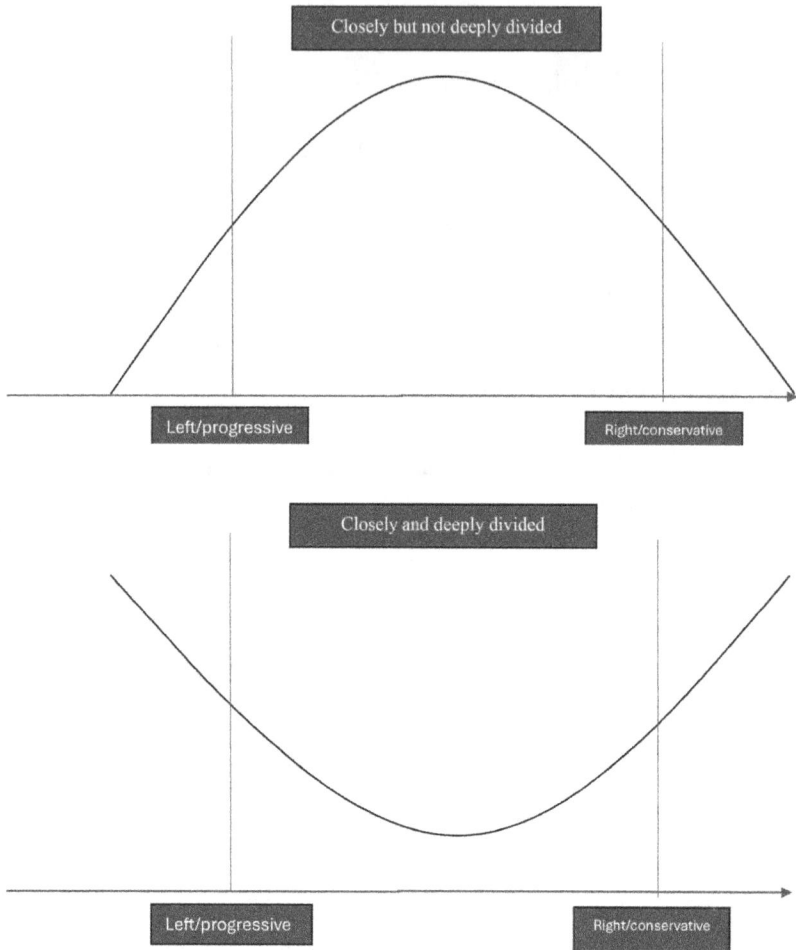

Figure 4.1 Two types of polarization
The horizontal axis of each chart represents political/social views.
The vertical axis indicates the share of people.
Source: Adaptation from Kenworthy. https://lanekenworthy.net/
political-polarization/.

deepening over issues of identity politics. According to Lane Kenworthy (2024), polarization has two dimensions: sorting into sharply distinct groups (closely divided) and moving away from the center toward the extremes (deeply divided). Society can experience either dimension or both. In Figure 4.1, we see two types of political/social polarization: "closely but not deeply divided" (e.g., in the US case: two big political parties) or "closely and deeply divided" (e.g., the cases of the Arab world and France, where many issues have polarized society with the presence of far left and far right). The latter is more dangerous, as it lacks a shared epistemic foundation and has the potential to spill over into other areas of life, generating excessive identity politics and favoring hybrid/tactical parties over traditional Right/Left parties.[1]

In his project on polarization, Mark Freeman (2023) argues that while the problem of polarization is nowhere near the scale of civil war, authoritarianism, genocide or other such evils, it can – if ignored – become their harbinger and accelerant. A wide array of qualifying adjectives is routinely attached to the word polarization (e.g., affective, ideological, symmetric, asymmetric, political, social, ethnic, religious, racial, elite, mass, pernicious, toxic, benign and so on). One might call it a hyper-problem, a type of issue that makes the solution to every other problem more difficult (Freeman 2023). Let me be clear: I acknowledge that conflict in society is normal, but polarization is more than that. As Freeman defines it, polarization is a prominent division or conflict that forms between major groups in a society or political system, marked by the clustering and radicalization of views and beliefs at two distant and antagonistic poles. It is often hierarchical, as it involves dimensions of power and domination.

Today, such a phenomenon is present everywhere, including on university campuses and in the media. It manifests through a high degree of intolerance in debates surrounding political, cultural and social issues, where *taking sides and positions has taken priority over making sound, explanatory arguments.* Interestingly, this intolerance is displayed by both the Left and the Right (with differences in their motivations and mechanisms), as evidenced by both camps subscribing to what is known as "cancel culture." This phenomenon has reached an unprecedented level, alarming many scholars and leading to the signing of the "Letter on Justice and Open Debate" (*Harper's Magazine* 2020). The letter was signed not only by conservatives but also by scholars known for their affiliation with the Left, such as Noam Chomsky, Martin Amis, Gloria Steinem, Salman Rushdie and Margaret Atwood. For the signatories, "cancel culture" is defined as "an intolerance of opposing views, a vogue for public shaming and ostracism, and the tendency to reduce complex policy issues to a blinding moral certainty." The call for a reckoning "has

---

[1] See the section, "Authoritarianism, Populism and the Rise of the Right," in the Introduction to this book.

also intensified a new set of moral attitudes and political commitments that tend to weaken our norms of open debate and tolerance of differences in favor of ideological conformity" (*Harper's Magazine* 2020).

Disqualification and diabolism (such as in symbolism of virus, illness, pandemic, Islamo-leftists, infiltrators, and so on) are heavily and easily used in reference to those opposing views. The outcome is the clustering and radicalization of views and beliefs at two distant and antagonistic poles. This has resulted in the subscription to a greater risk aversion by many academics, artists and journalists who fear for their livelihoods if they depart from the apparent consensus within their camp or even if they are seen to lack sufficient zeal in agreement.

The intolerance of debate is not only based on anecdotal information but on data. The renowned journal *Science* published an editorial arguing that researchers have experienced harassment, threats, prosecution or even violence for opinions or their work on high-profile issues, not only from the "outside world" but also within academia itself.[2] For instance, a survey among political scientists worldwide in 2019 (The World of Political Science Survey) revealed that the reply to the questions that constitutes the Cancel Culture Index reflects the "experience of growing restrictions on academic freedom of speech, pressures for ideological conformity, and the enforcement of politically correct speech. The results of the models confirmed *the significant effects of Left–Right ideology which consistently predicted scores on this index*" (Norris 2020, 16). In the same vein, in another global survey in 2022 in which 468 climate scientists were interviewed by Global Witness, it was found that 39 percent of scientists polled had experienced online harassment or abuse as a result of their climate change work, and that the level of exposure to harassment was linked to the number of their academic publications and the frequency of their media appearances (Global Witness 2023). This survey highlights the tremendous effect of social media (particularly X and Facebook) in incitement and harmful speech because of their business models and lack of moderation and transparency. The algorithmic systems that determine what content is shown to users are kept opaque by the companies.

Neoliberalism, which permeates every sphere, including academia, has reinforced polarization and cancel culture. The spread of the "culture of 'safetyism'" among administrators (particularly in the new managerial system, where they are not academics) has led to hasty decisions and disproportionate punishments against some professors, sometimes for merely quoting works of literature in classrooms or for failing to provide advance

---

[2]   See Gerards 2024.

warnings (trigger warnings) to students, all in a spirit of panicked damage control.

This chapter seeks to investigate how this hierarchical polarization is present everywhere, including on university campuses, the very places that are supposed to be safe for free expression, where such polarization should not occur. Thus, our focus here will be on the stifling of academic freedom. To illustrate this, I will provide three examples – not from the Arab world, where academic freedom is catastrophic (El Amine 2018; Hanafi 2021b)[3] – but from three liberal democratic countries: the United States, the UK and France. These examples will show how cancel culture, often driven by symbolic liberals (but not exclusively), has spread widely in places that pride themselves on their academic freedom. I will then present a case study related to the current War on Gaza, as it has revealed many contradictions regarding societal polarization and academic freedom, affecting not only campuses but also the media and political and judicial fields. As this case is loosely or partially related to symbolic liberalism and cancel culture, I will propose five factors that can explain the Western pro-genocidal Israeli position: 1) the instrumentalization of the memory of the Holocaust; 2) the transformation of Zionism into symbolic liberal and religious zionisms; 3) the false image of Israel as a secular state; 4) Islamophobia and the portrayal of Hamas as a fanatic religious organization, ignoring its anti-colonial agenda; and 5) the Euro-American colonial legacy. Before addressing these, however, I will outline some features of the debates on academic freedom.

Debates on Academic Freedom

Recently, numerous incidents have indicated the stifling of academic freedom under various surveillance regimes, where traditional repressive methods have been replaced by securitization and managerial logics (Aldrin et al. 2022). Some scholars were dismissed from their positions in Germany, the

---

[3] In many Arab countries, university autonomy is virtually nonexistent. The security sector often interferes with both teaching and research, frequently targeting professors who publicly criticize government policies or social issues. Some academics must obtain approval from security forces before traveling abroad, and stringent restrictions are imposed on hosting academic talks and conferences. Furthermore, student unions are heavily restricted, further stifling independent thought and expression within universities. For example, see the "Letter Concerning the Ongoing Deterioration of Academic Freedom in Egypt." https://mesana.org/advocacy/committee-on-academic-freedom/2024/04/04/letter-concerning-the-ongoing-deterioration-of-academic-freedom-in-egypt.

UK, and Israel due to their criticism of the Israeli genocide in Gaza, as seen in the case of the renowned and internationally respected anthropologist Ghassan Hage.[4] Students at many American universities were arrested in April 2024 for protesting against American foreign policy regarding the "War in Gaza." As a corollary, Laëtitia Atlani-Duault and Stéphane Dufoix (2014) have observed that the increasing number of defamation lawsuits against researchers has posed a tremendous challenge to the autonomy of the academic profession, placing researchers working on sensitive topics in precarious situations.[5] Greg Lukianoff and Jonathan Haidt (2018) clearly state that some stress can be beneficial for students' resilience, whereas coddling their minds is not. We no longer talk about risk as a positive force; only small risks are seen as manageable. To understand the current form of risk aversion in universities, Dina Kiwan (2023) highlights the role of neoliberal-driven *individualization* and *psychologization*, arguing that the "infantilization" of society in general, and particularly students, echoing Frank Furedi (2002), can be located within the therapeutic turn in Western contexts. This therapeutic turn is evident in the protection of the legal and market-oriented interests of higher education institutions.

To understand academic freedom, I address three fundamental issues: first, what distinguishes it from freedom of expression; second, the importance of academic autonomy; and third, the tension between this freedom and "diversity, equity and inclusion" (DEI).

For the first point, let me state clearly that there are differences between free speech and academic freedom. The latter demands a higher level of *social responsibility, intellectual integrity and professional ethics*. What a professor writes, which readings they select, for teaching or what they say in the classroom, should all be framed by these principles, while, in general, a layperson can make utterances in private and public spheres. Regarding the first principle, Alexander Meiklejohn, a founder of the American Association of University Professors (AAUP), wrote, "Our final responsibility, as scholars

---

[4] See "Statement Regarding my Sacking from the Max Planck Institute of Social Anthropology (February 9 2024)." https://hageba2a.blogspot.com/2024/02/statement-regarding-my-sacking-from-max.html.

[5] Stephen Ellis and Catherine Lutard-Tavard (2014) recount their experiences as researchers accused of defamation: Ellis for describing the cannibalistic acts of former Liberian president Charles Taylor in a book, and Lutard-Tavard for writing that a particular book on the Serbo-Croat conflict was a "call to hatred, racism, and national revenge." Although the outcomes of their trials differed – Ellis was acquitted while Lutard-Tavard was convicted – both authors reach the same conclusion: defamation laws tend to favor the wealthier party, posing a significant threat to both scientific research and democracy.

and teachers, is not to the truth. It is to the people who need the truth" (Kirk 1955, 31). In this vein, Stanley Fish (2014) places professionalism at the heart of academic freedom – an approach that requires submitting all values to scrutiny in the classroom. However, crafting exceptions to general free speech principles is often difficult. Hate speech is a category with no fixed legal definition (though some countries have established legal parameters, as seen in the *Brandenburg* v. *Ohio* case decided by the US Supreme Court). Therefore, I argue that it should be addressed more socially (depending on context) than legally (see the conclusion to this chapter). The scope of academic freedom extends beyond the classroom to off-campus activities as well. Ronald Dworkin (1998) underscores the importance of such activities and even equates politicized engagement with one's civic duty.

Concerning the second point, while the principle of intellectual integrity relates to how peers assess the robustness of research, the principle of social responsibility is more complex, as it requires moral deliberation to evaluate a statement, as I will outline below. The best discussion on this point I found in Gisèle Sapiro's *Peut-on dissocier l'oeuvre de l'auteur ?* (2020). Academic freedom is threatened by the lack of autonomy in higher education institutions. Historically, in the Global North, the primary threat often comes from donors, particularly in managerial universities, while in the Global South, it tends to stem from authoritarian governments and, to a lesser degree, conservative groups. However, the picture is far more complex when different university traditions (Humboldtian, Napoleonic and managerial) intersect. There is little evidence of a direct relationship between the type of funders (private versus public) and the extent of autonomy (El Amine 2018). Instead, there is stronger evidence that autonomy is influenced by the type of elite (liberal, conservative, symbolic liberal) and the nature of the political regime (authoritarian, liberal democratic, popular democratic). In her important book, *Academic Freedom and the Transnational Production of Knowledge* (2023), Dina Kiwan presents a nuanced analysis of how academic freedom is stifled beyond the North/South divide under the influence of transnational knowledge production. Her study, based on interviews conducted in four countries – the United States, the UK, Lebanon and the UAE – reveals a complex landscape of constraints on academic autonomy.

In authoritarian states, scholars often internalize "red lines" when producing "sensitive" knowledge on topics such as gender, sexuality, security and sectarian politics. However, such "forbidden knowledge" is not exclusive to these states; it also exists in many liberal democracies. According to Kiwan, this knowledge – what she calls the "knowable unknown" – is considered too sensitive, dangerous or taboo to produce. Scholars must be aware of what knowledge should not be pursued. Forbidden knowledge, therefore, encompasses not only specific content but also the structural and sociopolitical processes that regulate and suppress such inquiry. She identifies three dominant discourses surrounding forbidden knowledge: first, concerns about the potential misapplication of research findings; second, the revelation of "uncomfortable truths"; and third, the exploration of taboo topics.

In contrast to forbidden knowledge, Kiwan examines the concept of "legitimate" knowledge, where legitimacy is constructed through the "right to authority" and public acceptance. This leads to the final point: the ongoing polemical debates over whether the principles of academic freedom are in tension with the principles of diversity and inclusion. Drawing on philosophers of education such as Eamonn Callan and Sigal Ben-Porath, as well as Judith Butler, Kiwan argues that inclusivity is a threshold condition for academic freedom – or, in effect, a "precondition" for it. This preconditionality offers a way to navigate the politicized debates between right-wing conservative and liberal left-wing positions. While right-wing conservatives typically defend academic freedom, left-wing responses often view these arguments as disingenuous attempts to weaponize academic freedom against inclusive knowledge. Kiwan contends that the processes of forbidding and legitimizing knowledge operate through transnational mechanisms of publishing and dissemination. These processes impact individual researchers, either by enabling them to publish their work or by blocking them from giving guest lectures (Kiwan 2023, 137).

Building on Kiwan's call to balance free speech with inclusion, this equation becomes untenable in the chilling climate of polarization. Through this framework, most protests against the genocidal war on Gaza are suddenly reframed as acts of antisemitism. Such an "inference" would not be possible without the proliferation of "psychologizing" literature on harm and trauma, which mediates between free speech and inclusion. By adopting an expansive definition of violence and harm, this literature often advocates for restricting free speech and academic freedom, invoking "harms" or "rights violations" as justification. The question I raise here is: Harm or rights violations for whom and for what? In an era of excessive identity politics, group rights frequently come into conflict, and harm cannot be assessed without qualification. The problem is that the discussion has shifted from ethical considerations to legal ones, where crossing an invisible line – particularly regarding the holding of a certain political or gender-related opinion – can lead to lawsuits, exclusion from recruitment or even dismissal. While Dina Kiwan encourages an ethical approach to this debate, scholars like Ann Cudd (2019) extend the discussion to the legal realm, where the notion of harm risks undermining critical thinking:

Expressions that create a hostile environment oppose inclusion because those who are victims of this hostility are made to feel that they do not belong in the university and claim that it poses a threat to their safety and wellbeing...Trauma can be triggered by experiences that shatter our assumptions that the world is benevolent and meaningful, and that the self is worthy. Toxic and oppressive speech are harmful forms of speech because they shatter these assumptions about the world and the self. (Cudd 2019, 444)

How would a legal case evaluate "experiences that shatter our assumptions that the world is benevolent and meaningful, and that the self is worthy"? Uwe Steinhoff (2023) offers a compelling critique of Cudd's work, problematizing harm through the lens of the famous *Brandenburg v. Ohio* Supreme Court ruling:

that speech constitutes constitutionally punishable incitement only if the speaker intentionally incites imminent violent or otherwise illegal conduct that is likely to occur immediately. (Steinhoff 2023, 2)

For Steinhoff, First Amendment law is *highly* robust, and invoking "harms" or even rights violations caused by certain forms of free speech is insufficient to justify their restriction. Of course, applying the social responsibility principle of academic freedom (which, for me, distinguishes academic freedom from free speech) allows us to denounce certain "shattering experiences," but it does not warrant the legal restriction of speech as a blanket application of this conceptualization. The following sections explore this broad application in specific contexts.

Intolerance in the US and UK Academic Fields

According to the Academic Freedom Index,[6] there has been a global decline in academic freedom in many countries, including the United States and the UK,[7]

---

[6] This Index provides an overview of the state of academic freedom in 179 countries in 2023, and trends over time. It is produced through a collaboration between researchers at Friedrich-Alexander-Universität Erlangen-Nürnberg (FAU) and the V-Dem Institute in Germany. See https://academic-freedom-index.net.

[7] The Academic Freedom Index for these countries are, respectively, 0.69 and 0.79 over 1 – a decline compared to preceding years. See https://academic-freedom-index.net.

closely linked to both political and societal polarization.[8] In the United States, statistics from The Foundation for Individual Rights and Expression (FIRE) show that 149 professors were targeted for their speech in 2022, up from 30 in 2015, facing warnings, investigations, suspensions and terminations. Scholars were frequently targeted for expressing views on issues such as partisanship (25 percent of incidents), gender (23 percent) or institutional policies (25 percent).[9] A similar trend is evident in information provided by the National Association of Scholars (NAS), which tracks American academics who have been subject to campaigns calling for their dismissal. The database recorded 4 incidents in each year of 2015 and 2016, 9 in 2017, 13 in 2018, and a striking 65 in 2020 (Kaufmann 2021). This trend is increasingly covered by the media. For example, an art professor at Hamline University was fired in 2023 after a Muslim student complained about the professor showing ancient images of the Prophet Muhammad in a global art course. Similarly, the dean of Harvard's Kennedy School denied a fellowship to former Human Rights Watch executive Kenneth Roth due to his alleged "anti-Israel bias." And so on.

We have a great deal of evidence that this chilling climate of polarization reflects the general opinion of students and faculty. Pano Kanelos, President of the University of Austin, quotes a survey in the United States demonstrating that

> nearly a quarter of American academics in the social sciences or humanities endorse ousting a colleague for having a wrong opinion about hot-button issues such as immigration or gender differences. Over a third of academics and PhD students say they had been threatened with disciplinary action for their views. Four out of five American PhD students are willing to discriminate against right-leaning scholars. …The picture among undergraduates is even bleaker. In Heterodox Academy's 2020 Campus Expression Survey, 62% of sampled college students agreed that the climate on their campus prevented students from saying things they believe. Nearly 70% of students favor reporting professors if the professor says something students find offensive, according to a Challey Institute for Global Innovation survey. (Kanelos 2021)

---

[8]   Academic Freedom Index. https://academic-freedom-index.net/research/ Academic_Freedom_Index_Update_2024.pdf.

[9]   "Free Speech Makes Free People," FIRE (The Foundation for Individual Rights and Expression). www.thefire.org/. "REPORT: At Least 111 Professors Targeted for their Speech in 2021." FIRE. 2 March 2022. www.thefire.org/news/ report-least-111-professors-targeted-their-speech-2021.

I cite this quotation at length to show that the intolerance of the debate is not necessarily imposed from above, but it is also "popular." To further demonstrate its popularity, I will turn to disinvitation incidents.

Disinvitation Incidents

FIRE defines a "disinvitation incident" as a controversy on campus that arises when segments of the campus community demand that an invited speaker not be allowed to speak, rather than merely expressing disagreement with or protesting the speaker's views or positions. FIRE distinguishes between attempts to censor a speaker and the actual outcome of preventing a speaker from speaking. These incidents can include "unsuccessful disinvitation attempts," such as shouting down or intimidating speakers without formally banning them.[10] As of late 2023, FIRE's database recorded at least 574 disinvitation campaigns since 2000 across various higher education institutions, including public, secular and religious schools (accounting for 44 percent, 23 percent and 22 percent of cases, respectively). Roughly 60 percent of these campaigns were successful, with more than two-thirds originating from individuals politically to the Left of the targeted speakers (Tables 4.1 and 4.2). Additionally, between 2001 and 2022, the number of disinvitation campaigns increased tenfold (from 4 to 42) (Figure 4.1). The actual numbers are likely even higher, as some interviewees mentioned refraining from inviting speakers on controversial topics out of fear that such events would be blocked by the administration.

Incidents also include the cancellation of talks on American campuses about the Palestinian–Israeli conflict, justified by claims that such discussions would upset the "sensitivity" of certain students – without specifying who these students were or acknowledging the many others who would not be affected.[11] This intolerance of debate is not limited to the United States but also extends to Canada and, to a lesser extent, the UK, as reflected in surveys conducted in these countries (Kaufmann 2021), including official government reports,[12] and indeed, worldwide.

---

[10] "User's Guide to FIRE's Campus Disinvitation Database." www.thefire.org/research-learn/users-guide-fires-campus-disinvitation-database.

[11] We can see data from organizations other than FIRE, including "Steven Salaita, the Media, and the Struggle for Academic Freedom." www.aaup.org/article/steven-salaita-media-and-struggle-academic-freedom.

[12] See, for instance, "Academic Freedom in the UK," by Policy Exchange. https://policyexchange.org.uk/publication/academic-freedom-in-the-uk-2/. However, some argue that the call for "disinvitation"/"no platforming" is less acute in the UK. One survey indicates that a large majority of students (72 percent) showed

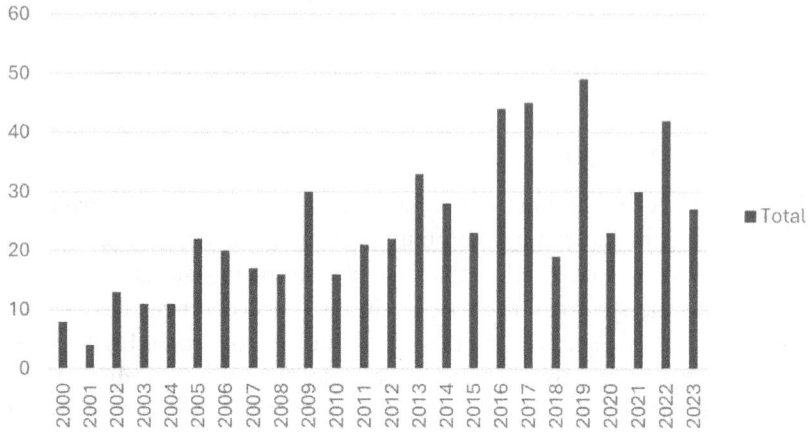

Figure 4.2 Disinvitation incidents per year
Source: FIRE database (my compilation).

Table 4.1 Disinvitation incidents by type of school and political orientation of protestors (Disinvitation coming from the left of speaker or from the right of speaker)

School type	Protestors from the left of speaker	Protestors from the right of speaker	Political orientation not known	Totals	Percentage of total protestors
Public	187	54	12	253	44%
Religious	56	70	6	132	23%
Secular	148	31	10	189	33%
Totals	**391**	**155**	**28**	**574**	**100%**

Source: FIRE database (my compilation).

Table 4.2 Disinvitation incidents by political orientation of protestors

Political orientation of protestors	Numbers	Percentage of total protestors
Protestors from the left	391	68%
Protestors from the right	155	27%
Political orientation not known	28	5%
Totals	**574**	**100%**

Source: FIRE database (my compilation).

Let me qualify how I interpret these figures using three points and two examples. First, I acknowledge that FIRE and the Center for the Study of Partisanship and Ideology (CSPI), for which Eric Kaufmann wrote his report, are affiliated with conservative circles and may produce these reports as part of their libertarian approach to academic freedom. This is why I have selectively used only some factual data rather than their opinion surveys, and I do not endorse their conclusions regarding the victimization of conservative faculty. I approach these sources critically, fully aware of how such organizations can advance a problematic agenda. At this stage, my aim is to demonstrate clear evidence of a chilling climate on academic campuses. I have used these data because there are no similarly comprehensive databases or figures from non-partisan centers. The trend they describe aligns with findings from other studies conducted by serious research groups, such as Alison Scott-Baumann et al.'s *Islam on Campus: Contested Identities and the Cultures of Higher Education in Britain* (2020), Wendy Brown's (2002) critique of higher education in the United States, as well as data from the Academic Freedom Index, the World of Political Science survey, Global Witness and the Challey Institute for Global Innovation survey in the United States.

Second, I used FIRE and CSPI data exclusively to illustrate a clear *trend* in academia toward restricting academic freedom. However, I recognize that such incidents and no-platformings must always be contextualized, as they may reflect broader societal intolerance driven by either symbolic liberals or right-wing populists – both of whom seek to reduce debates on the plurality of conceptions of the good into a single hegemonic framework – or, alternatively, may represent necessary measures to prevent racism and discrimination. However, *I do not automatically consider the disruption of talks to be inherently unethical.* Denouncing politicians with long histories of supporting wars can be justifiable. Universities should remain spaces for protest, open discussion and disagreement about the politics of hegemonic authorities, as they were during the Vietnam War and the struggle against apartheid in South Africa. However, many other cases I have observed align more closely with the definition of cancel culture and societal intolerance. Numerous examples could be provided to illustrate this point.

The first example, based on the work of Scott-Baumann et al. (2020), provides evidence of how the current counter-extremism measures known as "Prevent" are implemented in UK universities, raising significant concerns

some level of agreement that universities should never limit freedom of expression (Scott-Baumann et al. 2020).

regarding academic freedom. Religious identity is politicized by state actors through the erroneous conflation of perceived social conservatism with extremism, resulting in a chilling effect on free speech in universities. Attitudes toward Prevent were significantly negative, as expressed by more than half of the participants and interviewees, extending beyond just Muslim staff and students. According to these authors, students are often portrayed either as "snowflakes," who cannot handle controversy, or as proto-terrorists, who foment radicalization. The authors conclude that

> Instead of opening up debates on difficult issues there is undoubtedly a rising tendency to deal with controversy through silencing, marginalizing, and delegitimizing positions with which one disagrees. This is undeniable as a trend across the higher education sector in recent years. (Scott-Baumann et al. 2020, 132)

This securitization of campuses comes mainly from populist conservatives (such as the 2015 report of the Henry Jackson Society) claiming that campuses (such as SOAS) have given a platform to radical Islamists.[13]

Another example is the intolerance toward discussing issues related to gender identity or the refusal to hear different versions of feminism, which is common at many universities. At Oxford University, Professor Kathleen Stock, a gender-critical philosopher who was driven out of her position at Sussex University by trans activists (with both the university and the labor union failing to provide the necessary support and protection), required security to speak at the Oxford Union but still had her participation disrupted. Similarly, when Dr. Helen Joyce, an Irish academic and journalist, was invited to speak at Gonville & Caius College, Cambridge, on 25 October 2022, its senior leaders criticized the invitation, labeling her views as "hateful to our community."[14] There are numerous other cases of disinvitation in the UK, referred to as "no platforming."[15] Therefore, it is untenable to claim

---

[13] Again, Scott-Baumann et al. provide evidence against such accusations. According to them, "the School of Oriental & African Studies (SOAS) Students' Union received 2,645 room booking requests for events. Less than 2 percent of SOAS Students' Union events (forty-three) were judged to be 'extreme' by the Higher Judicial Service (HJS) in 2017–18. Of the forty-three, twenty-seven were given by the same speaker as part of a weekly course on the Qur'an" (Scott-Baumann et al. 2020, 57).

[14] Alumni for Free Speech. https://affs.uk/edi-and-free-speech.

[15] For example, feminist Germaine Greer, when students at Cardiff University tried unsuccessfully to "no platform" her – stop her from speaking on "Women & Power: The Lessons of the 20th Century."

that preventing these speakers is necessary to balance the power structure between a dominant group (e.g., conservatives in some countries) and a marginalized group, as these speakers often come from the Left and have specific interpretations of feminism. As long as a talk does not constitute clear hate speech (as defined by the US Supreme Court's *Brandenburg v. Ohio* decision), it should not be banned. In a similar vein, Dina Kiwan (2023) notes that, in the UK context, the production of knowledge offering alternative narratives on certain topics appears to be blocked from both public domains and academic forums. A UK professor of sociology recounts the difficulties he faced in publishing the widely publicized case of the 2019 protests in Birmingham against the inclusion of LGBT (No Outsiders) content in primary school curriculums. She quotes one professor of sociology in the UK, commenting on the No Outsiders issue in Birmingham schools at Parkfield Primary School:

> I've not been able to get anything published around the No Outsiders. Within newspapers, no letters to a newspaper, no offer to write something for a paper, article for *The Conversation*, which is like the house newspaper of universities, they were not interested in having anything on No Outsiders...They don't wish to publish on this topic with a view that is other than the mainstream view of a deficit in the attitudes of Muslim parents. (Kiwan 2023, 165)

Third, Zeina Al Azmeh and Patrick Baert (2025) provide insightful explanations for the increasing prevalence of cancel culture and the intolerance of debates, including de-platforming as a method of collective positioning. Drawing on positioning theory, they argue that considering only the intrinsic quality of intellectual interventions does not tell the full story. Intellectuals use various rhetorical devices to attribute certain qualities to themselves (self-positioning), thereby aligning with or distancing themselves from others.[16] Social media and digital culture amplify this phenomenon, fostering the formation of echo chambers and reinforcing divisive "us

---

[16] According to Baert, positioning can take two ideal-typical forms: "intellectual positioning" and "politico-ethical positioning." Intellectual positioning can be further divided into two types of claims: one concerning the general intellectual orientation of the agent (such as Habermas's description of his project as "critical hermeneutics" or Ian Hodder's (1986) "post-processual" archaeology), and the other regarding the significance of the intervention or the broader outlook. Politico-ethical positioning, on the other hand, can also occur within the academic context, either as a critique – such as Habermas's labeling of French postmodern authors as "crypto-conservative" – or as a more constructive

versus them" dynamics. At times, these platforms also serve as a space for individuals who have been academically canceled (e.g., the Canadian psychologist Jordan Peterson).

Intolerance in the French Academic Field

In the case of France, I focus on the intolerance directed toward the decolonial turn in the social sciences. First, I need to qualify this turn. Unequal access to publication has been a subject of debate, framed in terms of center-periphery (Keim 2010), or by emphasizing the working conditions of scientific communities, which leads to a separation between hegemonic and non-hegemonic countries in the global distribution of scientific knowledge (Losego and Arvanitis 2008). An influential article in *Nature* in 2010, for example, suggested that the vast majority of research in psychology was conducted in cultures that are "WEIRD" (Western, educated, industrialized, rich and democratic). It cited an analysis showing that 96 percent of study participants in top psychology journals were from Western industrialized countries, despite these countries accounting for only 12 percent of the world's population. In contrast, we question the canons in our discipline of sociology and why they are predominantly written by white male authors (Dufoix 2021; Hanafi 2019). Echoing Edward Said's *Orientalism* (1978), Stéphane Dufoix (2021) argues that epistemological issues must be addressed.

There is, indeed, a vast body of literature on the continuity of the colonial legacy in education and research,[17] including works by Aníbal Quijano (1992), Gurminder K. Bhambra and John Holmwood (2021) and Ali Meghji (2020). While one can critically engage with this scholarship (e.g., Hanafi 2019), a witch-hunt was launched in France against what was called *décolonialisme*, labeling it as pseudo-science. There was little argument or debate, only position-taking. Seventy-six academics (including sociologist of culture Nathalie Heinich), writers and journalists signed a petition against decolonialism, then established an *Observatoire du décolonialisme* to counter "pseudo-science." In 2023, the name of the observatory was

---

approach, as seen in Michael Burawoy's advocacy for "public sociology" (Baert 2012, 312).

[17] The research is not only about Western-centric theorization but also about data that is still drawn from Western industrialized countries. Pollet and Saxton (2019), for example, demonstrate that in some psychology journals, 91 percent of research is conducted in cultures that are "WEIRD" – home to only 12 percent of the world's population.

changed to *Observatoire des idéologies identitaires* and internationalized (offering articles in both French and English) to become the *Observatory of University Ethics*. On 7–8 January 2022, an international workshop titled "After Deconstruction: Reconstructing Science and Culture" was held at the Sorbonne, organized by the Collège de philosophie, the Observatoire du décolonialisme and the Comité Laïcité République, and inaugurated by the French Minister of Education, Jean-Michel Blanquer.

A few months earlier, the same participants in this workshop had signed a petition accusing Amnesty International, Human Rights Watch and French scholars of anti-Semitism for their analyses, which characterized Israeli practices in the Palestinian Territories as apartheid.[18] Later, those who criticized Israeli colonial practices in the territories were labeled "Islamo-leftists" and faced intense attacks orchestrated by the government and amplified by the mainstream media, with the support of apologetic academics such as Gilles Kepel and Florence Bergeaud-Blackler.[19] Germany, Belgium and other European countries cautiously and largely ineffectively followed this trend.

Unfortunately, the practice of criticizing scholarship through collective statements is no longer an isolated occurrence. In 2021, Michel Wieviorka became the target of a statement from the Observatory of University Ethics regarding his recent writings.[20] More recently, Fariba Adelkhah, a French-Iranian anthropologist, faced a harsh collective statement questioning her professionalism following the publication of her memoir, *Prisonnière à Téhéran* (2024) [*Prisoner in Iran*].[21] This statement came from a group associated with the French Left, *Les mots sont importants* [Words Are Important], and was signed by 16 individuals from academia and human rights organizations. This collective refused to acknowledge that even under authoritarian regimes, governments may sometimes concede to prisoners' demands to improve their conditions. Any fieldwork or narrative that seeks to introduce nuance and complexity becomes a target for denunciation. This once again demonstrates how intolerance in debates is perpetuated by symbolic liberals (as well as the

---

[18] See "Antisémitisme: 'La question israélo-palestinienne ne doit pas être l'exutoire des passions primaires.'" *Le Monde*. 3 September 2021. www.lemonde.fr/idees/article/2021/09/03/antisemitisme-la-question-israelo-palestinienne-ne-doit-pas-etre-l-exutoire-des-passions-primaires_6093200_3232.html.

[19] In addition, see www.liberation.fr/debats/2016/04/14/islamo-gauchisme-aux-origines-d-une-expression-mediatique_1445857/.

[20] See https://decolonialisme.fr/michel-wieviorka-nest-que-le-pompier-pyromane-de-lantiracisme/.

[21] "Des prisons en Iran." https://lmsi.net/Les-prisons-en-Iran-laboratoire-de-cruaute-et-matrice-de-la-violence-d-Etat.

Right), whether from academia or other sectors of the knowledge economy, including media, law and human rights organizations.

Academic Freedom Under Fire as Gaza Burns

During the war on Gaza,[22] we witness Western genocide-enabling silence, not only at the political level but also among the large sector of media and academia. Gilbert Achcar (2023) is right to consider that the refusal of Western governments to call for a ceasefire is making them accomplices to crimes against humanity. We can roughly speak of a division within the international community: the Global North – heavily dominated by the Israeli lobby – has mostly sided with the Israeli regime's ethnic cleansing of the Palestinian people (with perhaps the exceptions of Slovenia, Spain, Scotland and Ireland), while the Global South, including the heavyweights of Russia, China and Iran, are in favor of a permanent ceasefire and a serious peace process.

The pro-Palestine demonstrations – despite some bans – were massive in nearly all major cities worldwide, including in the West. These protests grew significantly following the Israeli bombardment of al-Ahli Arab Hospital in Gaza on 13 October 2023, which killed nearly 500 Palestinians and sparked global outrage over the massacre of civilians, many of whom had sought refuge from the relentless Israeli bombing of the besieged enclave.[23] Some Western countries – particularly Germany and France – not only support the Israeli colonial project but are also attempting to ban Palestinian flags and *kufiyas* at demonstrations against genocide. They claim that holding Israel accountable to international humanitarian law is antisemitic. In the United States, the government has taken measures to suppress pro-Palestine speech and criticism of Israel. A new bill (HR 6090) aims to stifle dissent on college campuses, threatens sanctions against the ICC and family members of its staff, seeks to ban TikTok, violates the Leahy Law and imposes further restrictions – examples of broader efforts to curtail free speech and undermine academic freedom in the United States. Since Trump took

---

[22] For my full analysis of why I consider the war on Gaza a genocidal one, see Hanafi 2024a.

[23] Despite independent verification (e.g., www.aljazeera.com/news/2023/10/20/what-have-open-source-videos-revealed-about-the-gaza-hospital-explosion), including articles from the *Washington Post* and French newspaper *Libération*, some Western media and politicians parroted the Israeli lie that the explosion did not come from them.

office in January 2025, many visas and green cards have been revoked from individuals who participated in pro-Palestinian demonstrations against the genocide in Gaza.

This is not limited to politicians who cater to interest groups essential for their funding and re-election but also extends to the media and academia. Today, more criticism of the Israeli genocide in Gaza can be found in *Haaretz* than in mainstream American, Canadian or European newspapers. Even some Israeli sociologists are more vocal in condemning Israel's violations of international law than academic associations in Europe.[24] In a disturbing turn of events, we recall how Robert Badinter rightfully led the abolition of the death penalty in France in 1981, while he and his wife, philosopher and feminist Élisabeth Badinter, now openly support a collective death sentence against the people of Gaza.[25]

Needless to say, in the West there are many honest scholars and human rights defenders, such as Craig Mokhiber, director of the New York office of the UN High Commissioner for Human Rights. He resigned his post on 31 October 2023 with a scathing letter attacking UN and Western complicity in Israeli abuses. We are also witnessing how – despite universities' institutional support for the Israeli colonial regime – university students demonstrate strong support for the struggle of the Palestinian people.[26] And in 2024, we have seen thousands of Western scholars and writers denounce the war on Gaza and call for an end to the Occupation, despite the witch-hunt that has been conducted since 7 October by the Israeli lobby and its allies. In these liberal democracies such as the UK, France, Canada, Germany and Australia, a researcher posting against genocide on Facebook and X can be considered an apologist for terrorism. In France, nearly 400 investigations for complaints linked to the Israeli–Palestinian conflict were launched between October and December 2023, according to the investigative website Mediapart.[27] Some 1,557 French jurists and scientists signed a statement "Defending Freedom of Expression on Palestine: An Academic Issue."[28]

---

[24] See, for instance, Lev Grinberg (2024).

[25] Christophe Oberlin (2020).

[26] See, for instance, "Student Protests for Gaza Targeted by Pro-Israel Groups for Alleged Civil Rights Violations." https://theintercept.com/2023/11/16/israel-palestine-gaza-student-protests/.

[27] "France's 'Apology for Terrorism' Law Used to 'Criminalise' Palestine Solidarity." www.middleeasteye.net/news/france-apologism-terrorism-offence-used-criminalise-palestine-solidarity-and-restrict-freedoms.

[28] "Defending Freedom of Expression on Palestine: An Academic Issue." https://docs.google.com/forms/d/e/1FAIpQLSfvJoKtwzoN_h_m7Bgbbo BUuJK5Wl9hZWCfjTgnX1DJpVtXCw/viewform.

Philosophically, censorship over Palestine may be viewed as a form of cancel culture. However, sociologically, it is a distinct phenomenon shaped by different forces and motivations. In broad terms, and in the following sections, I will outline five factors that explain not only the West's pro-genocidal stance toward Israel and its double standards but also the physical and legal violence used to silence dissenting voices.[29] These factors include: the memory of the Holocaust, oscillating between sincere remembrance and instrumentalization for guilt-washing; the rise of symbolic liberal Zionism; the perception of Israel as a secular state incapable of wrongdoing; Islamophobia and the portrayal of Hamas as a fanatical organization rather than a liberation movement; and the Euro-American colonial legacy. Of course, no single factor alone can fully account for the suppression of academic freedom and free expression. Other elements also play a role, albeit to a lesser extent, such as Israel's crucial position within the Western military-industrial complex. In the United States, the vast majority of military aid to Israel never leaves Washington – it goes directly into the coffers of arms manufacturing and distribution companies. The scale of these transactions is directly linked to military aid to Israel, which serves as the foundation of the military economy of scale that reinforces the overwhelming power of what Israeli political economists Jonathan Nitzan and Shimshon Bichler (2002) termed the Weapondollar–Petrodollar Coalition.[30] Beyond this militaristic and colonial liberalism, one must also consider the role of biblical narratives, particularly among Evangelicals.[31]

Memory of Holocaust: Sincerity and Guilt-washing

The memory of the Holocaust remains vivid. There is no doubt that the Hamas attack on 7 October, which did not distinguish between civilians

---

[29] Several international organizations and human rights groups have characterized Israel's military actions in Gaza as genocide. Notably, Amnesty International (5 December 2024); United Nations Special Rapporteur on the Occupied Palestinian Territories Francesca Albanese, in her March 2024 report titled "Anatomy of a Genocide"; Médecins Sans Frontières (MSF) (19 December 2024); International Federation for Human Rights (FIDH) (12 December 2024); Boston University School of Law (https://www.bu.edu/articles/2024/is-israel-committinggenocide-in-gaza/). These assessments are based on documented actions and policies that, according to these organizations, meet the criteria defined in the 1948 Genocide Convention.

[30] Personal communication with the American historian Mark LeVine.

[31] Personal communication with the American scholar Muqtedar Khan.

and combatants, evoked genuine historical trauma. Antisemitism also persists in some parts of the world and must be combated by all possible means. It manifests in "abhorrent conspiracy theories about Jewish control of the media, finance, and governments, blood libel accusations, Holocaust denial tirades, and dehumanising caricatures of Jews."[32] However, the working definition of antisemitism adopted by the International Holocaust Remembrance Alliance (IHRA), along with its illustrative examples, has become a key tool for addressing antisemitism in many Western countries.[33] This definition conflates antisemitism with anti-Zionism and criticism of Israeli actions and policies, including campaigns that seek to hold the Israeli government accountable under international law, such as the Boycott, Divestment and Sanctions (BDS) movement. It also deems it antisemitic to draw comparisons between contemporary Israeli policies and those of the Nazis. Although this definition is non-legally binding, it is being applied in legal contexts, effectively weaponizing antisemitism. Some US states have even passed legislation incorporating the definition into law, making it legally enforceable.

The UN Special Rapporteur on contemporary forms of racism, racial discrimination, xenophobia and related intolerance, E. Tendayi Achiume, has warned against the use of the IHRA definition "due to its susceptibility to being politically instrumentalized and the harm done to human rights resulting from such instrumentalization."[34] In the same vein, the European Legal Support Center and the British Society for Middle Eastern Studies (BRISMES) show in a 2023 report that "there is widespread agreement among genocide scholars and legal experts (including the lead drafter of the IHRA definition, Kenneth Stern) that the IHRA definition is not appropriate for academic settings where critical thought and free debate are paramount."[35] The report presents case-based evidence of infringements of staff and students' fundamental rights caused by the implementation of the IHRA's definition. The evidence is supported by 40 documented cases in 14 UK universities involving allegations of antisemitism that invoked the IHRA definition. The 2020 Jerusalem Declaration of Antisemitism,[36] was

[32] "Letter to Max Planck Society Regarding Professor Ghassan Hage." www.brismes. ac.uk/news/letter-max-planck-society-professor-ghassan-hage.

[33] "Working Definition of Antisemitism." https://holocaustremembrance.com/ resources/working-definition-antisemitism.

[34] "Report of the Special Rapporteur on Combating Glorification of Nazism." https:// tinyurl.com/yh2n66dw.

[35] "The Adverse Impact of the IHRA Definition of Antisemitism." https://tinyurl. com/2sewk8cm.

[36] "Jerusalem Declaration on Antisemitism." https://jerusalemdeclaration.org/.

drafted to counter the IHRA definition precisely because the majority of genocide scholars believe it is unfit for purpose.[37] This declaration states its opposition to the IHRA Definition:

> Because [it] is unclear in key respects and widely open to different interpretations, it has caused confusion and generated controversy, hence weakening the fight against antisemitism. The IHRA Definition includes 11 "examples" of antisemitism, 7 of which focus on the State of Israel. While this puts undue emphasis on one arena, there is a widely-felt need for clarity on the limits of legitimate political speech and action concerning Zionism, Israel, and Palestine.

Even more recently, hundreds of Jewish scholars, writers and artists have signed an Open Letter arguing that not all criticism of Israel is inherently antisemitic.[38]

The Israeli political scientist Neve Gordon traces the transformation of antisemitism from its traditional meaning to what is now called "new antisemitism." The logic of this shift can be expressed as a syllogism: (i) antisemitism is hatred of Jews; (ii) to be Jewish is to be Zionist; (iii) therefore, anti-Zionism is antisemitic. According to Gordon (2023), the flaw lies in the second proposition, which paves the way for banning any criticism of Israeli colonial practices. A striking example of the political instrumentalization of the IHRA definition can be seen in the actions of the former UK Secretary of State for Science, Innovation and Technology, Michelle Donelan. At the end of October 2023, she published an open letter to UK Research and Innovation (UKRI), an independent public funding body overseeing academic research. In the letter, Donelan criticized several academics appointed by the body, citing their "extremist views on social media," which she claimed included references to genocide and apartheid. In response, the UKRI swiftly launched an investigation, pledging "swift and robust action." In opposition to this crackdown, over 3,000 academics signed an open letter to the UKRI, denouncing what they described as "the current wave of repression and attempts at censorship led by the government against lawful expressions of solidarity with Palestinians and criticisms of the Israeli military's heavy bombardment of the Gaza Strip since 7 October."[39]

---

[37] "Letter to Max Planck Society Regarding Professor Ghassan Hage."

[38] "'All Criticism of Israel Is Not Inherently Anti-Semitic': An Open Letter From Jewish Writers." https://thewire.in/world/all-criticism-of-israel-is-not-inherently-anti-semitic-an-open-letter-from-jewish-writers.

[39] "Academic Freedom Under Fire as Gaza Burns." https://consortiumnews.

In Germany, the witch-hunt against scholars who criticize Israel began in the late 1990s, marked by incidents of disinvitation and public campaigns, which coincided with the emergence of the new definition of antisemitism (Younes 2020).[40] The media, for instance, opposed the participation of Achille Mbembe at the *Ruhrtriennale*, an international arts festival in Germany's Ruhr area.[41] The most compelling explanation for this phenomenon is offered by Anna Younes (2020) through her concept of the "War on Anti-Semitism" (analogous to the War on Terror), as well as by Esra Özyürek (2023), who argues that German politicians, journalists and academics "subcontract" the guilt of the Holocaust to newly arrived minority immigrants, particularly Arab Muslims. The "general German social problem of antisemitism" is thus projected onto this minority, which is then further stigmatized as "the most unrepentant antisemites" in need of additional education and discipline. As a result, the instrumentalization of "new antisemitism" becomes one of the avatars of Orientalism, i.e., how the 'Orientals' were historically portrayed as uncivilized. This subcontracting was further demonstrated by Al-Taher and Younes (2023) in the aftermath of an antisemitic attack against a synagogue in Halle in 2019.[42] Although the attack was perpetrated by a white supremacist German, the German Rectors' Conference issued a statement that, rather than directly condemning white supremacy, instead advised banning BDS activism from university campuses. While a pro-American/Israeli stance from the Right and Far Right is expected, what is striking is the position of the Left. Whether within leftist political parties (such as the Social Democratic Party and the Green Party) or among leftist academics, there has been a notable silence – and, in some cases, even apologism – regarding the Israeli genocide in Gaza.[43]

com/2023/12/04/academic-freedom-under-fire-as-gaza-burns/. In this article by Mick Hall, you can find more examples of recent censorship in New Zealand related to the growing solidarity with the Palestinian people.

[40] Recently, but this time in Germany, and not in the United States, I was invited to a university to talk about the war on Gaza. The organizer also invited an Israeli scholar whose position is apologetic to Israeli colonial practice. After a long negotiation with the administration, the talk was canceled because of my presence.

[41] Following the controversy surrounding his attendance, more than 400 scholars, including Judith Butler, Noam Chomsky and Etienne Balibar, signed a pledge "opposing ideological or political interference and litmus tests in Germany." See "Colonial Discourses Are Stifling Free Speech in Germany." www.aljazeera.com/opinions/2020/6/19/colonial-discourses-are-stifling-free-speech-in-germany.

[42] In fact, it was a white supremacist attack and not simply an antisemitic act. The alleged perpetrator went on to shoot people at a Turkish doner restaurant.

[43] "The German Left's Complicity in the Palestinian Genocide." https://mondoweiss.net/2024/09/the-german-lefts-complicity-in-the-palestinian-genocide/.

This goes beyond Germany. The Center for Security, Race and Rights' report "Presumptively Antisemitic: Islamophobic Tropes in the Palestine-Israel Discourse" is very compelling, arguing that "when Muslims and Arabs in America defend the rights of Palestinians or criticize Israeli state policy, they are often baselessly presumed to be motivated by a hatred for Jews rather than support for human rights, freedom, and consistent enforcement of international law."[44]

Pankaj Mishra (2024) refers to Andrew Port's *Never Again: Germans and Genocide after the Holocaust* (2023), to better understand the widespread indifference in Germany to the fate of the Palestinians in Gaza. Examining the German response to mass killings in Cambodia, Rwanda and the Balkans, Port suggests that the Holocaust "may have unwittingly desensitized Germans. The conviction that they had left the rabid racism of their forebears far behind them may have paradoxically allowed for the unabashed expression of different forms of racism."

In the same vein, Hamid Dabashi is right when he elegantly put it: "We must be forgiven if we thought what Germany had today was not Holocaust guilt, but genocide nostalgia, as it has vicariously indulged in Israel's slaughter of Palestinians over the past century (not just the past 100 days)" (2024). In Germany, prizes were recently canceled for Palestinian novelist Adania Shibli and Jewish Russian-American journalist and writer Masha Gessen. Gessen was awarded the prestigious Hannah Arendt Prize for Political Thought, but the award was revoked after she compared Gaza before 7 October to the Jewish ghettos of Nazi-occupied Europe. Samantha Hill (2023) rightly argued that Arendt, who was critical of the nation-state of Israel from its founding, would not qualify for the Hannah Arendt Prize in Germany today. On 14 December 2023, a group of students at Freie Universität Berlin occupied a lecture hall in solidarity with the Palestinian people. They later received letters from the police notifying them that the university administration had pressed criminal charges against them for "trespassing."[45] Referring to this incident, Omar Sabbour wrote:

> guiltwashing is leaning in the direction of anti-Semitism – as well as anti-Arab racism and Islamophobia – because it operates on a

---

[44] See https://csrr.rutgers.edu/issues/presumptively-antisemitic/ (co-authored by Mitchell Plitnick and Sahar Aziz).

[45] The same happened to Dr. Walaa Alqaisiya, who was "disinvited" for her talk (planned date 30 May 2022, Vienna University), where the administration gave as a reason in their public justification for the lecture's cancelation, a "transgression of boundaries" (Al-Taher and Younes 2023).

superficial level and does not genuinely internalize the lessons of the past...Germany has adopted a robotic, mindless, unidimensional reactive position. "Never again" is promoted in the narrowest sense – which is not altogether surprising considering the lack of education within Germany about its colonial past and other victim communities of the Nazi regime. It refuses to accept that never again should mean never again for genocide against any people.[46]

The German violation of academic freedom continues: on 5 February 2024, the outstanding Lebanese-Australian anthropologist Ghassan Hage was sacked from the German Max Plank Institute (MPI).[47] A Few days earlier, the rightwing newspaper *Welt am Sonntag* published a defamatory article against him, highlighting that, in social media, Hage had used racist or antisemitic material.[48] It is interesting to note that some academic bodies issued clear statements against the MPI decision, including the German Association of Social and Cultural Anthropology[49] and the European Association of Social Anthropology,[50] even with support from Israeli anthropologists.[51]

The British Association of Middle East Studies statement supporting Hage made it clear that the decision of sacking him was "based on a flawed definition of antisemitism that has been institutionalized in Germany, but is not legally binding according to the German government."[52]

Antisemitism, as a subject, shuts down debate and discussion. In the United States, while requesting a ceasefire in a war zone where tens of thousands of civilians were being slaughtered, university students chanted, "From the River to the Sea, Palestine will be Free." Many banners at their demonstrations explicitly stated that this was a call for a democratic and secular state for all its residents. Yet, this chant was rhetorically distorted as a "call for genocide of the Jewish people" by Republican Congresswoman

[46] "German Guiltwashing in Times of Genocide." www.aljazeera.com/opinions/2024/2/27/german-guiltwashing-in-times-of-genocide.
[47] "Statement of the Max Planck Society about Prof. Ghassan Hage." www.mpg.de/21510445/statement-ghassan-hage.
[48] "Antisemitismus-Skandal erschüttert deutsche Nobelpreis-Schmiede." www.welt.de/politik/deutschland/plus249881966/Max-Planck-Gesellschaft-Antisemitismus-Skandal-erschuettert-deutsche-Nobelpreis-Schmiede.html.
[49] "Statement of the Board on Academic Freedom in Germany." www.dgska.de/en/statement-on-academic-freedom-in-germany/.
[50] "EASA Letter Regarding Academic Freedom and Prof. Ghassan Hage." https://easaonline.org/outputs/support/mpso224.shtml.
[51] "Letter in Support of Prof. Ghassan Hage." https://tinyurl.com/5n7dx8ky.
[52] "Letter to Max Planck Society Regarding Professor Ghassan Hage."

Elise Stefanik during a congressional hearing on 5 December 2023. The hearing summoned the presidents of three Ivy League schools – Harvard, MIT and the University of Pennsylvania – to testify about "antisemitism on college campuses". Even though Stefanik may not be considered a symbolic liberal, some American Democrats participated in the hearing. Notably, many of these demonstrations were organized by Jewish Voices for Peace and Students for Justice in Palestine, meaning that many of the participants were Jewish themselves. I cannot help but reflect on the fact that the three university presidents called to testify were women, and one of them was Black. The outcome of this non-debate has been the banning of discussions on certain American campuses where speakers had merely called for a ceasefire – despite polls showing that 80 percent of Democratic voters and 56 percent of Republican voters supported an immediate and unconditional ceasefire in Gaza.[53]

Under the commodification of higher education, the issue at stake is high. Catherine Liu explains very well its meaning:

> University administrators are guided by the same playbook: First, invest in fundraising and development that would be attractive to billionaires looking for philanthropic opportunities to avoid taxes. Second, leverage your assets by taking on bond-funded debt for new buildings. Third, shrink your workforce down to the bone by reducing the number of tenured faculty positions, outsourcing food and cleaning services, and paying graduate student workers as little as possible. Then, get rid of unprofitable departments in the name of productivity. Finally, establish and copiously reward administrators who will execute those policies with alacrity.[54]

At a more theoretical level, this is how knowledge was transformed into what Burawoy (2015) calls "fictitious commodity," driven by colonial and corporate interests (Dolgon 2024). Under these transformations, certain major donors to Harvard University, for instance, have signaled that their funding is at risk of being pulled. In 2023, Bard College was subject to attack because of the

---

[53] "Nine Reactions to Professor Claire O. Finkelstein's Call for Restricting Free Speech on Palestine, Ahmed Bouzid." https://social-epistemology. com/2024/01/22/nine-reactions-to-professor-nicole-finkelsteins-call-for-restrict-ing-free-speech-on-palestine-ahmed-bouzid/#respond. This trend can be found worldwide and not only in the United States. See Mohamad Alsharqawi. https:// studies.aljazeera.net/ar/article/5826.
[54] "Academic Freedom Under Fire as Gaza Burns."

"Apartheid in Israel–Palestine" course taught by Jewish American researcher Nathan Thrall. Bard's decision to defend it provoked a concerted campaign and threats by donors to withdraw funding, including property developer Robert Epstein, who resigned from Bard's board of trustees.[55]

Transformation of Zionism into Symbolic Liberal and Religious Zionisms

The Zionist movement emerged in nineteenth-century Europe as a minority ideology among Jews, advocating for ethnic-national emancipation in contrast to the assimilation movement that Jews had either voluntarily or forcibly embraced. Over time, however, the movement underwent various ideological transformations, including the rise of socialist Zionist pioneers during the Second Aliya, who laid the foundations for the Israeli state. The movement shifted from its initial project to a colonial endeavor in Palestine, with socialist, liberal and religious Jews reshaping it in response to the specific historical contexts of the Holocaust and antisemitism in Europe.

As I show above, since the IHRA adopted its working definition of antisemitism in 2005, there have been attempts to equate anti-Zionism with antisemitism and even to redefine Zionism not as a national doctrine but as an ethnicity. According to this redefinition, Zionists are seen as a nationality, akin to Arabs, Mexicans or French, and any criticism of this "nationality" is labeled as racist.

In my view, Zionism is primarily a nationalist doctrine that can be colonial, chauvinistic, exclusionary or emancipatory – much like any other form of nationalism. However, I believe the major transformation of this ideology occurred within two contexts: first, how liberals came to violate liberalism itself, turning it into symbolic liberalism, and second, how religious forces radicalized it. I will focus here on "liberal Zionism," drawing on the seminal work of Egyptian-Canadian legal scholar Mohamad Fadel, who distinguishes between different iterations of this doctrine and heavily critiques its mainstream form, which he labels "liberal Zionism." I would argue that this form is more accurately described as "symbolic liberal Zionism."

Fadel defines liberal Zionism as "a recognition that Palestinians are victims of something, but that their victimhood demands only a humane response, not a legal response in line with general liberal principles of justice"

---

[55] "Academic Freedom Under Fire as Gaza Burns."

(Fadel forthcoming). This form of Zionism fails to take Palestinian equality seriously, and this failure manifests in three key ways:

1. **Historical**: Symbolic Liberal Zionists often ignore Palestine's history prior to the founding of the State of Israel. For instance, Eva Illouz (2024), in a recent interview, criticized the slogan "From the river to the sea, Palestine will be free," arguing that this was the first time a nation [the Israelis] was called to be eliminated. She conveniently overlooked that Israel had already effectively eliminated the Palestinian nation long before.

2. **Legal**: Liberal Zionists disregard the legal norms that existed in Palestine before and after the establishment of the State of Israel. Areej Sabbagh-Khoury (2023) gives the example of the leftist Zionist settlement movement, Hashomer Hatzair, which, by using specific new legal norms, transformed large portions of Palestine into sovereign Jewish territory. The Absentees' Property Law provided a legal mechanism for the state to expropriate the property of Palestinian individuals and businesses. This law treated Palestinians as subjects without rights, and the conflict between Zionists and non-Jewish Palestinians is often framed as one that takes place in a *terra nullius* (land belonging to no one). In this view, the historical fact of Jewish marginalization is seen as sufficient to exonerate the Zionist project from accusations of colonialism. Of course, they also ignore that the West Bank, Gaza Strip and Golan Heights are internationally recognized as occupied territories.

3. **Political**: Since the founding of Israel, liberal Zionists have pushed for a system of Jewish ethnic dominance over Palestine and non-Jewish, Arab Palestinians. They present their political aims as rational, focused on the security of the Jewish people, but "they are not reasonable because their proposals do not seek a common basis for reciprocal cooperation with non-Jewish Palestinians on the basis of mutual recognition of equal standing" (Fadel forthcoming). Ultimately, their symbolic liberal Zionism rests on the belief that what is good for Jews as a people is more important than the conventional liberal ideal of reciprocal freedom. More generally, Rawls refers to such an arrangement as a *modus vivendi*, which is inherently unstable. For Rawlsian political liberalism, the transition from the rational to the reasonable is crucial, and this shift is violated by symbolic liberal Zionism (Fadel forthcoming). This strand of liberal Zionism is governed not by classical civilian liberal elites but often by heavy

intervention from military and security establishments, which both disregard national justice for the colonized and shape how Israeli society negotiates competing conceptions of the good.

The problem today involves not only the prevalence of this non-reasonable form of liberal Zionism but also the rise of a religious version, which takes the form of a messianic strand aiming to realize the vision of Eretz Yisrael (Greater Israel) – an Israel stretching "from the river to the sea." However, in the original and current platform of the Likud Party, the "river" is not the Jordan River but rather the Euphrates River, meaning the vision calls for the annexation not only of Gaza and the West Bank but also parts of Syria and Jordan.[56]

Israel as a Secular State

For many in the West, Israel is a secular country that can do no wrong. However, if we look at one indicator alone – the expansion of illegal settlement in the Occupied Palestinian Territories – we will quickly realize that the Israeli leaders, both secularists and religious actors, both leftists and rightists, have engaged in this land theft (Hanafi 2013). I recall a public talk by Alain Touraine at the School for Advanced Studies in the Social Sciences (EHESS) in Paris, in 1993, where he evoked the Israeli "miracle" of absorbing 100,000 Russian Jews in a short lapse of time. When I contested this "miracle" with the fact that most of these Russians were settled illegally in Occupied Palestine, he replied: "Mister Hanafi, those migrants will change the equation: grown up in the Soviet Union, they are secular, so they will support the peace process."

Demonstrating perverse naivety, he didn't realize that these illegal settlers would establish some of the most fascistic political parties in the Israeli regime – such as Yisrael Beiteinu ("Israel Our Home") – and have allied themselves with the religious settlers' movement in the West Bank. After the time of this anecdote, we have met many times and from time to time I reminded him what he said, but each time I only received from him either a laugh or a big smile.

---

[56] It is important to note that analyzing the Palestinian–Israeli conflict as a settler–colonial and apartheid project does not imply that Palestinians should not also be reasonable in seeking a compromise with Zionists. Both peoples must cooperate to reach a stable, democratic solution through a process of negotiation, knowing that the colonized have the right of resistance as far as the colonizer refused to find a just solution.

This secularistic trend continues to flourish through the writing of scholars such as Elie Barnavi[57] and Gilles Kepel.[58] In an interview with *L'Express*, they asserted that contemporary conflict stems from two religious nationalist movements: Hamas/Islamic Jihad on the Palestinian side and Israeli religious parties. Consequently, they could not criticize Israel as a secular state, but rather the excesses of certain political fringes. Kepel even analogized Hamas to Al-Qaeda and ISIS, and compared 7 October to 9/11. This perspective fails to recognize Hamas as a national liberation movement, a view repeatedly expressed by François Burgat (2016), amidst what the international community and international law deem an illegal settler colonial and apartheid project in the occupied Palestinian territories (post-1967) (see ICJ judgment released 20 Jul 2024). This critique extends to hard secularists in the Arab world, such as Tunisian political scientist Hamadi Redissi, who overlook Hamas as an expression of Palestinian nationalism, using 7 October to denounce the organization's military *raison d'être* of this organization.[59]

Islamophobia and Hamas

The third factor in my formulation is that the position taken against Hamas is closely related to the creeping Islamophobia in many Western countries to varying degrees. In both European media and academic work, particularly in France, there is sometimes a denial of the rampant racism against Muslims, most of whom are integrated into national societies but who refuse to be assimilated into cultural majoritarianism. In the last decade, many social scientists in France have been using the word Islamophobia with quotation marks (i.e., "Islamophobia") – as if they do not believe that it constitutes a dangerous social phenomenon that even deserves a label (Hajjat 2021).

François Burgat (2020) and Nacira Guénif-Souilamas have emphasized

---

[57] "Elie Barnavi: 'De l'héritage de Netanyahou, il ne restera qu'un champ de ruines.'" www.lexpress.fr/monde/proche-moyen-orient/elie-barnavi-de-lheritage-de-ne-tanyahou-il-ne-restera-quun-champ-de-ruines-TJRX7GNFEVBDVBKZDHTL-NUMK2A/.

[58] "Gilles Kepel: 'Le Hamas a atteint une victoire encore plus grande que le 11 Septembre.'" www.lexpress.fr/idees-et-debats/gilles-kepel-le-hamas-a-atteint-une-victoire-encore-plus-grande-que-le-11-septembre-I6AHDSCN6ZCKTHMVKD-VQWAL52E/.

[59] "France/Tunisie: une position irréconciliable face à la guerre Israël/Hamas?" Interview on Radio France Culture, 25 October 2023. www.radiofrance.fr/franceculture/podcasts/les-enjeux-internationaux/france-tunisie-une-position-irreconciliable-face-a-la-guerre-israel-hamas-5611005.

that the tensions and rifts between Europe and the Muslim world, whether domestic or regional, can be analyzed as resulting from various historical dynamics.[60] The most important of these rifts has little to do with global religious affairs; rather, it is internal and political. It is by far the most structural – and the most decisive – as, over the past five years, this posture has no longer been the sole preserve of extreme-right political forces. From Italy to Denmark, Sweden, and Austria, it has become the position of a quasi-majority of the political landscape. For instance, in Denmark Sofie Aaltonen provides a detailed report on policies targeting Muslims in the country:

> The Danish parliament has ratified at least 58 bill proposals, in which the parliamentary debate has concerned Islam or Muslims in the past seven years alone, along with 38 resolution proposals aimed at disciplining religious practices within Islam and [being both] Muslim and Danish. ...These resolutions have sought to restrict practices and spaces such as wearing the hijab or niqab, establishing or maintaining prayer rooms, mosques, Muslim free-schools, performing circumcision, adhering to halal food practices, and even challenging the formal recognition of Muslim religious communities in Denmark. (Aaltonen 2024, 7)

The reading of the Arab–Israeli conflict remains dominated by an Islamophobic secularism that is obsessed with Hamas. It is a Schmittian moment of the Muslim problem, involving a stark friend/enemy distinction (Esmili 2024). By considering it to be ISIS, Hamas becomes a target to be eliminated, while the Palestinian Gazans are *homo sacer*, who can be murdered without holding their killers accountable. To achieve that, Hamas is represented as a militia that does not represent the Palestinian people.[61]

---

[60] See, for instance, her talk in the Sociology World Conference in Melbourne in July 2023. Some of the panel's questions commend the organizers of this congress for addressing a topic that has been largely underexplored in sociology.

[61] Hamas has significant support from some Palestinian people, both within Occupied Palestine and the diaspora. It was elected by the Palestinian people in 2006, and its ideology was made clear to those who voted for them. I know some Christian friends who supported Hamas in that election. Over the past five years, Hamas has continued to win student body elections in Palestinian universities in the West Bank. Their popularity stems from the lack of a political solution with the Israeli regime, and from their ability to inflict costs on the ongoing Israeli settler colonial project. This makes Hamas the only group that seems to genuinely work for Palestinian interests in a real and tangible way. Those who

If we look at the French and German media during the war on Gaza we so rarely find any Palestinian or Muslim voices. Academia joins the media in defining those who can participate in knowledge production, and those who should not, and all this is not without relationship to colonial legacy. Hanna Al-Taher and Anna-Esther Younes elegantly put it thus:

> Silence can be understood as a structural feature of colonially constituted forms of communication. Spivak analyzed the possibilities and impossibilities of 'being heard' in a colonial structure. According to Spivak, gender, colonial status, and class coproduce a subject that speaks but is not listened to. (Al-Taher and Younes 2023, 11)

In the same vein, Dina Kiwan argues (2023, 164) that "the production of knowledge on Palestine in the US and UK contexts attests to experiences of a hostile working environment and constraints on academic freedom in several interviewee accounts" that were given in her book.

Listening to the many debates in the French media concerning Gaza, one involves a slippery slope when talking about Islam, when "what is debated is not Islam as a phenomenon and as an object of investigation, but Islam as a filter and a criterion for demarcating the belonging to the political community" (Dupret and Ferrié 2024).

Euro-American Colonial Legacy

If I accept the saying that "The enemy of my enemy is my friend," I will not be surprised by those on the far-Right wing, who, being Islamophobic, have become very supportive of Israeli colonial practices. These positions are a continuation of the Euro-American colonial legacy and colonial method as it is described by Afreen Faridi (2023): "wait for a people to die, make a museum of their genocide, then set up departments of decoloniality over their mass graves."

Two focal points here are to be discussed: first, what counts for constructing universal categories, and second, the gap between liberal values and their application, particularly outside the confines of the

criticize Hamas should explain why the "moderate" Palestinian Authority failed to compel Israel to withdraw from the West Bank and end the Occupation. The Palestinian Authority had no leverage, as its leaders became dependent on renouncing violence against Israel in exchange for their own livelihoods and aid from Western and Arab countries.

nation-state. Regarding the first point, the outstanding Iranian-American literary critic Hamid Dabashi made a bitterly compelling criticism of European philosophy:

> those of us outside the European sphere of moral imagination do not exist in their philosophical universe. Arabs, Iranians and Muslims; or people in Asia, Africa and Latin America – we do not have any ontological reality for European philosophers, except as a metaphysical menace that must be conquered and quieted. (Dabashi 2024)

For me, it is more complicated, and each thought has its own (ideological) blind spot. Not only do the social sciences and humanities influence culture, but culture also influences knowledge production. Such observations explain how universal categories are influenced by the bias of an author's positionality. Yet, humanistic values and universal categories are salient for comparing social and political phenomena and for mobilizing humanistic solidarity.

Constructing universal categories is not an easy endeavor, particularly in relation to (il)legitimate violence. At the University of Pennsylvania, law professor Claire Finkelstein has made a "Call for Restricting Free Speech on Palestine."[62] She views the debate only in terms of potential "violence" and "(in) safety" on American university campuses, the violence in the form of genocide and war crimes in Gaza is apparently invisible.[63] Only debate and discussion can enhance our understanding of (soft) universalism, but the tension is not only between the Western world and the rest. For instance, some Arabs who are sensitive to the Palestinian cause simultaneously cheer the mass killings carried out by the Syrian regime against its own people (Haydar 2024). We see the Israeli war on Gaza as a crime against humanity, but we do not view the Syrian dictatorship in the same way (Mallat 2015).

Returning to the Western position on the genocidal war on Gaza, the problem does not lie in the universal values of human rights and international conventions,[64] nor in denying them and exposing their fallacious

[62] "To Fight Antisemitism on Campuses, We Must Restrict Speech." www.washingtonpost.com/opinions/2023/12/10/university-pennsylvania-president-magill-resigns-antisemitism-speech/.
[63] Some voices put emphasis on the question of safety. While student protesters cry out for the end to Israel's act of genocide of Palestinians, Harvard University has come under attack from alumni, including Utah Senator Mitt Romney, for supposedly not doing enough to keep Jewish students "safe." See "Academic Freedom Under Fire as Gaza Burns."
[64] In fact, many people write angry letters criticizing human rights but hinting at the double standards in applying them. See, for instance, what the human

nature, but rather in exposing how being emptied of their content through interpretations they are subjected to by vested interests and power relations (Bishara 2024). I fully agree with Azmi Bishara who observes that our criticism of the double standard should not lead the Arabs to talk about religious or civilizational conflicts with the West. Even if the West is motivated in its support of Israel by Islamophobia, this latter is a political phenomenon more than a religious one (for example, many Islamophobes are atheists).

Are liberal values applicable outside the nation-state or beyond European borders? Historically, and in the context of colonialism, not at all. Currently, the stark contrast between universal principles and their real-world application is evident in the selective enforcement and interpretation of international and human rights laws. The case of Jürgen Habermas is exemplary, as he strongly appeals to liberal theories of politics and ethics and provides a solid philosophical foundation for both democratic communication and the ethics of difference. Yet, he falters when it comes to the right of Palestinians to national liberation. He co-signed the Research Center "Normative Orders" at Goethe University Frankfurt's statement, "Principles of Solidarity: A Statement," which is entirely one-sided and expresses no regret for Israel's actions in Gaza.[65] He has demonstrated complete insensitivity to Israel's actions in the Palestinian territories, something I became aware of when I met him over dinner in Jerusalem during the period of the Second Intifada. I was taken aback by his position at that time, so his denial of Palestinian national rights is not merely a political faux pas. Regardless of one's interest in Habermas as a person and his political views, we must engage with his broader system of thought and his dialogical communicative theory.

Here, I would follow Michael Gill's two-part justification and expand it to three. First, the "conceptual isolation" of certain ideas from a problematic scholar, separating their valuable contributions from their racist or flawed views. Second, the "division of intellectual labor," meaning that some scholars will focus on the positive contributions of a problematic thinker to our knowledge, while others will critique their racist or flawed views (Gill 2023). For instance, some may analyze nineteenth-century America through

rights activist Mohamad Safa wrote: "Gaza has taught me that a lot of people who claim to be human rights activists are only active when it applies to people of a specific background or ethnicity. Human rights have a skin color, and the darker you are the less human rights you have." https://twitter.com/mhdksafa/status/1762789786807332969.
[65] "Grundsätze der Solidarität. Eine Stellungnahme." www.normativeorders.net/2023/grundsatze-der-solidaritat/.

Alexis de Tocqueville's *Democracy in America*, while others may provide a more inclusive and nuanced perspective using Harriet Martineau's *Society in America* as a critique of Tocqueville. Third, the "historical development of scientific and moral views," recognizing that humanity's conception of otherness has evolved over time and that what we consider ethical today may be deemed racist or flawed in the future.

I will, therefore, engage with Habermas's dialogical communicative theory even if I disagree with his political position on Palestine. Having said that, I can observe some patterns. With the partial exception of Herbert Marcuse, all the thinkers associated with the Frankfurt School project were just so utterly and radically inattentive to movements from what we today call the Global South. In that sense, Habermas is just simply being a good Frankfurt School theorist.[66]

I would apply the same reasoning when dealing with Heidegger, Foucault, Levinas, Locke, Kant, Hume, Marx, and others. This approach should also extend to both historical and contemporary politicians, celebrities, and public figures, allowing us to recognize their positive contributions while critically assessing their political positions, particularly with awareness of their colonial legacies. A good example is the National Museum of Fine Arts in Amsterdam, where each painting of historical Dutch figures includes an additional label explaining their role in the slave trade. I prefer this approach over the removal of David Hume's name from "David Hume Tower" at the University of Edinburgh.[67] Initially, it was suggested to rename it "Julius Nyerere Tower" in honor of the anti-colonial Tanzanian leader who graduated from Edinburgh University in 1952. However, it was later pointed out that Nyerere's leadership was marked by despotism and homophobia (Gill 2023). Similarly, one Arab sociologist suggested not teaching Durkheim due to his complete silence on French colonialism in Algeria, proposing instead to teach W.E.B. Du Bois. But can we imagine undergraduate sociology students not engaging with the founder of sociology? And what should we do knowing that Du Bois disregarded the plight of the Palestinian people while praising the establishment of the State of Israel? This endless cycle of exclusion, driven by dichotomous thinking – angel or demon, guilty or innocent – will never be resolved. Only the three-part justification suggested above offers a way to move beyond this self-defeating approach.

In brief, Euro-American knowledge production should be treated as

---

[66] See Global Dialogue's dossier about the Frankfurt School development, including its Eurocentric stance. https://globaldialogue.isa-sociology.org/uploads/imgen/3430-v13i3-english.pdf.

[67] Hume was known for his racist views, particularly in "Of National Characters." See https://davidhume.org/texts/empl1/nc.

Dipesh Chakrabarty (2007) described it – necessary but not sufficient. This is the ultimate meaning of provincializing Europe. We can question certain scholars' positions after Gaza in the same way that was done after WWII on the positions of some scholars. However, I fear a "populist" tendency that seeks to discard modernity and the universality of human rights in response to such inquiries and contradictions. However, I would remind any Western scholar advocating against domestic violence against women in the Middle East today that they should also have spoken out against Israel's mass killing of civilian women in Gaza (if they have not already done so). Similarly, because European politics and its organic intellectuals have lost their authority, referentiality and even credibility, I would now engage more with African and Latin American human rights scholars and activists, who better understand and address human suffering than their European counterparts – particularly those from Germany, the UK and France, who often fund human rights organizations in the Global South.[68] In this way, one can recognize the importance of certain topics that are particularly significant to Europeans (e.g., domestic violence), while other issues (e.g., mass human rights violations against colonized subjects) receive less attention. In this context, examining African or Latin American human rights agendas becomes especially relevant. Only by disentangling the univer- sality of human rights – embodied, for instance, in the *Universal Declaration of Human Rights* – from Euro-American mainstream politics, both past and present, can we preserve the former.[69]

Conclusion: Intolerance and Critical Dialogue

While conducting final checks on this chapter, I learned that the renowned French political scientist François Burgat, emeritus senior researcher at the French National Center for Scientific Research (CNRS), was detained by the French police on 9 July 2024, accused of being an "apologist for terrorism," and taken into custody. Suddenly, a conversation I had with Ghassan Hage about his fieldwork in Lebanon during the civil war in 1978 came to mind. One of his interviewees, a member of a right-wing

---

[68] See, for instance, how they gave compelling statements about the illegality of the Israeli occupation in the ICJ. They are mainly countries in Africa and Latin America.

[69] I fully agree with Gurminder Bhambra and John Holmwood (2021) and Syed Farid Alatas and Vineeta Sinha (2017) about the necessity of adding (past and ongoing) colonialism/coloniality as a sociological topic in our canon.

militia, claimed that the Palestinians in Lebanon aimed to take over the country and establish an alternative homeland for themselves. When Hage asked whether he had any evidence for this, the man fell into a glowering silence before angrily reproaching both the question and the questioner as politically heinous: "I will go to get my revolver from the car." Today, I feel that the level of discussion about the Israeli war on Gaza has reached this same standard of "evidence." In a similar vein, while giving a talk in Oslo about the war on Gaza, I encountered an audience member who repeatedly insisted that antisemitism is on the rise in Europe, attributing this to demonstrators calling for a ceasefire in Gaza and a political solution to the Israeli occupation. I could not stop him before asking whether it would have been considered normal during the Battle of Algiers in the 1950s or the German genocide in Namibia in the early 1900s to claim that Algerians were anti-French and Namibians were anti-German – or worse, that Algerians and Namibians were anti-Christian.

Despite this nightmare, it is more urgent than ever to create some shared perspective without alienating another group. How do we engage between two parties when one of them is so powerful? By becoming a moral community, does academia set norms that constrain the questions scholars may ask?

In this chapter, I show that the intolerance in the debate stems from polarization in a society where both symbolic liberals and conservatives contribute to this chilling political climate. Each group becomes rigid and dogmatic, reminiscent of the Progressive Patriotism of Woodrow Wilson's era or the McCarthy era campaigns against communism in the 1940s and 1950s. However, I emphasize, based on my findings, how campuses – the locus of the liberal arts – have shifted toward illiberal positions, eroding their autonomy amid extreme polarization among faculty, students and administrators.

Let us clarify: the three geographical case studies on stifling academic freedom in the UK, the United States and France, along with the specific case study on academic freedom and freedom of expression during the War on Gaza, are not always "caused" by symbolic liberals – whether university administrators, faculty, students, media actors or politicians. Instead, the broad framework provided in this chapter allows us to recognize a rising trend of intolerance in debates that coincides with the increasing power of symbolic liberalism and popular rights.

When it comes to the influence of symbolic liberals, its relationship to each case can be seen as follows:

1. Their disregard for the conception of justice either locally (e.g., the

right to dissent from the mainstream, as in the case of gender-critical feminism) or globally (e.g., the right to national liberation for colonized peoples; selective application of liberal principles due to pro-Israeli bias; and selective blindness violence only in US campuses and not in the mass killing in the Gaza strip).

2. Their imposition of a hegemonic and deculturalized conception of the good (e.g., the repression of some Muslims' conceptions of the good under the UK's Prevent policy).

3. Their framing of a group's aims as rational but not reasonable, on the grounds that these aims fail to seek a common basis for reciprocal cooperation with other groups (e.g., Liberal Zionist claims in Israel disregarding Palestinian claims).

I leave it to readers to use a narrower brush to analyze each case individually.

The great conundrum of academic freedom in the era of symbolic liberalism, excessive identity politics, guilt and guilt-washing is that both the absence of academic freedom and total academic freedom lead to political indoctrination. How to walk this thin line? In the line of Dialogical Sociology, I will advance four recommendations on how this sociology can resist labeling the other and challenge politics and media dominated by powerful and wealthy groups and lobbies while advocating for the inclusion of critical voices and resolving the tension between academic freedom and "diversity, equity and inclusion."

First, intolerance often begins with labeling the other. For instance, "woke" has become so divisive that it undermines support for the very issues it aims to highlight. It is used as a way to delegitimize any critique of dominant forms of knowledge production, but "anti-wokism" also plays this silencing game. This is why I refrain from using these terms, and even when I use the term "cancel culture," I emphasize that it is not a label for a specific group (not solely a product of the Left or the woke) but rather a phenomenon that also exists on the Right and among conservatives. How many times have I heard colleagues in academia and activists during the Arab Spring argue, "No democracy/dialogue for the enemies of democracy," particularly referring to Islamists?

Second, stifling academic freedom has serious consequences for undermining critical voices, which runs counter to the inclusivity of Dialogical Sociology and the Dialogical Liberal Project. The typical social science and humanities scholar often trades free speech for emotional safety. Elisabeth Noelle-Neumann's classic concept of the "spiral of silence," developed almost four decades ago through studies in social psychology and interpersonal communication, describes situations where people hesitate to express authentic opinions that contradict prevailing social norms due to fear of social isolation or loss of status (Noelle-Neumann 1974, cited by Norris 2020). However, the balance of public opinion is far from static; it evolves over time in response to societal development, as thoroughly documented in Pippa Norris and Ronald Inglehart's *Cultural Backlash* (2019).

Following this, Dialogical Sociology is not naïve about the power structures between groups and there is an issue of how to deliver critical thinking in the case of imbalance of power. While criticizing the powerful, we also need to simultaneously open up a dialogue with the very forces being critiqued. This is exactly how I can criticize all Israeli colonial practices in the Palestinian territories, but at the same time open the space for dialogue, for talking with some Israelis (Hanafi 2022). This is how the German literary critic Sonja Mejcher-Atassi (2024) criticizes the Israeli longstanding colonial regime but also shows us a possibility of friendship between Muslims and Jews historically, taking the example of a group of artists, writers and intellectuals. Among them are Wolfgang Hildesheimer, Jabra Ibrahim Jabra, Sally Kassab, Walid Khalidi and Rasha Salam, who came together across religious lines in a sensitive moment of possibility within the history of Palestine/Israel, working for the reasonable (and not simply the rational) way to live together. Even in times of extreme violence, Amaney Jamal and Keren Yarhi-Milo, two Palestinian and Israeli deans in American universities, remind us in a joint article that when the discourse is toxic, universities can only help free speech when there is vigorous counter-speech.[70]

More roughly, the role of Dialogical Sociology is to show that there is no pure evil or pure good. Sociology equipped with sociological imagination reminds us of the complex nature of social phenomena, the importance of the agency of actors and the logic of gift and love. This logic can defeat extreme polarization. Power cannot always come from authority and hierarchy (through domination and competition mechanisms), as many symbolic liberals think, but through collaboration and overabundance of care as it is theorized by the sociological school of social love (Iorio 2016). This school is sensitive not only to how people ethically justify their actions but also to how sociologists can take seriously this suffering and approach it as a hermeneutics of presence (Cataldi 2020).

Third, chilling polarization will persist as long as politics and media

---

[70] "The Discourse Is Tozic. Universities Can Help." www.nytimes.com/2023/10/30/opinion/princeton-columbia-israel-gaza.html.

remain dominated by powerful and wealthy groups and lobbies. Should the media be more regulated? What about digital media? According to Habermas (2023), digital media should be held accountable for published content, even if they neither produce nor edit it.

Let me develop this in relation to the Palestinian–Israeli conflict. We saw from the youth and student encampments how the old elite is completely destabilized in the United States and Europe, particularly among Jews. The latter curb the political tide against Israel's privileged status in the West and against the current Israeli colonial practice and apartheid. For the old elite, there should be no debate or discussion about the Israeli genocidal war. The goal is not to squelch critique of Israel but to outlaw it. In her blog, "Can the Palestinian speak?" Ruba Saleh wrote:

> Such ascription of Palestinians to a place outside of history, and of humanity, goes way back and has been intrinsic to the establishment of Israel...The tricks of DARVO (Denying Attacking and Reversing Victim and Offender) have been unveiled. We are now desperately in need of re-orienting the world's moral compass by exposing the intertwined processes of humanisation and dehumanisation of Jewish Israelis and Palestinians.[71]

The War on Gaza is a paradigm shift not only in the Palestinian–Israeli conflict but definitely in the crisis of Western liberal democracy and the relationship between North and South – more populism, Islamophobia and antisemitism. It reveals tensions and polarization, not only between different generations concerning the decolonization of Palestine but also the relationship between mainstream media and different neoliberal centers of power, including the Israeli lobby. It shows how much the new generation mistrusts mainstream media and relies on social media (including the Chinese TikTok). The outcome of this paradigm shift is neither fully negative nor positive. Many factors will be at work to swing toward privileging the negative or the positive. However, the salient factor is the organized social movement. What is heartening is that these groups who demonstrate in the streets in support of the ceasefire in Gaza, are mostly the same ones who defend the rights of oppressed minorities, including LGBTQ+, and who defend the environment.[72] In the language of Rana Sukarieh (2024), there is "a

---

[71] "Can the Palestinian Speak?" https://allegralaboratory.net/can-the-palestinian-speak/.

[72] It is worth noting that some of the ecological movements such as Fridays for Future (FFF) took a clear position against the genocidal war on Gaza. FFF is a

continuum between an anti-colonial Third World Internationalist imaginary and a pragmatic rights-based imaginary as central to the trajectory of the [BDS] movement." Therefore, they deserve to be described as moral groups, but we must acknowledge that their weight in the political arena is limited as long as they are not organized within influential frameworks, such as political parties, or at least politically organized. The emergence of young new actors, faculty and students, in campuses challenging the injustice or business-as-usual of the old elite formation (whether from symbolic liberals or conservative) is a major breakthrough in the direction of the Dialogical Liberal Project.

Fourth, both Dina Kiwan and Tariq Modood (2022b) were interested in resolving the tension "between academic freedom and 'diversity, equity and inclusion'" (DEI). Kiwan considers DEI more as a prerequisite for academic freedom, while Modood treats them equally by considering that "neither commitment can be absolute, because each must be open to being qualified by the other, and; the two sets of commitments will clash at times." For me, Dialogical Sociology and the Dialogical Liberal Project need to keep renegotiating a stretch of the border between these two regions through dialogue and not legal action or recourse to disinvitation/no platforming in order to hear all views (including all forms of dissent) and not commit what Miranda Fricker (2009) calls "epistemic injustice." It is more complicated when it comes to the content of speech (critique versus prejudice); what to do with speech or writing that is not unlawful, but which our commitments to DEI call upon us to censure? In other words, how to distinguish between criticism of Islamophobia and antisemitism? Modood suggested that the answer could not be determined solely by examining the proposition itself. Rather, it requires consideration of a broader context: Does the proposition stereotype the other? Does it invite a dialogue with the other? Is the language civil and contextually appropriate? Are there insincere criticisms for ulterior motives? It depends on how we reply to determine whether we are indeed dealing with racism/Islamophobia/antisemitism or not (Modood 2022b).

In brief, working against intolerance and for the reconciliation between academic freedom and DEI is a long process that needs to engage parties in critical dialogue – the dialogue that I advocate by addressing the illiberal trend of symbolic liberalism and the populism of conservatives.

---

youth-led and -organized movement that began in August 2018, after 15-year-old Greta Thunberg and other young activists sat in front of the Swedish parliament every school day for three weeks, to protest against the lack of action on the climate crisis.

CHAPTER 5

Secularism as Religion vs. Multicultural Secularism

Bobos [Bourgeois Bohemian] abandon questions of identity in favor of an empty talk about laicism. They are the gravediggers of their own culture and the young "Arab" population, which is overwhelmed by the alternative truths of conspiracy theories, antisemitism, and communitarianism, has no difficulties swiping away the body of this dying France.

Thorsten Botz-Bornstein, *The New Aesthetics of Deculturation* (2019)

Introduction

In 1992, while studying for my Ph.D. at EHESS in Paris, a close Tunisian friend, writing a Master's in anthropology, was shaking while telling me what happened to him that day. He had an appointment with his thesis director at her office in EHESS. Her secretary asked him to call the director at her home as she was tired. On the phone, she proposed to him to come to her home, that they have a light lunch and talk about his thesis. When my friend told her that it would be a pleasure to come but that he was fasting (it was the month of Ramadan), she angrily replied: "You cannot be an anthropologist while you fast" (meaning being religious), and she ended the call.

This story is not an extreme case of how some French scholars understand secularism as anti-religion. If you read *La religion en miettes ou la question des sectes* (2001) by *the* leading French sociologist of religion, Danièle Hervieu-Léger, you will have the same feeling. Hervieu-Léger shows how minimalism has become religiosity, relating it to ceremonies (like marriages and funerals) rather than everyday ritual practice. Then, if the degree of religiosity of a group is excessive, it becomes a *sect*, undermining societal cohesion and laicity, hinting of course at the religiosity of Muslims in France. I had the same conversations with sociologists in China about the Muslims there and how difficult it is for a light-religious society to understand that. Even in the Arab world, a Palestinian religious friend who belongs to a leftist Palestinian faction told me that his leader one day told him how much he was suspicious of seeing him praying – and being a good leftist. Is there a paradox? This will be the subject of this chapter.

In this chapter and the next, I focus on the consequences of imposing a hegemonic conception of the good by symbolic liberals in two areas related to religion – secularism and sexuality – through two contradictory movements. One movement involves the shift of religion from the public sphere to the private, while sexuality moves in the opposite direction. This would not be problematic if there were a societal dialogue on how both should be positioned. However, the intolerance displayed in debates on these issues has led to severe polarization. I ultimately advocate for a Dialogical Sociology that embraces soft secularism – a sociology that balances the collective and individual dimensions of the political liberal project.

Five Features of Symbolic Liberals' Secularism

Secularism is essential for the success of any liberal project. I define it in my Dialogical Liberal Project, drawing on the work of the French philosopher Cécile Laborde (2017) and the Indian-American political scientist Rajeev Bhargava (2019). It is a conception of justice that maintains a safe and principled distance between religion and the state, with minimal state neutrality. The term "minimal" refers to neutrality regarding competing conceptions of the good but not with respect to the conception of justice. This is why Rawls does not use the concept of neutrality in this context (Kchaou 2019). Secularism, in this sense, is a mechanism for achieving a political liberal project and *not* as a value by itself.

Symbolic liberals are often intolerant of religion, viewing it as a relic of the past that has no place in the public sphere. A major research program by the International Panel on Social Progress (Davie and Ammerman 2018) suggests that religion and religiosity can just as easily foster social progress and resistance to colonization and tyranny as they can unleash violent forces, encourage conservatism and sectarianism, and sustain forms of social and political oppression. In other words, the same religion can play different roles in different contexts. Yet, symbolic liberals have primarily focused on the negative role of religion. While religious individuals may hold some socially conservative views, they can also be more humanistic than symbolic liberals. The philosopher François Dosse (2024), a specialist in French intellectual history, demonstrates that the Christian humanist movement avoided the ideological Cold War trap among (liberal/leftist) intellectuals by positioning itself in relation to both blocs (East and West). Christian intellectual journals strongly denounced the brutal French war in Algeria during 1956–57, particularly opposing colonialism and the systematic use of torture, as evidenced by publications in *Esprit* and *Témoignage chrétien*. In the Arab world, an additional issue arises: the virulence of conflicts between elites is such that much of their academic research remains insensitive to norms and values as they manifest in the practices of social actors. Fundamentally, this problem is reduced to a polarization between universalists and cultural relativists/particularists/contextualists, or between symbolic liberals and (il) liberal religious actors.

Although symbolic liberals often understand religion as a separate social sphere, I argue, following François Gauthier (2020), that society should not be seen as differentiated into separate compartments, with religion being one of them. The spheres of religion, culture, politics, economy and the social are interconnected by a common logic that allows a given society to be understood in its totality, in line with the theorizations of Marcel Mauss and Karl Polanyi. However, due to an absolutist and exclusive distinction between religion and the secular, symbolic liberals have often conceived of secularism as a unitary model (primarily the French style) that should be replicated identically.

Their positivist paradigm views religion as a system diametrically opposed to rationality, a minor sub-phenomenon or superstructure that would be superseded by the development of an industrial economic structure and its associated scientific culture, as if religion were inevitably destined to be shelved like antiquity. In this paradigm, secularization is defined as the process by which religion is confined to the private sphere. The supposed irreducible contradiction between the sacred and the secular, as well as the presence of a clerical class, has been projected from the Christian context onto the Islamic one (Asad 2003; Hermassi 2012). All of this has led symbolic liberals to lose touch with the substance of religion and personal religious experience. As a result, they have been unable to recognize the coexistence of the sacred and the secular in the era of multiple modernities, within the paradigm of pluralism (Berger 2014) and the ethos of pluralization (Connolly 1995), or within a more nuanced understanding of the process of separating religion and state (Cipriani 2017), which challenges many scholars' assumptions about the inevitable decline of religion in modernity. The secular, in its relationship to the religious, can take different forms. Many countries in the Global South, particularly in Asia, can be described as spaces of "traffic" between the religious and secular spheres. For Prasenjit Duara,

> Traffic belongs to the family of circulation within a society and refers to the redistribution of qualities and attributes associated with religion in earlier periods in the process of creating the secular. We recognize Max Weber's concept of the penetration of the Protestant ethic into capitalist practice and Carl Schmitt's concept of confessional principles shaping the nation as prime instances of traffic. (Duara 2014, 123)

For Duara, secularization, as understood in the dominant Western paradigm, represents alienation from the cosmos, spirit, and transcendent sources. Using the traffic metaphor, we can even challenge the notion of Muslim exceptionalism (i.e., the idea that Islam is not secularizable) by demonstrating how the secular permeates Muslim individuals through their everyday practices and worldview, rather than focusing on Islam as an unchangeable entity. Abdolmohammad Kazemipur (2022) has revealed this presence in contemporary Iran.

In the Arab world, the problem manifests itself in different ways. While conservatives in the region refuse to acknowledge that changing patterns of religiosity are driven by transformations inherent to local contexts rather than by a "Western invasion" of the Muslim world, symbolic liberals attribute these new patterns of religiosity to the influence of foreign Muslim powers (e.g., the International Bureau of the Muslim Brotherhood). This simplistic binary reasoning has also shaped the perspectives of symbolic liberals, who contrast the West – associated with materialism and rationalism – with the Arab world, which they perceive as rooted in indigenous knowledge based on revelation.

Here, I examine the symbolic liberals' interpretation of secularism, which reduces it to a universalist, one-size-fits-all concept that often aligns closely with the French model. The recent exclusionary policies in France have led many to question the new French secularism and the challenges posed by its imposition both within and beyond the country.

French laicism is no longer exactly what it was at the beginning of the twentieth century. However, let us dispel any ambiguity: its core principle – ensuring both individual freedom and freedom of conscience, as well as equality of rights and duties in both private and public spheres – remains fully (though subtly) universal. There is no question here of opposing or even merely criticizing this secular state, which, while respecting the citizenship of all – believers and non-believers alike – is defined by its separation of political and religious institutions. Nor is there any question of criticizing the laws that establish citizenship, which, within the nation-state, extend rights and benefits beyond religious believers, ensuring a minimal neutrality of the state despite the existence of competing conceptions of the good. Due to the widespread adoption of this secularization process, this model of the secular state has become dominant globally (Zuber 2019), including in many Muslim-majority countries. This is evident even in nations governed or co-governed by Islamic political parties, such as Turkey, Malaysia, Tunisia (before the coup of July 2021) and Morocco under the "Commander of the Faithful," as well as in smaller Asian countries, including former Soviet states with Muslim-majority populations.

Indeed, historical secularism has several virtues that give it universal significance, particularly in differentiating religion from politics, protecting religion from state authority and shielding the state from the hegemony of the religious clergy – a long history that Azmi Bishara (2013; 2015) has written about extensively. However, there is no sociological evidence to suggest that secularization necessarily leads to a decline in religiosity, nor that believers should be prevented from infusing political action with morality, as is the case in many countries worldwide, not just in Muslim-majority ones. With this essential clarification in place, five key reasons emerge as to why this version of secularism promoted by symbolic liberals is not only unsuitable for export beyond France but also problematic within the country itself. This observation is based on my research (Hanafi 2024c) on the influence of French secularism among the Arab secularist Left and on symbolic liberals' efforts to impose their particular interpretation of secularism.

Ethnocentrism

Underpinning symbolic liberalism, secularism has an "ethnocentric" character rooted in the Christian reformist conception of religion. The works of American anthropologist Talal Asad (2003), Cécile Laborde (2017) and French historian Jean Baubérot (2014; 2017) have all demonstrated that symbolic liberals' secularism has approached religion in the Christian manner, more specifically in the manner of reformed Catholicism, by reducing it to individual belief and freedom of conscience and confining it to the home and the church. As a result, rituals (e.g., displaying fasting during Ramadan, as in the case of Muslim football players in France) and other public forms of religious affirmation (such as wearing the Islamic headscarf) are often regarded as unacceptable forms of proselytism.

In the name of defending the ideals of this secularism, symbolic liberals have no hesitation in transforming themselves into *faqihs* (Muslim jurists) or *muftis* to prove that the veil "is not part of Islam,"[1] or that it is a "symbol of the slavery of women," as "the Arab/Muslim women always submitted to Arab/Muslim machos," critically denounced by Guénif-Souilamas and Macé 2004; Puar 2007; Shahrokni 2019). In a completely ethnocentric display, they project meaning and cultural interpretation onto Muslim societies that emanate only from European culture. Such arguments clearly violate the most basic freedoms accorded to all, since it is up to each individual to define and give meaning to their social behavior, as far as they do not harm others. Of course, this is also related to communitarian social norms – establishment, conformity, violation, rewards and punishments.

The French law banning headscarves in schools and for civil servants in public institutions passed on 15 March 2004, can legitimately be seen as an explicit violation of the freedom to practice religion.[2] Driving this legislation more than anything appears to be the sheer rejection of, and genuine obsessive disgust for, the headscarf by the majority of French citizens. Martha Nussbaum (2009) argues for the condemnation of any legislation built on the subjective rejection of the actions of others. She further asserts that moral or legal judgments cannot be justified or legitimized by feelings of disgust or other forms of subjective rejection.

The symbolic liberals' exclusionary secularism à la française has, alas, been replicated in some European countries (e.g., Belgium and Denmark), while others resist. Where French lawmakers enforce such bans on what is part of the conception of the good, their counterparts in Great Britain (not to mention the United States, Canada and Australia, where the famous "Burkini" originated) see no contradiction in a Muslim policewoman wearing a hijab or a Sikh policeman wearing a turban. Very recently, this radical opposition was once again expressed in at least two ways. A campaign launched by the Council of Europe to promote the recognition and acceptance of diversity among women, including the freedom to wear the headscarf, was met with virulent criticism, leading to its cancellation.[3] The French anthropologist

---

[1]   See, for instance, "'Point de vue.' Le voile, une obligation pour les musulmanes?" www.ouest-france.fr/reflexion/point-de-vue/point-de-vue-le-voile-une-obligation-pour-les-musulmanes-7136815.

[2]   "France: Headscarf Ban Violates Religious Freedom: By Disproportionately Affecting Muslim Girls, Proposed Law Is Discriminatory." www.hrw.org/news/2004/02/26/france-headscarf-ban-violates-religious-freedom.

[3]   "Hijab Campaign Tweets Pulled by Council of Europe After French Backlash." www.bbc.com/news/world-europe-59149035.

Florence Bergeaud-Blackler viewed the campaign as part of a romanticization of the veil that ignored the fact that some women are "raped, vitriolized, and burned if they do not wear the veil" (2023, 143). Of all the members of the European Union, only France – through the voice of Sarah El Hairy, in her capacity as State Secretary for Youth at the time – officially protested against the Council of Europe's campaign, despite the fact that some of her relatives wear the headscarf.[4] This intolerant secularism is expressed in different ways. Recently, Valérie Pécresse, President of the Île-de-France Regional Council, asked her council (in March 2023) to rename a secondary school in Seine-Saint-Denis, named after Angela Davis, on the pretext that the American philosopher and activist had signed a petition criticizing the ban on veils in public schools. This "secular identity," to use Jean Baubérot's (2017) words, transforms Islam into a religion "alien" to European culture and one that is supposedly "incompatible" with democratic values.

More than Just a Mechanism, Secularism as a "Value in Itself"

Symbolic liberals consider secularism not simply as an instrument of governance but as an objective in itself. In their view, secularism is no longer a means of implementing the values of political liberalism – freedom, equality and pluralism – within the framework of a democratic state. Rather, they see secularism as an intrinsic bearer of universal values, regardless of the consequences for society.

I argue here that while the concept of justice should be shared by all citizens, the notion of (liberal) pluralism should allow for the multiplicity of ideas of the "good" and, therefore, a good life for different groups in society and the individuals within them. In its "new" sense, however, secularism takes into account the historical conditions and cultural environment of only one segment of society (albeit a majority).

For example, while the presence of a cross in public school classrooms is considered contrary to secularism, a cross in the public square of a country with a Christian architectural heritage cannot be seen as such. When liberal conceptions of justice and the good compete, society debates them in the public sphere using public reason or moral justifications derived from culture, tradition and the influence of globalization. The affirmation of secularity poses no problem as long as the reasoning does not extend beyond a sphere that is audible and acceptable to all or most citizens. It is difficult to distinguish in these reasonings between what is merely a composite vestige

---

[4]   "EU-Funded Hijab Campaign Sparks Outrage." www.dw.com/en/eu-funded-hijab-campaign-sparks-outrage/a-59725546.

of religious teaching and cultural practice, and other sources or moral references. For instance, is the presence of a statue of the Virgin Mary at a street corner part of a religious conception of how a neighborhood can be protected, or a simple secular view of heritage? This is not really important as long as no social group feels excluded by the presence of this statue.[5]

Secularism, therefore, is not an end in itself. Rather, it is a means – it is the grammar – that makes it possible to control the shape of this debate and respect the concept of (multicultural) citizenship while accepting, for example (in the area of religious or ethnic cults, rituals, and festivals), exceptions for the benefit of minorities, as long as these exceptions do not harm society as a whole. In a society where Christians make up the majority, it is natural that certain official holidays would have Christian origins. But this should not preclude citizens of other faiths from celebrating their own holidays. Unlike France, Germany grants such rights to other religious minorities.[6]

We should, therefore, emphasize here the difference, too often overlooked, between two very different dynamics – one, where a society with a low level of religiosity pushes the state to secularize it further, and another, in Arab and Muslim societies, that resists a politically "illiberal" separatist secularism that seeks to reduce religion to the simple rituals of birth and death. Numerous prescriptions relating to the "respect for secularism" should, therefore, take into account the diverse terms of these two societal dynamics.

Let us take the example of Lebanese society, which has relatively strong religiosity, at least for some of its confessional communities, making it very different from French society. When it comes to widespread attitudes toward the institution of marriage, what should be done if the population clearly expresses a preference for maintaining the various confessional courts (dealing only with personal status norms – birth, marriage, death, inheritance) alongside the civil court? A recent survey I conducted in 2021–22 of a non-representative sample of 412 male and female students in Lebanese universities showed that more than two-thirds of those surveyed were against the abolition of confessional courts, despite the urging of many civil society associations and symbolic liberals. Does this mean that

---

[5] People can be sensitive to religion even when they themselves are not religious. According to a survey conducted by Scott-Baumann et al. (2020), in the UK, most university students agree that religion can be an important source of moral values, even among non-religious people.

[6] "German Official's Proposal for Muslim Holidays Gets Rejected." https://apnews. com/article/0937a90b4d644d8f8e3c2e4fd84d1497.

religious courts have the right to adopt legislation that could be in direct contradiction with the *Universal Declaration of Human Rights*? There is no reason to think so. Based on the results of other opinion surveys conducted using a representative sample in four Arab countries (Hanafi forthcoming), the answer is clearly negative, by a large majority. I argue here that such an attitude toward keeping these courts should not result in maintaining the status quo but rather accommodate all the genuinely universal components of the concept of secularism. In the Lebanese example of the marriage issue, the state must therefore ensure that citizens have the right to choose between a religious court and a civil court. At the same time, it remains essential for the state to have the right to oppose certain judgments by religious courts if they contradict the concept of justice adopted consensually by society. For example, the state must be able to punish all domestic violence and ensure that there is a minimum sentence to be handed down by religious courts, as well as that any citizen has the right to appeal to a civil court if they feel that the religious court is undermining the principles of justice. It is interesting to note that the marriages of some Lebanese (whether involving mixed religious marriages or not) are conducted outside Lebanon, mostly in Cyprus, to escape the confessional courts – but not for long, as their family affairs (e.g., inheritance, divorce) will be subjected to the confessional court of the father.

A Secularism That Excludes a "Foreign" Religion

Symbolic liberals' secularism has been weaponized for passing restrictive legislation against minority religions.[7] In place of any public debate on aspects of the prevailing majoritarian culture, minorities with different lifestyles (including all religious practices and rituals that go into forming the "good life") are legislated against unilaterally.

After its legislation on the headscarf, France introduced additional legislation specifically against wearing the *burka*, and then yet more against wearing the burkini, even though it is very difficult to establish that these

---

[7] Symbolic liberals are not only weaponizing secularism against those perceived as the Other but also weaponizing sciences like psychology. In his outstanding book, *Doing Harm: How the World's Largest Psychological Association Lost Its Way in the War on Terror* (2023), Roy Eidelson examines how and why the American Psychological Association failed to align with human rights groups in efforts to curb the US government's unchecked pursuit of security and retribution in the two tumultuous decades following 9/11. This failure has had significant consequences, including the stigmatization of minorities and their religions.

practices would in any way harm the majority or the social contract. This normative frenzy has continued in France with more recent cases – for example, the French Football Federation's barring of breaks during matches for Muslim players to break their fast during the month of Ramadan, or the education minister's use of the notion of "religious symbols by destination" to ban long dresses worn by some schoolgirls (September 2023). Is this concept of "religious symbols by destination" not extraordinary? It means that anything can be banned as if it were a real (negative) symbol because it "alludes" to something. I am sensitive to this, as I have heard from some of the audience when I have given talks about the Palestinian–Israeli conflict that criticizing Israel "alludes" to antisemitism. This reminds me of some Sufi interpretations of the Quran, where exegesis is unrelated to the text!

The lifestyle choices of Muslim French individuals, as part of their conception of the "good," have been identified as a site for potential radicalization. In 2019, the French Ministry of the Interior, led by Christophe Castaner, outlined several markers that could be indicative of radicalization. These markers include: distancing oneself from family and old friends, dropping out of school, changing behaviors related to food, clothing, language, and finances, as well as changes in identity-related actions such as making asocial remarks, rejecting authority, and rejecting community life (Esmili 2024, 72). Hamza Esmili highlights that between 2014 and 2019, more than 72,000 reports were filed as part of the effort to combat radicalization, though most of these reports were not connected to any violent incidents. Esmili notes that radicalization is viewed as something that can affect almost anyone, without necessarily targeting a particular community. While this approach is presented as liberal, it reflects the way symbolic liberals frame the issue: "It is not a problem of a whole community, despite the potential incrimination of all its members" (Esmili 2024, 73). This means that while the French government's approach is intended to address individual behaviors, it risks stigmatizing entire communities, particularly Muslim communities, based on these markers.

As I showed in Chapter 2, all this has led French political scientist Olivier Roy (2022) to warn against such laws and an "extension of the domain of the norm" in several Western countries, and against the shrinking of the public space for negotiation, debate and dialogue. How to overcome this majority/ minority secularism comes best from the Bristol School of Multiculturalism (BSM). Established by Tariq Modood, Bhikhu Parekh, Nasar Meer and Varun Uberoi, this school understands multiculturalism not just as accommodating of minorities but as recognizing them institutionally in the framework of national identity. As Geoffrey Brahm Levey put it,

Even if a national identity were to be defined in political terms, it would not stop cultural minorities from contributing to and being part of a national-cultural identity, just as it does not stop the lingua franca from being part of that identity. A national-cultural identity is the dynamic outcome of the myriad interactions among all members of a political community (and often of geopolitical and cultural forces outside it). (Levey 2018, 210)

A Secularism Against Imbuing Political Action with Morality

In secular settings, the dissociation of politics and religion certainly makes sense whenever it is a question of limiting the exercise of political power by clerics whose actions are exclusively in the interests of their believers. Yassin al-Haj Saleh (2011) makes it clear that secularism means a separation of religion from sovereignty (coercion and public jurisdiction), and not from politics itself. The politicization of religion and the moral role it intends to play, negatively or positively, has become evident in many countries, including secular ones.

The electoral influence of the churches has become clear in many democratic countries, where it affects both the Left and the Right. In Brazil, the same Pentecostals who voted for Lula (and got 100 MPs in 2016) went on to vote later on for Jair Bolsonaro.[8] Yet no one has called for a ban on "political Christianity." So, it is no longer acceptable to focus solely on the negative role of religiosity – politically and socially – because of its possible role in trajectories of radicalization, sectarianism or social and political subjugation.

In other contexts, religiosity can serve social progress, civic solidarity and/ or resistance to colonialism and authoritarianism. Some Islamist movements have become "neo-Islamist" in the sense that politics has tamed the rigidity of their ideology, which the exercise of power sought to contain. These new political actors have given themselves the means to distinguish between the sacred nature of the object of their belief and the apparent profane and impure nature of political work, which requires above all the mastery of various techniques and wisdom in management. This is, importantly, how the separation between political action and preaching has gradually come

---

[8] For insights into the diverse voting patterns of Pentecostals in Brazil, see "'It is not a sin to vote for Lula': The Left and Evangelicalism in Brazil." https://peoplesdispatch.org/2022/09/29/it-is-not-a-sin-to-vote-for-lula-the-left-and-evangelicalism-in-brazil/.

about. Therefore, while the preacher and the religious jurist (*faqih*) will try to convince believers not to drink alcohol, the politician and the jurist will not try to prevent its sale, because it is the right of Christians and non-believers/lightly religious people alike to choose whether or not to drink it.

In light of all the above, the term "political Islam" loses most of its meaning. It is a stereotyping generalization that does not account for the heterogeneity of Islamic political thought, from the moderate to the extremist (held by certain individuals), from Islamic movements to official Islam. The term "political Islam" is now used only to stigmatize a minority – an important and respectable component of French society; its use suggests that all Islamist trajectories are identically reducible to the influence of Sayyid Qutb's followers – from the Muslim Brotherhood to Al-Qaeda and Daesh, a point regularly emphasized by François Burgat (2008; 2016) (who stresses the diversity of the broad political spectrum stretching "from Ghannouchi to Baghdadi"). This criminalization of "political Islam" can be found in France, where, since the Mureaux speech on 2 October 2020,[9] President Macron and his former Minister of the Interior (Gérald Darmanin) have undertaken de facto to outlaw (and dissolve) any Muslim associations wishing to take part in political debate on an oppositional basis. Effectively, some associations were dissolved (e.g., Collective Against Islamophobia in France) and some imams were deported even though they had lived in France for more than four decades. The newly appointed Minister of the Interior, Bruno Retailleau, considers that when he talks about "political Islam," it is the Islam that expresses lifestyles different from the Cultural majoritarianism.[10]

It is interesting to note that while anthropology is supposed to be sensitive to cultural pluralism, some of its French contributions seem to be quite insensitive. Two works in particular stand out: the book edited by Bernard Rougier, *Les territoires conquis de l'islamisme* [Territorial Conquest of Islamism] (2022), which introduces the notion of Islamic separatism, and the book by Florence Bergeaud-Blackler, *Le Frérisme et ses réseaux: L'enquête* [The Muslim Brotherhood Network in Europe] (2023), which has the obsession that political Islam is everywhere in France and Europe and undermines the values of the Republic. Added to which is the growing Islamophobia in France, where simply defending the view that Muslim

9   "La République en actes: Discours du Président de la République sur le thème de la lutte contre les séparatismes." www.elysee.fr/emmanuel-macron/2020/10/02/la-republique-en-actes-discours-du-president-de-la-republique-sur-le-theme-de-la-lutte-contre-les-separatismes.
10 See his first meeting with the French Commission of Law at the French parliament: www.youtube.com/watch?v=78LXIbbQre8.

women have the right to wear whatever they see fit is considered contrary to the "values of the Republic." It is a striking example of the instrumentalization of the defense of human rights as it is portrayed as a weapon designed to strike at a minority accused of having a particular conception of the good or the good life that is "incompatible with the French republic." These incitements are acts to prevent any Muslim constituents in Europe (apart from the most strictly "domesticated" fraction, in the mode of colonial Islam) from organizing and expressing any vision of political ethics.

By labeling all these Islamic expressions "political Islam," and as such illegal, symbolic liberals are in fact calling for a pure and simple ban on all dissent, but also pluralism in the conception of the hegemonic republican "good." This shortcut fails to take into account a reality that has been confirmed year after year, namely, that nowhere in the Arab region can purely security-based solutions resolve the fate of the most conservative Islamic political parties. It is only through dialogue conducted within the framework of the rule of law that these parties can be challenged and integrated. Why do symbolic liberals ignore the rooted causes of jihadist extremism and violence? One of the salient contributing factors is the absence of political space among the tyrants of the Arab world. Then the despots will call their European governments to repress "political Islam," who will listen to them looking for lucrative commercial contracts with them.

A Secularism Where the "Foreign" Religion is Being Coopted by Politics

The distinction between the political and religious spheres should simply mean the autonomy of religious institutions vis-à-vis political ones. However, the reality today is quite different, particularly where the Muslim minority is concerned. Under symbolic liberals' conception, temporal authority exercises dominance over religious institutions. This is whether symbolic liberals are from the Left or from the Right. Usually, the European Left is against Muslims who don't submit to cultural majoritarianism, while the far Right is against Islam, period. When former President Nicolas Sarkozy called for the organization of the Muslim community in France,[11] it was clear, even before elections were held, who would lead such an organization. Instead of facilitating genuine representation of the community through associations that would express their aspirations and organizing their activities (as is quite naturally the case for the Jewish communities), he mandated that he

[11] "Sarkozy's Muslim Group Criticised." www.aljazeera.com/news/2007/4/24/ sarkozys-muslim-group-criticised.

alone would nominate 30 percent of the council. The France of Emmanuel Macron has similarly discouraged any attempt at genuine representation of the Muslims of France.[12] It considers that freely elected representatives of the Muslim community would necessarily constitute obstacles to their assimilation policy. However, I am focusing here on the problems of exclusionary secularism, but there are other factors related to absence of democratic political representation, such as the pathological fragmentation of Muslim communities in Europe resulting from the interference of the security services of the Maghreb countries, Turkey and the Gulf States.

While the principle of state neutrality (in terms of competing conceptions of the good) is necessary for the autonomy of religious institutions, this does not mean that the state can refrain from fairly managing and regulating religious pluralism, especially in a multi-ethnic and multicultural society. If we look at a wide range of political systems – from the most repressive authoritarian states to liberal democratic regimes – we see that most of them are involved in managing religious pluralism (Modood and Sealy 2024). In such a configuration, the state may have different roles, depending on its vision of the moral dimension of religion. It can be positive with policies of integration and inclusion, policies of recognition, or negative with policies of exclusion, prohibition of religious manifestations, cultural indifference, policies of non-recognition or misrecognition (Turner 2011).

The symbolic liberals' secularism of exclusion focuses only on the negative vision and has become the fatal weapon of the (extreme) Right. It is a secularism described by Jean Baubérot (2014) as falsified and by Jean-Fabien Spitz (2023) as misguided and liberticidal (*dévoyée* et *liberticide*). It has thus turned into an ideology as totalizing as the one it seeks to denounce, with the ambition of seizing control of all aspects of religiosity in society, a kind of civil religion (Baubérot 2017). Just as there is a call to recognize the existence of non-believers in society, and with them their civil moral system, it should be just as important to recognize those who hold values with religious roots, or those who hold the same values, but expressed in religious terms.

Yet, from Rachida Dati to Fadela Amara, French political parties have never chosen political actors of Arab or Muslim origin to be ministers or Members of Parliament (MPs), other than those who are supposed to have

[12] A former unofficial advisor of President Macron, Hakim El Karoui, calls for a French Islam and proposes creating three bodies: the Foundation for Islam in France, the Muslim Association for French Islam and the "Grand Imam of France," who would be responsible for promoting doctrinal sources reinterpreted in line with French republican principles (El Karoui 2016; Kostić 2024).

distanced themselves as much as possible from the culture of their ancestors, which is nonetheless a culture of a large part of the Muslim community in France.

However, the institutionalized state Islamophobia (in the sense of J.-F. Bayart)[13] displayed in the law on Islamic separatism does not explain everything. The Islamophobia of a large part of French society (under the influence of symbolic liberalism in the media) must also be considered. In his book *Who Is Charlie?* (2016), Emmanuel Todd suggested that Islamophobia in France often masked the social conservatism of Catholicism. He noted that demonstrations with Islamophobic overtones were far more frequent in provincial France, such as in Ouest Bretagne or cities like Lyon, where, even if Catholicism was no longer really practiced, the old foundations of the Catholic order were still active. Todd, however, has probably overemphasized the role of classical Catholicism. Nothing should obscure the fact that, in other segments of the French population, it is an old and very classic racism, rooted in the trauma of decolonization, that seems to be the main source of hostility to expressions of Muslim religiosity in the public space.

Conclusion: Soft/Multicultural Secularism in the Dialogical Liberal Project

The objective of this chapter is to save the liberal project (thinly understood) from those who want to impose their conception of the good on society and alienate conservative and religious groups. Following Cécile Laborde, I am not analogizing religion with the category of "conceptions of the good," but disaggregating it into a plurality of normative dimensions, some of which are related to the conception of justice and others to the conception of the good. The Dialogical Liberal Project, focused on soft secularism, or what Modood and Sealy (2024) call multicultural secularism, is based on the minimum standard of human rights set out by the *Universal Declaration of Human Rights*, as well as other international conventions. There are mainly three: the *Universal Declaration of Human Rights*, together with the International Covenant on Civil and Political Rights, plus the International Covenant on Economic, Social and Cultural Rights, form the so-called *International Bill of Human Rights*, ratified by the vast majority of countries

---

[13] "Jean-François Bayart: 'Que le terme plaise ou non, il y a bien une islamophobie d'Etat en France.'" 31 October 2020. www.lemonde.fr/idees/article/2020/10/31/jean-francois-bayart-que-le-terme-plaise-ou-non-il-y-a-bien-une-islamophobie-d-etat-en-france_6057987_3232.html.

and fundamental to post-World War II international law. This should be understood abstractly.

At the same time, to maintain viable national and communitarian systems of human rights, these concepts need to be contextualized locally according to existing normative systems and societal norms. Indeed, each country that ratifies a UN convention should pass national legislation commensurate with the convention, so that the UN committee for the convention can oversee and audit the implementation of the convention. This, I think, is the means to overcome the "non-binding" aspect of international conventions. For instance, the Universal Declaration notes the equality of humans and, in the framework of the nation-state, the equality of citizens. This cannot be without a principled distance between the state and religion. Let us conceive an appropriate system of secularism that is not inherently anti-clericalist and fits each local context.

Dispelling these misunderstandings is essential if we are to establish a soft/multicultural secularism that is not so divisive.[14] This is necessary, indispensable, to each society – a multi-secularity that cannot be set up as an end in itself, sacralized and blind to the conditions under which it is implemented in each national or communal context.

Another point to be raised is that in the case of disagreement between different perceptions of rights, the state should be recognized as the ultimate arbiter, a point that is consistent with Cécile Laborde (2017). The qualification is that the state must truly respect the *Universal Declaration of Human Rights*, for sovereignty is not absolute. Yet when "state sovereignty, economic interests, and power monopolies were privatized and were not accountable to any form of public scrutiny" (Mbembe 2001), it is very difficult to keep the state as the ultimate court of appeal.

Secularism is merely a mechanism – albeit to a great extent – capable of effectively affirming the values of the Dialogical Liberal Project. By this, I mean that the major battle is not about how to deal with Islam or Arab traditions but how people in their everyday life manage complex moral reasonings – what I call partial secularization from below (Hanafi forthcoming). This concurs with the work of Rasheed al-Haj Saleh (2023), who argues that there are two (culturalist) camps in contemporary Arab ethical thought through the lens of the relationship between ethics and politics: "The first considers ethics as an ideal fixed in time that transcends

---

[14] For example, consider how I addressed the importance of the concept of secularism for the Arab layperson in a one-hour program on Al-Araby TV in 2021 (www.alaraby.com/program/show-12244), which was recently translated into English (Magout 2024).

society and politics," thus religious reform precedes political reform, or secularism precedes liberal democracy. The second camp "assumes that 'ordinary people' are responsible for the alleged decline in morality" (Saleh 2023, 7), that is, high religiosity precedes liberal democracy. Both camps are indeed wrong.

CHAPTER 6

Sexual and Gender Diversity: Embracing vs. Celebrating

The road to hell is paved with good intentions.

(Proverb)

First and foremost, I want to emphasise that I hold the highest regard for every individual, regardless of their personal preferences, gender, religion, or background. … Respect is a value that I hold in great esteem. It extends to others, but it also encompasses respect for my own personal beliefs. Hence, I don't believe I am the most suitable person to participate in this campaign.

French football player, Zakaria Aboukhlal, www.thepinknews.
com/2023/05/16/toulouse-fc-football-homophobia-zander-murray/.

Introduction

The epigraph is the 14 May 2023 tweet of Zakaria Aboukhlal, after a decision by the French Federation of Football to celebrate sexual diversity, including LGBTQ, requesting each player to wear shirts with rainbow-colored numbers. Toulouse Football Club benched players who refused to take part in this campaign and gave them a warning. The French media strongly criticized these players, requesting their clubs not renew their contracts and even sack them.

I would like to thank Eric Macé for his insightful comments into an early version of this chapter and also many Indian colleagues who discussed part of this chapter when I delivered my keynote in the Third Annual Lecture of the *Contributions to Indian Sociology*.

This is one of multiple incidences we find in the media about the conflict between those who clearly declare that they *embrace* sexual and gender diversity, while refusing to *celebrate* some sexual orientations. How to apprehend embracing (to accept, tolerate and not to discriminate) versus celebrating (to campaign for and/or to consider something as good for society) in liberal thought? Replying to this question is the objective of this chapter and also many Indian colleagues who discussed part of this chapter when I delivered my keynote in the Third Annual Lecture of the Contributions to Indian Sociology. As in the previous chapter on religion and secularism, we need to disentangle the discourse on gender and sexuality (sexual freedom, gender equality, gender fluidity, anti-gender campaigns) by distinguishing between justifications related to the conception of justice and those related to the plurality of conceptions of the good.

Since the beginning of the twentieth century, sexuality was conceived "as the province not of religious morality but rather of human nature...[and]... as the scientific domain of biology and medicine, of psychiatry and the emerging discipline of sexology" (Parker 2009, 252). It was only from the late 1980s onwards that the social sciences in general, and sociology in particular, showed an interest in sexuality and intimacy, their transformation, and later on the impact of emotional capitalism on them. In 1992, the outstanding British sociologist Anthony Giddens published his influential book, *The Transformation of Intimacy* (2013 [1992]), which became the reference for any further studies on this topic, and particularly for symbolic liberalism. The following is a brief critical overview.

Giddens provides an optimistic assessment of the modern condition, showing how in the twentieth century (high modernity), the "pure relationship" (defined as the relationship of sexual and emotional equality between two partners) forces individuals to negotiate rights and responsibilities. It is a relationship that replaces the concept of traditional marriage. The success of modern marriages, therefore, depends increasingly on the satisfaction felt by each partner, inducing a shift in the relationship between sex, love and reproduction. For Giddens, this "plastic sexuality" is decentered sexuality, freed from the needs of reproduction, while "confluent love" is active, contingent love, which jars with the "forever" and "one-and-only" qualities of the romantic love complex. In this view, the "self-reflective self" guarantees that monogamy must be "reworked" in the context of commitment and trust. In the area of reproduction, effective contraception, sophisticated reproductive technologies and genetic engineering increase the dislocation between reproduction and nature. As opposed to Foucault's bio-politics, Giddens argues here in terms of emancipatory life-politics.

For me, this description of modern subjectivity fails to account for social and cultural factors. This is why we see Giddens's bias toward the urban middle classes. The issue is particularly exaggerated when he argues that this subjectivity creates a particular "reflexive" identity. For Riggs and Turne (1997), it resonates more in terms of pragmatic accommodation to the vicissitudes of ordinary life events than being expressed in terms of reflexive identity. Thus, for the majority, the development of a sense of identity is an ongoing process throughout the life course. The self-reflexive nature of Giddens's interpretation of self-identity denies the centrality of the self as a social being, while the participants in Riggs and Turne's study have a very strong notion of themselves as the product of social processes.

Giddens is broadly optimistic about the emancipatory consequences of the emergence of a discourse of sexuality and sees a "possibility of a radical democratization of the personal" (2013, 182), and to a large extent, this is true today in the second decade of the twenty-first century. Like many, mostly from the progressive side of the political spectrum, he sees sexuality as the key to modern civilization. Drawing on structural, Marxist and feminist accounts of culture, Steven Seidman is more cautious, arguing that "while sex can and should be an agent of romantic bonding, exaggerating its role in creating and sustaining intimate ties threatens to conflate sex and love and to neglect other powerful sources of emotional and social bonding" (2003: 198).[1]

However, to be fair to Giddens, it is not only about sexuality. The structural source of this promise is the emergence of pure relationships, not only in the area of sexuality but also in those of parent–child relationships, and other forms of kinship and friendship. We could envisage the development of an ethical framework for a democratic personal order, which in sexual relationships and other personal domains conforms to a model of confluent love.

For other critics, even Giddens's pure relationship is a problematic concept. While Lynn Jamieson (1998) and Eva Illouz (2019) question the optimism of the concept of the pure relationship (not only fulfillment and authenticity but also commercialization of intimate practices under capitalism), and for Zygmunt Bauman (1993, 106) this relationship that becomes contingent with the now fleeting nature of commitment is devoid of moral quality and responsibility for the other as it depends on mutual satisfaction (reciprocity).

For me, Giddens seems to portray the transformation more in the Global North than in the Global South and more in urban and big cities than in

---

[1]   Like Seidman, other critics questioned Giddens's claim that the sexual revolution of the 1960s had been a liberating force for women. See, for instance, Singh (1996).

small towns and villages.[2] One would accept some normative stance in the conclusion of his research after conducting his observations. However, early in the book, in its second chapter, Giddens writes, "once sexuality has become an 'integral' component of social relations... heterosexuality is no longer a standard by which everything else is judged" (2013: 34). Is this a sociological observation, a statistical conclusion, or a value judgment? It is not clear, but it seems more suggestive that an observation. I don't think it is a good sociological observation given that we know today that in the UK, according to the Census of 2021, only 3.2 percent (of which 1.28 per cent identified as bisexual) identified with an LGB+ orientation ("Gay or Lesbian," "Bisexual" or "Other sexual orientation") against 89.4 per cent that identified as straight or heterosexual.[3] If the standard in Giddens's mind is normative and not descriptive, the statistics reflect what is most generally conceived of as normative sexuality, which should be related to the conception of the good. When he wrote "heterosexuality is no longer a standard," he suggests that there is a progress from injustice to justice, but it is not clear if those who think that heteronormativity as the normative standard violates the principle of the *Universal Declaration of Human Rights* principle of no discrimination on the basis of sexual orientation. By that, I mean that both those who think of heteronormativity as standard and those who see the diversity of sexuality as standard are expressing their conception of the good, and their position should not be packed normatively as a conception of justice.

Having said that, I simply argue that we always need mediation between what we conceive of as the natural, the social and the cultural in order to make a theoretical reassessment of gender and sexuality. If we admit that, should we accept that some people (in a given society) conceive reproduction as more natural than social or cultural? In that case, can one claim a certain mutuality between men and women? Some Islamists use and abuse what they call "complementarity" to undermine gender equality. However, others are more careful, like the Lebanese philosopher Nassif Nassar (2022), who argues in favor of complementarity in the sense that while a woman, in essence, is equal to a man, she can have complementary tasks in some domains (e.g., reproduction, care, heavy physical work) and this should not inherently imply unequal power. I am not necessarily advocating for the complementarity paradigm, but this paradigm does not preempt us from

---

[2]   I don't want to extend here some sort of Eurocentrism in the writing of Giddens. Readers can refer, for instance, to the work of Ray Jureidini (2006).

[3]   Some 7.5 percent did not answer the question concerning sexual orientation. See www.ons.gov.uk/peoplepopulationandcommunity/culturalidentity/sexuality/ bulletins/sexualorientationenglandandwales/census2021.

addressing the conception of justice, that is, situating male/female within gender relations and how "saying the difference" sometimes means "saying the hierarchy." A gendered division of labor does not have to be hierarchical. "Complementarity" entails also a conception of the good; males and females interdependent in the family unit. When childcare or care of the elderly becomes a compulsory activity of women, and when we split off economic production from social reproduction and treat these as two separate things, we can then talk, along the lines of Nancy Fraser (2016), of a domain of women's subordination that should be denounced.

My critique of Giddens can be extended to symbolic liberals who impose their conception of the good on society and prevent others from having their own conceptions of the good. Today, some strands of the LGBTQ+ movement fall into this trap. Let me expand.

Is Gender Fluidity Part of the Conception of Justice or the Good?

I am so glad that LGBTQ+ movements in Western Europe, North America and some other regions of the world have made significant progress in securing LGBTQ+ rights, especially institutional recognition for same-sex couples and their families. Yet, one should distinguish between what is related to the conception of justice (e.g., acceptance, social and institutional recognitions) and that of the pluralistic conception of the good. With regard to the conception of justice, despite major changes in laws and norms surrounding the issue of same-sex marriage and the rights of LGBTQ+ people around the world, public opinion on the acceptance of homosexuality in society remains sharply divided according to country, region, religion and political leanings.

Generally speaking, the societal acceptance of homosexuality is always greater than acceptance of same-sex marriage.[4] As the 2023 Pew survey, carried out in 32 countries, showed, for many countries outside Europe and North America, recognition of homosexuality does not also accord with recognition of same-sex marriage (Figure 6.1). The same survey shows a strong correlation between attitudes to homosexuality and religious affiliation (except in Mexico, Thailand, Brazil, Cambodia and India) (Figure 6.2) and political leanings. Muslims are in general against same-sex marriage, but this

---

[4] The question in the Pew survey was whether the interviewees think that homosexuality should be accepted in society. "How People Around the World View Same-Sex Marriage." www.pewresearch.org/short-reads/2023/11/27/how-people-around-the-world-view-same-sex-marriage/.

Views toward same-sex marriage across 32 publics

% who say they ___ allowing gays and lesbians to marry legally

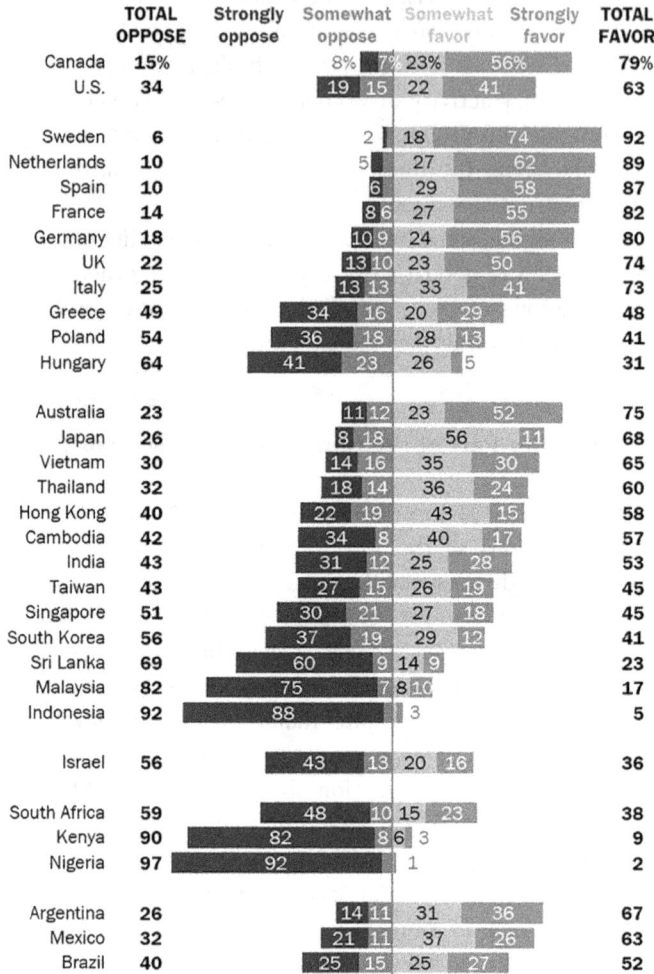

	TOTAL OPPOSE	Strongly oppose	Somewhat oppose	Somewhat favor	Strongly favor	TOTAL FAVOR
Canada	15%	8%	7%	23%	56%	79%
U.S.	34	19	15	22	41	63
Sweden	6	2		18	74	92
Netherlands	10	5		27	62	89
Spain	10		6	29	58	87
France	14	8	6	27	55	82
Germany	18	10	9	24	56	80
UK	22	13	10	23	50	74
Italy	25	13	13	33	41	73
Greece	49	34	16	20	29	48
Poland	54	36	18	28	13	41
Hungary	64	41	23	26	5	31
Australia	23	11	12	23	52	75
Japan	26	8	18	56	11	68
Vietnam	30	14	16	35	30	65
Thailand	32	18	14	36	24	60
Hong Kong	40	22	19	43	15	58
Cambodia	42	34	8	40	17	57
India	43	31	12	25	28	53
Taiwan	43	27	15	26	19	45
Singapore	51	30	21	27	18	45
South Korea	56	37	19	29	12	41
Sri Lanka	69	60	9	14	9	23
Malaysia	82	75	7	8	10	17
Indonesia	92	88			3	5
Israel	56	43	13	20	16	36
South Africa	59	48	10	15	23	38
Kenya	90	82	8	6	3	9
Nigeria	97	92			1	2
Argentina	26	14	11	31	36	67
Mexico	32	21	11	37	26	63
Brazil	40	25	15	25	27	52

Note: Those who did not answer are not shown. Figures may not add to the totals indicated due to rounding.
Source: Survey conducted June 2-Sept. 17, 2023, among adults in five East Asian publics, spring 2023 Global Attitudes Survey; and survey conducted June 1-Sept. 4, 2022, among adults in six South and Southeast Asian publics.

PEW RESEARCH CENTER

Figure 6.1 How people view same-sex marriage
Source: Adapted from the World Inequality Report 2023. World Inequality Database, https://wid.world/ (2023), licensed under CC BY 4.0: https://creativecommons.org/licenses/by/4.0/ Graph modified only for clarity and black-and-white printing; all data remains the same.

Support for same-sex marriage is lower in more religious places

% who say they favor allowing gays and lesbians to marry legally

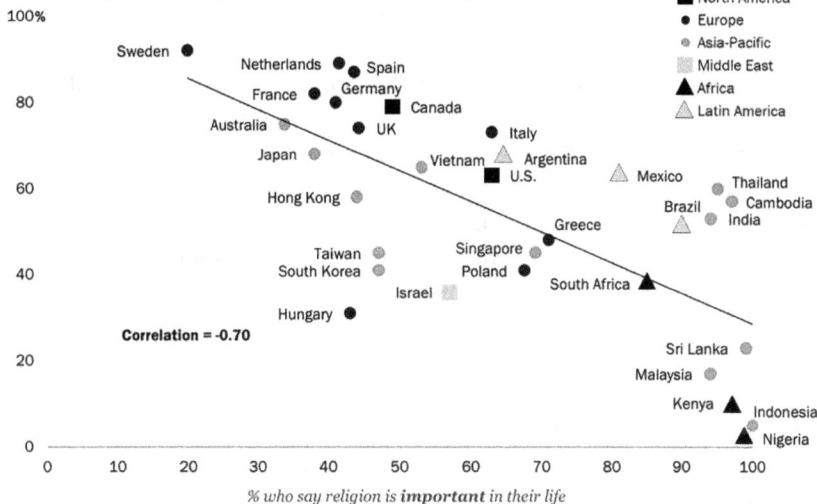

Figure 6.2 How attitudes about same-sex marriage vary by religion
Source: Adapted from an image taken from the Pew Survey 2023. Graph modified
only for clarity and black-and-white printing; all data remains the same.

could be the case among Christians as well. For instance, in Nigeria, Christians and Muslims are equally likely to oppose same-sex marriage (97 percent and 98 percent, respectively).[5] While same-sex marriage is legal in 30 countries in the world (as of 2021), it constitutes quite a low percentage of total marriages, varying from 0.4 percent in Ecuador to 3.3 percent in Spain.[6]

Some countries embrace full visibility for multiple sexual orientations in the public sphere, while others do not. Visibility (including for heterosexuals) is indeed part of the conceptions of the good and how this will be regulated in the public sphere. One could argue, what would be the difference between the Muslim veil and the Sikh turban? Should this also be regulated? I don't think so, as it is considered by many Muslims and Sikhs as part of

[5] "How People Around the World View Same-Sex Marriage."
[6] "In Places Where Same-Sex Marriages Are Legal, How Many Married Same-Sex Couples Are There?" www.pewresearch.org/short-reads/2023/06/13/in-places-where-same-sex-marriages-are-legal-how-many-married-same-sex-couples-are-there/.

their comprehensive doctrine, and so society should allow it as part of the conception of justice.

Take the case of the World Cup in Qatar. While caring about justice means denouncing the criminalization of the sexual practices of the LGBTQ+ community, many argue that carrying the Rainbow flag, a representation of the LGBTQ+ community is part of the conflicting conceptions of the good, that required that Qatari society debate the issue publicly, which it refused to do. The Qatari authorities announced that although the country's laws were based upon the principles of Sharia, they would not be concerned about what same-sex couples did inside their hotel rooms – as long as there were no public displays and agitation challenging the culture and laws of their host country. Some in the Qatari media denounced how foreigners sought to impose their conception of the good in Qatar and considered it a form of cultural imperialism.[7]

In this regard, Joseph Massad's *Desiring Arabs* (2008) is particularly interesting. As a disciple of Edward Said and a professor at Colombia University, he argues against the institutional recognition and public visibility of LGBTQ in the specific context of the Arab world. He criticizes Western-driven activism as constructing "homosexuality" in societies that traditionally have not seen sexual desire as fitting neatly into binary categories on the basis of the gender of the sexual object-choice and envisioned sexual preferences as the basis for social identity. For him, all too often, gay activists simply dismiss this as false consciousness and as "homophobia." The consequences are harmful, as activism triggers a reaction against what is frequently perceived as the dissemination of Western indecency and lack of modesty. State persecution, often spurred by animated public opinion, is intensified, replacing traditional and more benign notions of tolerating private sexual idiosyncrasies, as long as they are carried out discreetly.

One should read Massad carefully, as he protests against the Eurocentric conception of sexuality that denies the possibility of the Arab LGBTQ movement to genuinely make a case for getting "out of the closet" and for some forms of visibility that can be negotiated.[8] I find it interesting to argue for a culturally driven model of non-discrimination on the basis of sexual orientation and how the identitarian choice enforced on them harms them more than it serves them.

For seven years, I have regularly walked along the Beirut sea-front

---

[7]   Of course, when we see the call of French authorities that they will not tolerate "inappropriate" political flags during the event of the Paris Olympics (July 2024), they think of the Palestinian flag, and this demonstrates the double standard.

[8]   For critique of Massad's work, see Dalacoura 2014.

corniche outside my residence at AUB, where all Lebanese social classes – couples, boyfriends and girlfriends, and families spend social time there as *flâneurs* or passers-by. No more than three times have I seen people kiss each other on the mouth. This kind of cultural shyness is related to sexuality even if *flâneurs* can transgress the dress code (e.g., short skirts or transparent T-shirts). Here is where culture intervenes to set some rules of what could be a *common good* –that is, as much as there are no police enforcing such public morality as exist in other Muslim countries. Among the Lebanese, there is always the possibility of keeping pluralistic conceptions of the good. This means sexuality and gender should be discussed in terms of (culturized) social relations and not as an autonomous category. This is how Sara Mourad made her analysis of "appearing as women" in the Lebanese 2919 October uprising. Feminists and non-feminists coalesced against the Lebanese neoliberal regime:

> There is no single female gender identity that defines the social experience of womanhood. And yet, in particular times and places, a certain provisional unity among women manifests itself. Even as we question the cohesiveness and universality of gender as an identity, even as we deconstruct it to show its limits and its normative effects, we still feel the pull of "women" as a label that we cannot afford to abandon. (Mourad 2022, 146)

More generally, and in the vocabulary of Eric Macé:

> As soon as gender is no longer defined by categories but as a social relation, it leaves the relativity of the actors' experience to become a general sociological concept...Contestations of this modern patriarchy and gender coloniality by broadly defined feminist movements...based on non-patriarchal cultures are part of the historicity of gender relations around the world according to agendas and forms of mobilization and conflict specific to each context in the global North and South. (Macé 2024, 160)

In the same vein, one can question whether gender fluidity and the delinking of gender roles from sex roles should be celebrated in all regions and whether pleasure and desire can be deculturized. Pleasure is indeed part of the conception of the good. Can parents claim the right to educate their children on what constitutes the good life for them? If a community wants to celebrate heterosexual normativity, is this against the conception of justice if there is no discrimination against the "queer" community? Can one argue that behind gender fluidity is a conception of the good that has its own metaphysics, celebrating ephemeral gender identity (and sex as a spectrum) based on a hedonistic project of absolute pleasure and self-expression? In the name of absolute pleasure, can a society tolerate polygyny and polyandry, as Melanie Heath (2023) problematizes, particularly in the context of postcolonialism? Are Giddens's "pure relationships" and polyamory ("many loves," once referred to as "serial monogamy") (Olson and Brussel-Rogers 2022) not a form of polygamy, open marriages and swinging? Can conservative families defend marital-centered sexual ethics as a conception of the good without it being criminalized by the social service labeled in Sweden as "honor-related repression"?

All these questions I raise require careful reflection and debate without conflating the conception of justice. This should be agreed upon societally with the pluralistic conception of the good and how culture (and by consequence religion) matters in their conception of sexuality and gender identity. This must be done with consideration of what is the common good. Again, I don't mean here to essentialize any culture nor assume their uniformity. Unlike nation-states, cultures have no rigid borders. They are more dynamic and meandering, open to influence, and translatable. I argue that if one considers that elements of cultures change because they are not set in stone, then we should reflect on how culture is shaped by power and emotion in the structure of our feelings, so influenced nowadays by social media. Thus, some aspects of symbolic liberals' scientific and normative conceptions of sexuality and gender fluidity should be culturally bounded and not packaged as an inherent part of the conception of justice.

How Scientific is the Conception of Sexuality and Gender Fluidity?

Between 2012 and 2021 in the United States, LGBT identification among young people tripled. While many studies show increasing gender noncon-formity and transgender, there remains uncertainty about the reasons for this increase. Is it due primarily to psychological or behavioral changes? If so, how have the two domains interacted? Is it nature or nurture, sociali-zation or imitation, seeking LGBT identity or just adopting non-heterosexual experiences? Is the increase in LGBT identification among the Left/liberal/non-religious due to the fact that they may be more liberated? Or is it tied to a new political identity and a more modernist, transgressive youth culture, particularly among Generation Z and Millennials?[9]

---

[9]   For a more detailed discussion, see Kaufmann 2022, Habib 2021 and recent

As many surveys concur, what seems settled, at least in the United States, is that there is a growing divergence between sexual behavior and sexual identity among Americans under the age of 30. In 2008, attitudes and behavior were similar, but by 2021 LGBT identification (16.3 percent) was twice the rate of LGBT sexual behavior (8.6 percent). It was found that there is a strong correlation between sexual identity and political beliefs/ideology influencing each other (Kaufmann 2022). What is established, is evidence of a larger rate of mental health among LGBT people, compared to their heterosexual peers – LGBT people being more anxious and depressed than others in multiple surveys across the United States.[10]

My claim here, again, is that these issues go beyond the legitimate conception of justice regarding individual choice of sexual orientation. There are conflicting normative conceptions of the good that society should debate when it comes to shared spaces (e.g., the public sphere, early school curriculum, health regulations for puberty blocker treatment for adolescents). For instance, if a group in society were to defend heteronormativity as a conception of the good life, this position does not have to be inherently homophobic. However, at the same time, not only should those who identify as heterosexual accept and tolerate other sexual orientations, but they should also, in line with the conception of justice, protect those who identify with them – even showing empathy and compassion (while awaiting more egalitarian recognition). This is a very important principle when legal and cultural homophobia is pervasive.

At a time of polarization in the debate between the conservative right and symbolic liberals, I argue in favor of Dialogical Sociology, which calls us to debate controversial issues such as sex versus gender identity in a way that facilitates how, strategically, the abstract conception of justice (e.g., no discrimination against LGBTQ+ individuals) can be advanced within a given society. Without this critical dialogue, we succumb to what Wendy Brown

research such as the Pew survey: "Americans' Complex Views on Gender Identity and Transgender Issues."

[10] According to the Centers for Disease Control and Prevention (CDC), data indicates a significant rise in emotional problems among young people since 2015. A major study of nearly 40,000 teens in Wisconsin found that the mental health of LGBT youth deteriorated significantly faster than that of their heterosexual peers between 2012 and 2018. During this period, the percentage of heterosexual young people reporting anxiety in the previous month increased from 32 percent in 2012 to 35 percent in 2015 and 41 percent in 2018. In contrast, among gay and bisexual teens, the rate soared from approximately 55 percent in 2012 to 65 percent in 2015 and 72 percent in 2018. See Parodi et al. 2022, cited in Kaufmann 2022, 88.

(2002) calls "progressivist moralism," a concept also used by the French feminist activist Elsa Deck Marsault (2023) to criticize certain strands of French feminism and civil liberty movements.

I raise these questions because they are rarely discussed openly in academia. Non-orthodox research on sexuality is pushed to the margins. The *Journal of Controversial Ideas* is one of those margins where one can find many articles about gender and sexual identity. On 7 February 2023, the Department of Philosophy at my own university invited Holly Lawford-Smith, feminist and professor of philosophy at the University of Melbourne, to present her book, *Gender-Critical Feminism* (2022). The Gender and Sexuality Club used Title IX (office of DEI enforcement) to call off the invitation. Some administrators feared that such an invitation would endanger USAID funding to the university. After failing to stop it, the Club and its partner student societies issued a statement the following week. Here are some excerpts:

> In accordance with the club's values and principles, Title IX's anti-discriminatory policies, and AUB's Diversity, Equity, and Inclusion (DEI) statement, we condemn the talk and the speaker and denounce any opinions or statements issued by the speaker that come at the expense of the LGBTQ+ community, specifically the trans community. ...Trans rights are human rights, *no one should ever have to debate the validity of their existence.*[11]

I highlight the last sentence, as the book by Lawford-Smith is not really questioning trans existence but pointing out some conflicting rights between trans and other sexual orientations.[12] Thus, it is not about no discrimination

---

[11] The post was published on Instagram on 14 February. www.instagram.com/p/ Copiy-iMzlD/?utm_source=ig_web_copy_link. AUB is a liberal oasis. When it comes to an illiberal context, the problems are different. See, for instance, the cases of the Saudi historian, Hatoon al-Fassi or the Jordanian Dean, Rola Kawas (Elsadda 2024).

[12] For instance, the gender-critical feminist position on women-only spaces is that they should be reserved for women based on sex rather than gender identity, for multiple reasons – not solely to exclude trans women. This stance is also upheld by penitentiary authorities in many countries. Thus, anyone has the right to transition – physically, medically or simply through self-declaration. However, cisgender women have the right to maintain their spaces. The French psychoanalyst Claude Habib has also joined this movement (Habib 2021). Concerned about gender fluidity, she wrote a book arguing that it does not advance women's freedom or the feminist cause.

against LGBTQ+ community but about how to manage conflicting claims of different variants of this community – and this is a typical problem of symbolic liberals in which some groups will use identity politics against other groups.[13]

Dialogical Sociology calls for debating controversial issues such as sex versus gender identity, and facilitates how strategically, in a given society, the abstract conception of justice (e.g., no discrimination against LGBTQ+) can be advanced while allowing for the plurality of the conception of the good. One of the heated debates about sexuality and gender identity is focused on the school curriculum.

Gender Identity School Curriculum

In an interview, former British MP George Galloway defended his support for same-sex marriage during his 2016 campaign to become Mayor of London while simultaneously opposing the inclusion of a sexuality and gender identity curriculum in schools.[14] Is there a contradiction? Many research studies and surveys show that this attitude is common among parents. They do not deny LGBTQ individuals the right to institutionalize their relationships, but they believe that the timing and manner in which sexuality and gender identity are taught in schools are either too early for students or that certain curriculum materials are more appropriately addressed within the family rather than in the school setting.

The inclusive curriculum encompasses various approaches and topics, including diversity and anti-bias training, LGBTQ-inclusive sexual health education and LGBTQ history (Burdge et al. 2013). Its implementation varies by location, but a toolkit originating in the United States often influences countries that adopt such training. This includes lessons such as "Drag Queen Story Hour," "The Queen Hour," and "Pink, Blue, Purple," which emphasize the concept of gender fluidity through the idea of feeling

---

[13] Coming from a sexual minority group, the American Lebanese philosopher Raja Halwani remains unconvinced about the heuristic possibilities of gender identity. For him, "attraction on the basis of sex makes sense from an evolutionary perspective; that it helps explain the basic human pursuits for procreation, sexual pleasure, and love; that it accommodates attractions on other bases, such as gender presentation and age; that it handles other purported sexual orientations; and that it does not prohibit our ability to politically and morally advocate for the recognition of various sexual preferences and identities." The reasons on offer for adding gender, "are not convincing unless we are willing also to admit other bases, such as race, ethnic belonging, and body size" (Halwani 2023, 22).

[14] See www.youtube.com/watch?v=sw4cjsiBLw8.

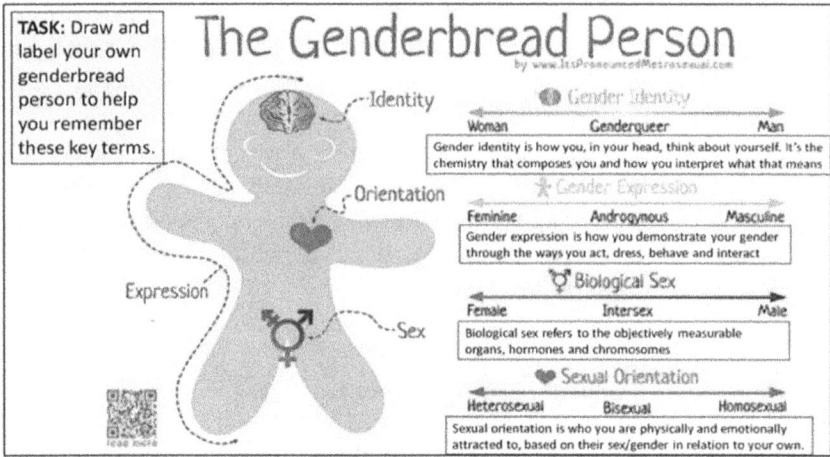

TASK: Draw and label your own genderbread person to help you remember these key terms.

The Genderbread Person
by www.ItsPronouncedMetrosexual.com

Identity

Gender Identity
Woman   Genderqueer   Man
Gender identity is how you, in your head, think about yourself. It's the chemistry that composes you and how you interpret what that means

Orientation

Gender Expression
Feminine   Androgynous   Masculine
Gender expression is how you demonstrate your gender through the ways you act, dress, behave and interact

Expression

Biological Sex
Female   Intersex   Male
Biological sex refers to the objectively measurable organs, hormones and chromosomes

Sex

Sexual Orientation
Heterosexual   Bisexual   Homosexual
Sexual orientation is who you are physically and emotionally attracted to, based on their sex/gender in relation to your own.

Figure 6.3 The Genderbread Person
Source: https://care.org.uk/cause/transgender/
the-shocking-truth-about-what-is-being-taught-in-schools.

different from the gender assigned at birth (Greenberg, cited by Albitar 2024) and the principle that "no one should influence others' sexual orientation."[15] Additionally, "The Genderbread Person" (Figure 6.3) is included in elementary school curriculums in many countries, including the UK and Norway. This international toolkit is often supplemented by country-specific curriculums. Critics, such as Julie Maxwell (cited in Albitar 2024), argue that these lessons encourage children to disregard biology, teaching that "women can have male organs" or that "all genders can have menstrual cycles."

In the United States, each subject approached LGBTQIA+ inclusion in its own way. For instance, in health classes, students learned about sexual orientation and gender expression, along with related terminology such as "heterosexual," "transgender" and "bisexual" (Snapp et al. 2015). In history and English classes, the focus was more on exploring LGBTQIA+ history, particularly topics related to gay men (Snapp et al. 2015).

When an LGBTQIA+ inclusive curriculum was implemented, it was typically found in social science and humanities courses, where topics

[15] "Støtte til undervisning om kjønn og seksualitet" [Support for Teaching about Gender and Sexuality] – a supported resource for school staff containing short and overarching texts that address various topics of gender and sexuality within the Norwegian LK20 curriculum. See www.udir.no/laring-og-trivsel/lareplanverket/ stotte/Stotte-til-undervisning-om-kjonn-og-sexualitet/seksuell-orientering/.

included delinking biological sex from socially constructed gender and the use of different pronouns. Some key principles emphasized for students, parents, teachers and administrators included the idea that "diversity in identity, race, religion, culture, and sexual orientation should be celebrated" (Kocsis 2019, 34).

Beyond celebrating LGBTQ individuals and themes, school curriculums also integrate LGBTQ topics into classroom discussions (Moorhead 2018). Whether this is seen as a form of celebration or something else depends on one's perspective – a point that will be clarified in the conclusion.

Let us take the case of Norway. In 2020, the country introduced a renewed school curriculum that incorporated topics related to gender identity. While the curriculum aims to "cultivate inclusivity and respect for diverse identity groups," particularly regarding gender identity, it has faced criticism and concerns about its potential role in indoctrinating children. Researcher Rim Albitar (2024) conducted a content analysis of 18 textbooks used in Norwegian primary schools (grades 3–5) and conducted 15 in-depth interviews with parents about their experiences with the new curriculum. She observed, for instance, that 5th-grade students were taught lessons from the Social Sciences textbook *Arena 5* (2020) that encouraged them to explore their own gender identity. It clearly stated, "the parents are no longer the child's hero." For the parents,

> The majority of the interviewees expressed feelings of alienation towards the gender identity curriculum, while a minority signified support for its inclusion in the school curriculum. The moral reasonings for this alienation include undermining family authority, perceived threats to religious beliefs, individual expression and concerns for the children's and parents' well-being. Conversely, supporters of the curriculum emphasize its contribution to tackling societal issues like racism, through its promotion of tolerance, respect, individualism, and freedom as integral components of the Norwegian policy initiatives. (Albitar 2024, 4)

Newspapers in many countries reported heated debates and a striking contrast between parents who are in favor of the new curriculum and those who feel alienated. While one finds some research studies and surveys about how gender identity should be taught, academia's contribution to the debate remains one-sided, that is, not giving the arguments pro and con. Let us now take the case of the United States.[16]

---

[16] This case is based on an unpublished literature review carried out at my request by Giselle Jaffa from the American University of Beirut. I am so grateful to her. I

Gender Identity Curriculum in the United States

The United States is particularly relevant for analysis due to the extensive research data available. The incorporation of LGBTQIA+ themes into school curriculums has been a persistent topic of debate, driven in part by the rise of anti-LGBTQIA+ bills and legislation across the country (SIECUS 2023). Between 2022 and 2023, SIECUS, an organization advocating for sexual and reproductive health education, identified over 749 bills addressing LGBTQIA+ rights, sex education and access to reproductive and gender-affirming health care. Of these, 236 bills aimed to enhance inclusive education by incorporating sex education, while 125 bills opposed sex education (SIECUS 2023). This issue has led to sharp polarization in the United States, a divide largely influenced by religiosity, political affiliation (Left/Right) and geography (state-level policies).

Broadly, the United States can be categorized into four types of legislative approaches: (1) LGBTQIA+ inclusive curriculums, (2) parental rights, (3) restrictions on LGBTQIA+ themes and (4) anti-LGBTQIA+ education. In most cases, states have enacted legislation requiring school curriculums to include LGBTQIA+ individuals, themes and history within subjects such as social studies and history (MAP 2024).

There are different approaches to curriculum inclusion. Some schools integrate LGBTQIA+ themes directly, while others require parental notification before teaching LGBTQIA+-related content, allowing parents to opt their children in or out of these classes (SIECUS 2023). Such "parental rights" bills can be found in states like Arizona (opt-in), Arkansas (opt-out), Florida (opt-out), Montana (opt-out), Tennessee (opt-in/out) and Wyoming (opt-in) (MAP 2024). A lasting effect of these parental rights bills has been the restriction of discussions on gender identity and sexual orientation in classrooms.

While several states incorporate LGBTQIA+ themes into their curriculums in an educational manner, others – such as Louisiana, Mississippi, Oklahoma and Texas – address homosexuality in a restrictive way. For instance, some schools may reference homosexuality as a criminal offense within the context of sexual or health education. In other cases, discussions on LGBTQIA+ topics may be deliberately vague, aiming to minimize their inclusion (MAP 2024). It is important to note that these restrictive laws are not recent developments but rather continuations of policies dating back to the 1980s and early 1990s (MAP 2024).

should also thank Rim Albitar for her excellent Master's thesis about the Gender Identity School Curriculum in Norway.

On a similar note, rather than restricting discussions of homosexuality in the classroom, several states (Alabama, Arkansas, Florida, Indiana, Iowa, Kentucky and North Carolina) completely censor discussions of LGBTQIA+ themes and individuals within the school curriculum. Also known as the "Don't Say Gay or Trans" laws, these bills ban school teachers and staff members from introducing discussions on LGBTQIA+ issues and themes, from including books on such themes or from implementing other learning materials on the themes (MAP 2024). In 2023, 42 book ban bills were introduced to restrict materials related to sexual themes and discussions, including books related to the LGBTQIA+ community (SIECUS 2023).

When it comes to perceptions towards inclusive or restrictive curriculums, the recent debate on the implementation of LGBTQIA+ themes into the curriculum has stirred a mixed reaction from K-12 teachers. Around 71 percent of K-12 teachers stated they do not have influence over the topics being taught in public schools and around 40 percent believe that the current debates have had a negative impact on their jobs (PEW 2024).[17] Around 58 percent of teachers said that their state government holds "too much" influence over the integration of certain topics into the school curriculums (PEW 2024).

Moreover, when it comes to teaching about gender identity, one-third of teachers believed that students should be taught that an individual's gender identity can be different from the sex they were assigned at birth, while 14 percent stated that students must learn that an individual's identity is determined by their sex at birth (PEW 2024). On the other hand, the majority of elementary school teachers, around 62 percent, stated that students should not even learn about gender identity in schools (PEW 2024). On this note, Pew research found that Democrat teachers were more likely to say that students should be taught that a person's gender identity may differ from the sex they were assigned at birth, while most Republican teachers (69 percent), stated that students should not learn about gender identity in schools as a whole (PEW 2024).

Feelings of hesitation by teachers were further expressed due to the confusion of how to approach LGBTQIA+ topics, particularly with the enactment of recent anti-LGBTQ laws (Viles 2023). Teachers may also feel afraid of tackling such topics due to the lack of support from administrators and parents, thus, avoiding LGBTQIA+ topics as a whole (Viles 2023).

A further survey amongst 5,029 adults by Pew Research Center in 2023 showed that only 31 percent of parents would rather have their children

---

[17] See "Teachers' Views of Current Debates About What Schools Should Be Teaching." www.pewresearch.org/social-trends/2024/02/22/teachers-views-of-current-debates-about-what-schools-should-be-teaching/.

learn that one's gender can be different from sex assigned at birth. A similar percentage stated that they would rather have their children be taught that their sex is determined at birth. Conversely, 37 percent of parents stated that their children should not learn about gender identity in schools at all.[18]

When it comes to students, it has been found that inclusive curriculums have positively impacted all students' safety, well-being and achievements (Burdge et al. 2013). The corollary is that by avoiding LGBTQIA+ inclusive curriculums, LGBTQ issues are seen as shameful, thus hindering school safety, and alienating students (Burdge et al. 2013). Furthermore, students attending schools with an inclusive curriculum, hear less anti-LGBTQ slurs and remarks than those without (Burdge et al. 2013). Students acknowledged that learning about LGBTQ issues in their school reduced bullying incidents, as students become aware of related issues in a more serious way (Snapp et al. 2015). These studies are *in sharp contrast* with another PEW 2023 survey (based on 1,453 teens), according to which 48 percent of teenagers stated they should not learn about gender identity in schools. Some 26 percent of teenagers said they would prefer to learn that gender identity is determined by the sex assigned at birth, while a quarter stated they would rather learn that one's identity may differ from the sex they were assigned at birth.[19]

In summary, it is clear from the above how a percentage of parents (sometimes the majority) feel the new gender identity curriculum is alienating for them. On this issue, they feel there is an imposition of the school to a specific conception of the good on their children. They are not convinced that this is in favor of giving justice to LGBTQ+ but it is a way of promoting gender fluidity, when the parents believe in the gender binary as the *basic* characteristic of society. Again, however, being basic means allowing other forms of social structures to co-exist (gay, lesbian, trans families). When parents feel that schools are undermining their parental authority, it becomes a problem for political liberalism where the state (and the public school) should not impose controversial conceptions of the good. For them, it should be left to the family and perhaps delay such exposure to a later stage in schooling or beyond.

In some countries, including Canada, schools allow pupils to change their pronouns and to sexually transition without family knowledge or consent. Rather than fostering collaboration between schools and families, this approach creates a divide between the two authorities. This issue is further amplified by the widespread influence of social media, which is often accused

---

[18] "Race and LGBTQ Issues in K-12 Schools." www.pewresearch.org/social-trends/2024/02/22/race-and-lgbtq-issues-in-k-12-schools/.
[19] "Race and LGBTQ Issues in K-12 Schools."

of "convincing" children to transition. Is this phenomenon driven by cultural change or influenced by the pharmaceutical industry lobby?

In this context, concerns over the excessive use of puberty blockers have recently alarmed UK health authorities, prompting a report by Dr. Hilary Cass.[20] Since its publication in April 2024, the report has sparked both local and global debates. David Bell, former President of the British Psychoanalytic Society, commented on the report, referring to the promotion of gender transition in schools as "the policy of affirmation." He described this as "speedily agreeing with a child that they are of the wrong gender...[it is] an inappropriate clinical stance brought about by activist groups," warning that it places children on a potentially harmful medical pathway with serious risks of sexual dysfunction and sterility. Similarly, Bell argued that labeling a child as "transgender" is problematic, as it prematurely defines their experience and suggests a singular condition requiring a singular "treatment." Instead, he proposed that the appropriate description should be that "the child suffers from distress about gender/sexuality," which should be carefully explored within the broader context of the child's life experiences, including histories of abuse, trauma and confusion about sexuality.[21] The report was generally well received in the UK but met with resistance in Australia, illustrating the broader instability and deep divisions that arise in discussions on this issue.

In this polarized climate, it is evident that moral panic exists among conservatives. While some materials in the gender identity curriculum align with the conception of justice and the embrace of gender diversity, their controversy might have been mitigated if they had been discussed and negotiated with various constituencies. An example of this comes from a conversation I had with a Norwegian parent with a low level of religiosity, who contested the new curriculum for her 8-year-old child. Her objection was not to the presentation of diverse family structures but rather to *how* they were introduced. For her, the issue wasn't with the idea that a family can consist of either a male–female couple or same-sex parents – or a variety of other configurations. Rather, she suggested that children be taught, "statistically, a family is most often composed of heterosexual couples, but it can also be made up of same-sex couples." This subtle distinction is important and should not be dismissed as "anti-gender" ideology. Her view reflects a

[20] "The Cass Review: Final Report." https://cass.independent-review.uk/home/publications/final-report/.

[21] David Bell, "The Cass Review of Gender Identity Services Marks a Return to Reason and Evidence – It Must Be Defended." *The Guardian*. 26 April 2024. www.theguardian.com/commentisfree/2024/apr/26/cass-review-gender-identity-services-report.

belief in her (liberal) right to educate her children according to her own conception of the good, while recognizing that the school where her child is enrolled has the right to teach a plurality of family forms (as part of its conception of justice).

This kind of disentanglement – separating elements of the school curriculum related to the liberal conception of justice from those related to conceptions of the good – is crucial if we are to reach a minimal liberal consensus on what schools can teach in the context of sex education. That said, I take very seriously the work of David Paternotte and Roman Kuhar (2017), who have documented the surge of anti-gender campaigns in Europe, Latin America and beyond. Their discourse and strategies have targeted certain elements of gender diversity and fluidity, which are part of the liberal conception of justice.

Below, I provide an example of how community leaders may offer moral justifications for a conservative position, which, for me, is compatible with political liberalism. This example is the case of Yasir Qadhi, a prominent Muslim leader in the United States. Addressing the issue of compatibility is critical for dialogue that can challenge or mitigate its effects. Simply labeling the position as homophobic or bigoted does not advance the conception of justice for LGBTQ individuals. On the contrary, such labeling can backfire in the Arab world and many liberal democratic countries, where the rise of the Right and the far-Right expresses strong disapproval of imposing a metaphysical concept such as gender fluidity on their children.

Are the Writings of Yasir Qadhi on LGBTQ Incompatible with Liberal Democracy?

In December 2023, a friend from the United States read the speech I gave in Melbourne where I addressed the issue of gender fluidity. He asked for my evaluation of the writings of Yasir Qadhi, a well-known Islamic scholar with a Ph.D. from Yale University, and an influential member of the Fiqh Council of North America (FCNA) on LGBTQ. In fact, Muslim communities in the West have been raising their voice against state-backed school curriculums "imposing" this new organizing principle of social relations. Qadhi wrote and/or co-wrote three documents of relevance: (1) a statement of advocacy mobilizing Muslim community leaders: "Navigating Differences" (May 2023)[22] (hereafter referred to as the "Statement"); (2) a fatwa addressed to Muslim

---

[22] "Navigating Differences: Clarifying Sexual and Gender Ethics in Islam." https://navigatingdifferences.com/clarifying-sexual-and-gender-ethics-in-islam/. This statement was signed by more than 300 scholars and imams in North America.

believers: "FCNA Fatwa Regarding Transgenderism" (June 2022)[23] (hereafter "Fatwa"); and (3) an article speaking to the broader public, published on Aljazeera: "Muslims Opposed to LGBTQ Curricula for Their Kids Aren't Bigots" (June 2023).[24] I will later use excerpts from these texts, referring to them respectively as "Statement," "Fatwa" and "Article." The question I raise here is whether Qadhi's stance on LGBTQ issues is compatible with liberal democracy.

My reply, in brief, is Yes. Qadhi expresses a classical *fiqh* position that I qualify as conservative, and he could have made more space for ethical justifications to complement his literal reading of the Islamic religious corpus.[25] However, his position is framed in a way that respects the basic tenets of human rights and the rules of political liberalism by appealing to non-authoritarian practical reasoning. Let me first highlight some quotes from these three documents and comment on them.

Individual Rights

While acknowledging that some people are born with sexual dysphoria, Qadhi holds that it is acceptable to feel outside a male–female binary but he does not condone *acting* on such feelings: "Islam distinguishes between feelings, actions, and identity. God holds individuals accountable for their words and actions, not for their involuntary thoughts and feelings" (Statement). Acting and promotion are thus considered a sin.

Qadhi argues against de-linking gender from biological sex: "The contemporary claim that gender is an imaginary or cultural human construct, with no necessary link to biological sex, is untenable in light of Scripture, the Shariʿah, biology, common sense, and the cumulative history of mankind" (Fatwa). The problem here is that he does not provide any evidence from the social sciences or history on the dynamic between gender and sex, a question that has already been the subject of relentless literature, both scholarly and non-scholarly, fiction and non-fiction.

Qadhi does not propose any punishment but provides advice for family

---

[23] "What is Islam's Position on Transgenderism?" https://fiqhcouncil.org/fatwa-regarding-transgenderism/.

[24] "Muslims Opposed to LGBTQ Curricula for Their Kids Aren't Bigots." www.aljazeera.com/opinions/2023/6/19/muslims-opposed-to-lgbtq-curricula-for-their-kids-arent-bigots.

[25] Conservatism exists in varying degrees. For an extreme form that opposes basic liberal values, see the late Hezbollah leader Sayed Hassan Nasrallah's 2023 Ashoura commemoration speech, in which he made particularly harsh remarks about the LGBTQ movement. www.youtube.com/watch?v=TeVr71jtglQ.

and friends. He also calls for individual members of the LGBTQ movement to be accepted in society: "We also acknowledge their constitutional right to live in peace and free from abuse" (Statement). In other words, there should be no "preaching hatred against persons. Disapproving of a particular act or lifestyle does not translate into hating or sanctioning acts of violence against an individual who practices those acts" (Fatwa). Also, he does not consider those who express LGBTQ sentiments as outside of the Muslim community:

> We welcome anyone intent on living an Islamic lifestyle to our masjids and communities, regardless of their personal temptations and desires, and we encourage all Muslims to provide others any spiritual help and support they need and to accommodate all people of all backgrounds as reasonably as possible...Islam does not ask us to mistreat anyone, and we advise Muslims to demonstrate to all people the kindness, compassion, and good manners emblematic of our faith, regardless of their personal practices. (Fatwa)

Right to Disagree

Qadhi is aware that in a liberal democracy, holding and advocating for any doctrine to the exclusion of other doctrines is a right: "We emphasize our God-given and constitutional rights to hold, live by, and promote our religious beliefs in the best manner" (Statement). The language used to address believers is mainly religious and only a few arguments are accessible to other faiths. Accessibility to the understanding of the moral arguments justifying a position is so important for public reason. However, for his article on Aljazeera, tackling the issue of LGBTQ curriculums for children, Qadhi uses straightforward moral reasoning against such curriculums. He reminds us that Muslims are part of a larger social movement against these curriculums and their voice should be heard and not dismissed as "bigoted or homophobic." He articulates his respect for differences of opinion and freedom of religion (as part of the conception of justice) but emphasizes that Muslims have a right to hold to their *communitarian* conception of the good. While he does not rely on the *individual* conception of the good, he does make use of non-authoritarian practical reasoning as conceptualized by Maeve Cooke (2007). He does not claim Islamic exclusivity for his moral justification but instead addresses them to the general public. He does not consider those who are against *fiqhi* rulings as being outside of the Muslim community: "To be clear, we cannot overstate the detrimental spiritual consequences for those who intentionally reject, advocate the rejection of, or misrepresent the will of God, as in doing so they endanger their status as believers" (Statement).

It seems to me that Yasir Qadhi's position correlates with that of Joseph Massad (as above) in considering sexuality as a private act. Both argue for a culturally driven model of application of non-discrimination on the basis of sexual orientation.

Conclusion

Over the last few months of 2024, it seems that not a day passes without reading about conservative criticisms of gender fluidity and the complete de-linking of gender roles from sex. These arguments often claim that some LGBTQ rights conflict with the rights of other groups, including feminists, whether this comes from my region or globally.

I would like to revisit the incident I mentioned at the beginning of this chapter, where wearing a pride kit by all footballers was seen as an inherent part of the conception of justice, while some, like Zakaria Aboukhlal, who refused to do so, were stigmatized as homophobes. My argument is that Aboukhlal embraces gender diversity, according to his tweet, but he does not wish to celebrate every form of this diversity. This is a matter of the conception of the good, and Aboukhlal has the right to celebrate some forms and not others. This is exactly what we ask of people to embrace religious diversity without asking them to attend mosques and synagogues to celebrate Islam and Judaism in times of Islamophobia and antisemitism.[26]

This distinction is not anecdotal. It is a strategic necessity for advancing the rights and societal recognition of vulnerable sexual and gender groups. I see how people in Western democracies move to the right as they feel that symbolic liberals, often located on the Left but not exclusively, are forcing them and their children to accept gender fluidity and non-binary gender identity as the principle for reorganizing society, and packaging this as a conception of justice (no discrimination against LGBTQ).

Many conversations I have had with colleagues in sociology and other disciplines (particularly in the West) confirm my observation, but at the same time, they express the fear of speaking out publicly about these issues. Some highlight how the Italian Prime Minister Giorgia Meloni has undermined the Left in her electorate because of her conservative position on what constitutes a family. I see in the Arab world how campaigns have

[26] I would like to thank Tariq Modood for maturing the reflection on this issue while discussing it with him.

been organized against the LGBTQ community today, partly because of the German, European and Canadian campaigns against the World Cup in Qatar, which sought to impose what some described as aggressive (some even called it Orientalist) visibility of LGBTQ issues in the stadiums.

After a violent incident in Asharafiyeh (Beirut) in 2008, I asked my students if they wanted to join me in a protest planned by an organization that defends LGBTQ rights in Lebanon. Six out of 20 students went with me. Last year, I asked my students if they would go to such a protest, and only 2 out of 15 replied positively. For me, this shows how conflating the conception of justice with that of the good has backfired against the vulnerable LGBTQ community, as participating in a protest against violence is about "embracing" more than "celebrating."

Discussing with students more recently, some argued that the AUB had moved to accommodate trans students by creating "all-gender restrooms" in the new building. This was favored by the university over the establishment of a prayer room for Muslims, even after 98.4 percent of an online survey of 1,000 students approved the need for a prayer room on campus.[27] One female student justified her position as follows:

> I don't mind having all-gender restrooms on the campus where I doubt to have more than one or two trans students in the whole university, but I see a double standard in how "Diversity, Equity and Inclusion" have been implemented. The demand of hundreds of Muslim women and men want to find a place to pray during the 10 minutes' break between courses was rejected. Of course, there are two mosques close to campus but they are only for males and they are at 6 minutes from the upper campus and 14 minutes from the lower campus. I don't want to be in solidarity with LGBTQ community, with all my respect to them, when all the power today is behind their cause.

Looking at the 2023 proposal for the Muslim prayer room, it is interesting to show their liberal argument. The proposal started:

[27] I refer to "Proposal On Campus Prayer Rooms," submitted by students to the American University of Beirut Students' Council on 28 February 2023. It is interesting to note that the proposal reminded the AUB administration that their request had been accepted and implemented in prestigious universities around the world where Muslim prayer rooms have been established (Harvard, Princeton, Yale and Columbia, along with UCL, Oxford and Cambridge).

> AUB is a liberal university that believes deeply in and encourages
> freedom of thought and expression and seeks to foster tolerance and
> respect for diversity and dialogue

as quoted from its mission statement.

> As an institution, it has repeatedly attended to students' needs and
> concerns and it has accommodated students accordingly. However,
> concerns have been heavily raised by Muslim students regarding the
> lack of adequate prayer spaces on campus which has left them feeling
> marginalized, underserved, and discriminated against.

This is how, today, DEI has been seen as an instrument for those who are
allowed to be visible in the public sphere. Those whose religiosity requires
such visibility are denied. This is an example from the previous chapter
to show how symbolic liberals push religion into the private sphere while
sexuality is allowed to enjoy both the public and private spheres. These
contrasting movements started in the West but then moved everywhere, with
some external pressures. For instance, USAID today does not subsidize any
university building construction unless the university respects regulations
that include a very precise one about the inclusion of all-gender restrooms
(their number in 100 square meters).[28]

The Dialogical Liberal Project that I advocate for seeks to accept culturally
influenced sexuality and gender identity. It is grounded in the minimum
standard of human rights outlined by the *Universal Declaration of Human
Rights* (and other international conventions), which are understood as
abstract, universal rights. At the same time, to maintain viable national and
communitarian systems of human rights, these concepts must be contextualized locally, according to existing normative systems and societal norms.
The Declaration also emphasizes that individuals should not be discrim-
inated against based on their sexual orientation and should receive certain
forms of social and institutional recognition as LGBTQ+ members of society.

In light of this broad guidance, some countries have embraced comprehensive and previously unimagined forms of legal recognition and full
visibility of all sexual orientations in the public sphere, while others have not.

Academic gender studies and feminist movements have been crucial
in this progress. Gender as a concept is vital for understanding political
economy, social reproduction, care and male domination. Therefore, one

---

[28] Interview with the person responsible for AUB's Cyprus campus, currently under
construction.

should not disregard these advances. However, what is controversial today is how the delinking of gender from biological sex has become excessive identity politics, which has been mainstreamed and is perceived as universal. I cite Raewyn Connell (1994, cited by Kiwan 2023), who argues that in the field of gender, some of the most creative work in the Global South arises from the critical appropriation of Northern ideas, combined with ideas stemming from radically different experiences. Let us, therefore, mediate between the natural, the social and the cultural to reassess composite-type gender arrangements, a concept that Eric Macé (2018) describes as a contingent combination, and sexuality, in order to disentangle the conception of justice from the plurality of conceptions of the good.

CHAPTER 7

The Demise of Family Authority: The Case of Swedish Compulsory Child Removal

God could not be everywhere, so he made mothers.

(Attributed to Rudyard Kipling)

Introduction

When I published my presidential address at the International Sociological Association's Congress in Melbourne in July 2023, I received a protest from some Swedish sociologists outraged by my brief remarks on Sweden's policy of compulsory child removal from biological families. Later, I noticed that whenever I speak about family authority, someone accuses me of playing into the hands of the right or echoing the rhetoric of Italian Prime Minister Giorgia Meloni. Perhaps I need to reiterate on every occasion that I am not advocating for the traditional family. I do not long for the past family structure that embodied patriarchy. However, the family and filial love, as interstitial practices, also serve as centers of care and personal affection. Do symbolic liberals truly seek to undermine the family as a social structure and source of authority? This chapter will explore that question through a specific case study.

The family remains the fundamental unit of society, though it is now more fragile and ephemeral than before. For a long time, it has been not only a locus of love and tenderness but also the foundation of civic education and public virtue. While families exist in various forms and their functions have evolved, they are more important than ever in an era of neoliberalism, where individuals are increasingly vulnerable to market forces. Across different regions, the family has traditionally been the primary site of elderly care. In Algeria, for instance, although the state provides residences for the elderly, fewer than 1 percent make use of them (Abderrahmane 2023, 245).

Patterns of family interaction have shifted to varying degrees – parent-child relationships, patriarchal authority, paternal and maternal affection and the mutual responsibilities of husbands and wives in the domestic division of labor. The transformation of kinship and friendship structures has altered family organization, yet the significance of affection remains pronounced. Its power is both distributive and generative, derived not from dominance but from restraint – the non-use of power. Some, such as the Moroccan philosopher Taha Abderrahmane, go even further, reclaiming the family as an essential institution. He argues that without ethics within the family, which serves as the nucleus of society, there can be no ethical foundation at the societal level (Hashas and al-Khatib 2020).

Many scholars contend that family authority is being eroded by both the liberal state and the forces of neoliberal and emotional capitalism. In this chapter, I will examine the consequences of this phenomenon, focusing on Sweden's policy of compulsory child removal from biological families and highlighting specific aspects of this issue.

For a century, capitalism has facilitated cheap mobile labor by making the family fragile as a salient social structure. Countries like Sweden, Denmark and Norway (Blix et al. 2021; Hovde 2022), Canada (Bennett and Blackstock 2005),[1] Australia (Cunneen and Libesman 2000),[2] and the United States became known for removing children from specific lower-class, aboriginal and migrant families and placing them in "culturally advanced" families, including by means of child auctions.[3] Some governments have since given recognition and apologies to persons maltreated under such arrangements

---

[1]   I quote from a 108-page report titled, *Indigenous Children: Rights and Reality of the First Nations Child and Family Caring Society of Canada*: "In Australia and Canada, the forced removal of children to residential schools for several generations corroded the traditional child-rearing values and practices of many Indigenous individuals and communities. ...In both countries, very high rates of child removals continue within the child welfare system, and this continues to corrode Indigenous parenting skills, the passing on of culture and identity, and the very institution of the family." In addition, see Indigenous Foundations, "Sixties Scoop." https://indigenousfoundations.arts.ubc.ca/sixties_scoop/ and Louise BigEagle, "New Series Tells Story of Sixties Scoop Survivor Learning about Her Past." CBC. 25 May 2023. www.cbc.ca/news/canada/saskatchewan/little-bird-sixties-scoop-new-series-1.6853171.

[2]   See also the report of Human Rights Watch: "Commission to Investigate Abuses Against Australia's First Nations." www.hrw.org/news/2021/03/10/commission-investigate-abuses-against-australias-first-nations.

[3]   A Human Rights Watch report in 2019 shows how indigenous and Black children are removed from their families at the highest rate. www.hrw.org/the-day-in-human-rights/2022/11/17.

(Höjer and Kjellberg 2020). Current research and human rights reports show how problematic it becomes when the state undermines family authority. Many families in Sweden are alienated from the bureaucratic power of the Swedish Board of Health and Welfare, which has been acting without due legal process.

Sweden, for long a social welfare state, has an excellent record of social justice and human rights, and a functioning Ombudsman. Particularly to be praised is the country's hospitality to the major wave of refugees in 2015, taking 163,000 at a time of extreme distress for Syrian refugees (Kubai and Mtetwa 2021). The country should also be praised for its work against gender inequality and for a comprehensive child protection system. Yet, these reforms have been tarnished by evidence of abuse. This resulted from the way the bureaucracy and political system were affected by symbolic liberalism that imposed their conception of the good by using social services as a means of undermining parental authority in its relationship to the child.

From the outset, let me clarify this statement. I am not fetishizing the family as a social structure. One can appreciate that the feminist movement, and scholars have pushed the state into the private sphere, addressing domestic violence – not only by combating it but also by advancing children's and women's rights. This has included opposing systematic parental violence against children, female circumcision and forced marriage, as well as recognizing unpaid domestic and care work and addressing gender discrimination in pay and opportunities. I support the state's intolerance of such practices and consider such interventions part of the liberal conception of justice, where society operates within a unified system. However, while unpacking the social construction of children's rights, I will argue that Swedish social services have extended beyond these legitimate actions, employing excessively heavy-handed interventions, particularly in the forced re-homing of children.

Methodologically, in addition to conducting three exploratory interviews with family members whose children were removed and analyzing Swedish official documents,[4] I examined numerous research-based publications and

---

[4] I worked with three research assistants who helped me with Swedish documents and interviews. As they are from migrant backgrounds, they requested I not disclose their names. My collaborators who are Swedish by naturalization also asked me not to disclose their names for fear of possible legal action against them. I would like to thank them and to thank my research assistant Jana Moussa, and those who commented on my early version of this chapter: David Thurfjell, Ruby Harrold-Claesson, Dalia Abdelhady, Lena Hellblom Sjögren, Ulrika Maria Mårtensson, Azril Bacal, Annika Rabo, Fanny Christou, Juan Piovani, Gabriel Kessler, Abdullatif Mohammad, Tonje Gundersen and Nina Drange.

human rights reports related to child and adolescent re-homing in Sweden. Through an extensive literature review, I found diverse perspectives within this discourse, including those who downplay the seriousness of child re-homing. There is a lack of sociological work on this issue, particularly in English, but a substantial number of articles and books have been written by social work scholars. From this body of research, many Swedish human rights reports were highly critical of compulsory child removal.

Given the sensitivity of this topic, I will include extensive quotations from the literature I reviewed. My conclusion will not only assess Swedish (symbolic liberal) social services but also highlight how Dialogical Sociology can contribute to the reform of such essential social services.

Some Statistics

According to the 2020 Swedish official statistics from the National Board of Health and Welfare, 3,486 children and adolescents were taken from their families and re-homed in the care sector without their families' consent. This practice, known as "compulsory care," falls under the Care of Young People Act (LVU).[5] While this seems like a significant number for a country of 10 million inhabitants, it is two-thirds of what it was in 2008, when approximately 15,800 children were placed outside their homes.[6] Of these, 4,800 were in compulsory custody (LVU care) (Edvardsson 2010). Notably, this figure could be much higher if one considers the hidden coercion embedded in officially classified voluntary placements (Svensson and Höjer 2016). The frequent removal of children from their parents through coercion is not unique to Sweden; similar practices exist in other countries, particularly Norway and Germany. According to Steven Bennett's 2016 article, "10.1 per 1,000 children [are] placed in foster care by the [Norwegian Child Welfare Services]...In 71% of cases, this occurs without the consent of the biological parents. In Germany, the corresponding figures are 9 per 1,000 and 10%, and in Sweden, 8.2 per 1,000 and 26%."[7] These Nordic countries and Germany differ significantly from the French case, where the rate of child removal is

---

[5] "Fact Check: What Is Sweden's LVU and How Does It Work?" *The Local*. 22 February 2022. www.thelocal.se/20220222/fact-check-what-is-swedens-lvu-and-how-does-it-work.

[6] In this chapter I use the term "children" for those who are under 18 years of age.

[7] Steven Bennett, "Secrets and Lies Inside Barnevernet." 18 May 2016. www.barnefjern.org/secrets-and-lies-inside-barnevernet/. For a more comprehensive comparative analysis of child welfare removals by the liberal states, see Burns, Pösö and Skivenes (2016), and for the errors and mistakes in child protection, see Biesel et al. (2020).

very low and compulsory removal is rare. According to Join-Lambert and Séraphin (2020, 195), parental authority is withdrawn only in cases of serious breaches of responsibility or prolonged abandonment. Returning to Sweden, a governmental report states that "physical abuse was routine and sexual abuse was common. Of 798 young people placed in foster homes, 763 (96%) reported abuse or neglect; of 665 placed in institutions, 462 (69%) reported abuse or neglect" (Höjer and Kjellberg 2020, 139–40).

Beyond these broad figures, not many statistics are available that show the consequences of re-homing, or a breakdown by ethnicity. Norway publishes statistics on children and young people who die in foster homes every year[8] and have produced a report on custody cases and ethnic minorities.[9] Sweden's Social Service claims that they do not have any such statistics. One of my informants explained that they do have statistics, but the authorities will not divulge them. Another said: "We in Sweden do not get statistics on ethnicity." This is not really true. For example, both the Crime Prevention Council (BRÅ) and the police have recently presented statistics where the perpetrators' ethnicity has been indicated.[10] Indeed, the ethnic background of the people concerned is always of interest when it comes to crime, as evidenced by media coverage and political speeches,[11] but information is withheld when it comes to whether people with an ethnic background other than Swedish are exposed to the authorities' exercise of power or when they become victims of crime and discrimination.

The lack of official statistics fuels rumors. Accounts circulate of children being removed. Instead of explaining that they were hit or had minor injuries, the category of "extremism" is used as a justification for removing children from Muslim families. These stories are widely shared on social media.[12]

---

[8] See, for instance, "Dør 150 barn hvert år under barnevernets omsorg hvert år?" [Do 150 Children Die Each Year under the Care of Child Welfare Services?]. www.ung.no/oss/343074.

[9] "Omsorgsovertakelser og etniske minoriteter. En gjennomgang av saker i fylkesnemnda." [Care Transfers and Ethnic Minorities. A Review of Cases in the County Board]. https://oda.oslomet.no/oda-xmlui/handle/20.500.12199/5130. I would like to thank Tonje Gundersen who provided me with a long summary of this report.

[10] See, for instance, "Crime Prevention Agency Warns of Risk for Ethnic Discrimination in Police Stop and Search." https://sverigesradio.se/artikel/crime-prevention-agency-warns-of-risk-for-ethnic-discrimination-in-police-stop-and-search.

[11] See the latest speeches and posts of the leader of the Sweden Democrats, Jimmie Åkesson.

[12] "Child Custody, Racism, Conspiracies and Swedish Social Services." www.cost-of-living.net/child-custody-racism-conspiracies-and-swedish-social-services/.

After three protests and rallies in three cities, followed by a social media campaign under #kidnappingkidsinsweden, Swedish authorities responded on 6 February 2023, accusing certain social media accounts of being linked to *violent Islamist organizations*.[13] They issued warnings about disinformation, violent threats against social services and a potential risk of terrorist attacks as a consequence. Government measures to counteract disinformation include proposals to increase penalties for violence or threats against public officials. Insulting a public official should be criminalized, along with a proposal to the Council of Legislation to expand the use of security officers in more settings, such as social services offices.[14]

As the problem does not concern only children from migrant origins, I will divide this chapter into two sections: one about the problem in general and then of children from migrant origins.

Social Services vs. Family

Contemporary Western European societies are characterized by globally standardized processes that include children's rights, individualized subjectivities and high-consumption styles of living (Castro 2020). Different countries have different ways of realizing them.

In Sweden, the standard procedure for social services interventions, including child removal, begins with a report submitted to social services by a neighbor or school, highlighting concerns about a child's behavior. Such concerns typically involve violence (whether physical or verbal), abuse, neglect or any form of harm against minors. Social services then dispatch investigators to interview family members. A report is subsequently submitted to the social welfare committee, which is attached to the elected municipal council. The committee discusses the case in a special meeting, which guardians can usually attend. The committee may decide on a course of action, which could range from ordering psychological therapy – often for both the child and the parents – to issuing a compulsory care order or petitioning the court for a care order. The court reviews the social services' investigation and holds an oral hearing, which includes the guardians. It then

---

[13] See example of such accusation in "Interview: Why Immigrant Families in Sweden Might Distrust Social Services." www.thelocal.se/20220222/interview-why-immigrant-families-in-sweden-might-distrust-social-services.

[14] "Government Taking Strong Action Against Disinformation and Rumour-Spreading Campaign." www.government.se/press-releases/2023/02/government-taking-strong-action-against-disinformation-and-rumour-spreading-campaign/.

decides whether to issue a compulsory care order, though the guardians have the right to appeal the court's decision.[15] As a result, the process can take several months if an appeal is filed or if the decision by either the social welfare committee or the court is contested, while the child remains with a foster family.

Scholarly work and human rights reports challenge how this process has been applied and highlight the significant role played by social services bureaucracy, particularly since the mid-1990s. The introduction of the neoliberal-style New Public Management (NPM) in social work in Sweden "has resulted in a fragmented and instrumental view of social work...and in many municipalities in a division of responsibilities where politicians 'order services by performers'" (Espvall 2018, 149). Some services were subcontracted to private companies, effectively turning them into "care for sale" (Höjer and Forkby 2011).[16] In 2020, there was an initiative to audit social services through an evaluative report.[17] However, in my interview with a Swedish criminologist, the report was criticized as "bland" and ineffective, failing to bring about any meaningful change.

The literature on child removal largely reveals a process that legitimizes the perspective of investigators while sometimes delegitimizing that of the family. Bo Edvardsson, a professor of psychology at Örebro University, with extensive experience training social workers at various Swedish universities, has provided sharp criticism of child protection investigations in Swedish social services. Below, I summarize some of the key points he raised extensively in his book and later in a monograph, "Child Protection Investigations in the Swedish Social Services" (2010), published by his university:

- [The objective of the social workers is to] accumulate as much negative data as possible, irrespective of their importance for the questions at hand.

- The perspectives of the investigator are not made explicit in the text, e.g., why so many small and trivial defects of the parents and the children are accumulated and not the strengths or why the knowledge of the clients is not worth taking into consideration. A negative and

15 See www.socialstyrelsen.se/om-socialtjansten/engelska/compulsory-care-of-children-in-accordance-with-swedish-act-lvu/.
16 It is interesting to note that Norway did not use private companies for that.
17 "Hållbar socialtjänst – En ny socialtjänstlag." [Sustainable Social Services – A New Social Services Law]. www.regeringen.se/rattsliga-dokument/statens-offentliga-utredningar/2020/08/sou-202047/.

pessimistic view of humans is one of the foundations of the child protection investigations.

- Background information is thin and to a large extent vague, often without specification of sources, and not reliable. Critical thinking about information is weak or non-existing.

- The family members that are investigated are not given the opportunity to reply to what other sources have said about them BEFORE the investigator formulates analysis and judgments in the investigation. Without control from all source persons and without replying from the persons (including children old enough to be interviewed) the information is not reasonably certain to use.

- Hypothesis work is not mastered in the investigations. The investigators work with fixed beliefs and bias in the selection and interpretation of data. One-sidedness and confirmation bias is a rule and falsification of the investigators' conviction is avoided.

- It is standard procedure to consciously withhold important material of different kinds that is contrary to the implicit agenda, which is to prove that the child/children in the particular case need compulsory care. This has been admitted by many social workers. This means lying and committing perjury in the courts. Concealing information is of course incompatible with Swedish constitutional law, but is a rule in the child protection investigations.

- Uncertainty is seldom expressed in the texts, e.g., words like "probable," "perhaps," "possibly" or longer statements of uncertainty are rare.

- The data is often changed, fabricated (e.g., by bolstering trivialities), fantasized (e.g., from preconceptions) or even created by gossip or lying. There even exists proved instances of forging of parts of documents in the social services.

- Judgments and conclusions often do not follow logically from the data. Concluding statements are often made without support in the data. More probable, alternative interpretations of common phenomena are often ignored. Contradictory evidence is often hidden.

- The Swedish child protection investigations are constructed as persuasive documents and according to some of the principles in propaganda texts, e.g., ideological and conformity conceptions about humans and human relations, biased selection, repetition, evidence fabrication, emotive expressions etc. Several investigators have mentioned to me that the intention is to persuade the decision makers on the social service board and in the court to make a decision about compulsory care. The board and the court are manipulated by the investigator by these so-called "investigation reports," but why is the investigator manipulating? What is the underlying process? (Edvardsson 2010)

In their study investigating family violence against children, Kubai and Mtetwa concurred with this observation with more recent fieldwork. Some families they interviewed, "complain that social workers do not listen to the parents' explanations or concerns. They stick to their own story without regard for the necessary evidence to support the allegations of violence or maltreatment of children" (Kubai and Mtetwa 2021, 348).

Kubai and Mtetwa highlighted the case of Pastor Daniel Edire, whose son was removed, as an example to illustrate the workings of the social services system:

Although the court did not find any evidence to support the allegations that Edire was violent to his children, the authorities did not allow him to be near them. Until proven innocent, he was viewed as a danger to them. The reports from doctors concluded there was no evidence of violence on the children's bodies, and a psychologist confirmed that the children had no evidence of psychological trauma. The police, too, submitted their report confirming the lack of evidence of violence in the family and closed the case. These results were presented during the court sessions that sought to decide whether the children should remain in foster care or be returned to their parents. Surprisingly, the court ruled in favour of the child welfare officials. The children's father explained that it was clear they suspected that violence had taken place in the family, and that this may have escaped detection during the investigations. As if to show lenience, the social services offered a parenting course as a condition for the children to come back home to the family. ...when the social services invited Pastor Edire and his wife for further interrogation sessions...they told them unequivocally that African parents, especially fathers, are authoritarian and that they suspected that the pastor was strict with his children. (Kubai and Mtetwa 2021, 348–49)

These two social work researchers bring another flagrant example from an interview with the former school counselor, who described a case of a child:

[She] came home and told the parent that she was bullied and beaten by other kids at school. The father told her to "beat them back" if they beat her again. Then the school contacted social workers and claimed the father told the child to beat other children. When the school contacted social workers about this, the child was taken away from the parents. Furthermore, when social services calls for a meeting with all the parties concerned, the parents tend to take it personally. In their view, being called to a meeting with "the Social" officials suggests that "your home is not your domain and that they have the power to tell you how to raise your children." The parents do not understand. They wonder why they cannot decide over their children and shape them as they grow up and why they should not yell at the children if they make mistakes. Apparently, parents do not understand that if they upset the children, "they need to apologise to them, to beg them...you must say you are sorry." However, according to the African cultural norms to which African parents are accustomed, age is accorded respect. Therefore, begging small children for forgiveness for yelling at [them] when they make mistakes is alien to the cultural understandings of respect. Evidently, such norms clash with the provisions of the Swedish Parental Code Act. (Kubai and Mtetwa 2021, 349–50)

For Kubai and Mtetwa, this reflects an apparent negative stereotype of African culture. Despite these critiques, the situation has not changed. The Health and Social Care Inspectorate (IVO), in its 2023 report, found that 4 in 10 children (37 percent) said their social worker did not speak to them before they were moved into a new home.[18] Additionally, according to the 2013 Report to the European Parliament Petitions Committee, "Lena Hellblom Sjögren [...] has found through extensive research into 25 Swedish case studies of parental alienation that the child's right to family life is being violated, with no redress, in Sweden."[19] Journalist Leila Nezirevic cites forensic psychologist Lena Hellblom Sjögren, whose book *Barnets Rätt Till Familjeliv* [*The Child's Right to Family Life*] (2013) argues that the Swedish

[18] "IVO kritiserar socialnämnder vid omplacering av barn." [IVO Criticizes Social Welfare Boards When Relocating Children]. www.ivo.se/aktuellt/publikationer/rapporter/ivo-kritiserar-socialnamnder-vid-omplacering-av-barn/.

[19] The Nordic Committee for Human Rights (NCHR) for the Protection of Family Rights in the Nordic Countries, Report to the European Parliament Petitions Committee, "Child Removal Cases in Denmark, Finland, Norway and Sweden." 2013. www.nkmr.org/docs/Report_to_the_European_Parliament_Petitions_Committee.pdf.

system is unfair to children because, "the child's rights – the human rights and legal rights and the child's needs – are violated, and if you have a very sound investigation that the child needs to be protected, then you can take that last step to move away a child from his or her family, but not before [having sound investigation]." Hellblom Sjögren further stated, "it is quite wrong that there are companies earning money from taking children in their homes. I think that it should be a last resort, and then you should recruit adults who love children, not adults who are in need of earning money." In contrast, Swedish law states that children should first be placed with a family member. However, according to Hellblom Sjögren, "This law is not followed, and that goes with many laws in Sweden. It looks very good on paper, but in practice, it doesn't. They don't follow the law."[20]

In a more detailed elaboration in 2016, Hellblom Sjögren wrote to the European Parliament's Committee on Petitions in Brussels.[21] Here are some quotes (my emphases):

- Placing children in need of love, acceptance, and proper care with total strangers – who are paid and **take orders from social services, and increasingly from consultants employed by a growing number of stock market companies profiting in this field** – may not be the best way to support these children.

- I would like to explain the background of **the ongoing violation of the human right to family life that occurs daily** in Sweden.

  o The results can be summarized as **systemic malpractice** within social services, **making it the rule rather than the exception**.

  o When a child is believed to be in need of protection (without clear signs of harm or fear), social services often take protective measures **before conducting any investigation**. Before any physical, psychological, or sexual abuse – or other severe harmful living conditions – have been observed or verified, authorities may remove the child from their family. In many cases, a mother who claims the father has abused her and/or the children is placed together with the children in a women's shelter. This intervention itself can be highly harmful and traumatic.

---

[20] "Experts, Families Say Sweden's Social System Mistreats Muslim Children." www.aa.com.tr/en/europe/experts-families-say-swedens-social-system-mistreats-muslim-children/2580019.

[21] She communicated this to me in a letter.

o   Research-based knowledge indicating that children placed with strangers are worse off than adopted children – and even worse off than those who remain in risky homes – seems to be largely ignored. **In a longitudinal study** [Bohman and Sigvardsson 1980] of approximately 700 children identified as needing removal from a risky home environment, about one-third were placed in foster care, another third were adopted, and the rest remained in their original homes. Years later, follow-ups examined school performance, psychiatric care records, drug addiction, criminal activity, and suicide rates. The results showed that children who remained at home fared the best. Adopted children ranked second on all measurable outcomes, while **foster children had the worst results**.

o   **The European Court in Strasbourg** has repeatedly stated in its child care verdicts: "**The State must unceasingly make efforts to reunite the children with their families.**" However, reunification verdicts are not implemented. Children suffer. Parents suffer. Grandparents suffer. High suicide rates and stress-related deaths have been observed among families affected by child removal and restricted visitation rights. However, it is difficult to obtain precise statistics, as such data is not systematically collected.

To conclude this section, I would say that compulsory child removal alienates some families and undermines their parental moral authority vis-à-vis their siblings, which makes their education more difficult. Fieldwork among parents, conducted by Mahama, Eriksson and Ellingsen, revealed that parents felt differently about the concept of forced child removal by social services:

> Some parents felt it was an extremely bad decision to remove children from home forcefully whilst others thought it offered a way out for children who might otherwise be living in adverse situations. All participants were, however, of the view that forced child removal should be the last resort after a thorough and fair investigation in a child protection case. (Mahama, Eriksson and Ellingsen 2024, 227)

Some parents say that they cannot discipline unruly children for fear of losing custody.[22] This issue is aggravated more when the child is removed from a migrant family, as we will see in the next section.

---

[22] "Child Custody, Racism, Conspiracies and Swedish Social Services." www.cost-of-living.net/child-custody-racism-conspiracies-and-swedish-social-services/.

Child Removal Among Migrant-Origin Families

No country in Europe has changed demographically as significantly as Sweden, which until recently was exceptionally socially and religiously homogeneous.[23] Now it is a country with a large migrant population, as much as 25.9 percent with an immigrant background, including people born in Sweden with both parents or one parent identified as "foreign-born" (Kubai and Mtetwa 2021, 333). Swedish authorities moved between two migrant policy poles: assimilation and multiculturalism. This policy was mainly driven from above and did not leave sufficient space for the self-integration of the migrants into Sweden's society (Christou 2019). The process of adaptation and negotiation of conflicting sets of values is at work. For instance, Mahama, Eriksson and Ellingsen (2024) show how some African families in their study shifted from an *authoritarian* kind of parenting that they were used to in their country of origin towards a more *authoritative* kind of parenting in destination countries where the autonomy of the child is valued either by freewill or as an effort to meet up with what is required of them in Swedish child welfare policy. But the issue at stake is how much Swedish child welfare is multicultural and how much family rights are respected as stipulated by the *Universal Declaration of Human Rights*: "The family is the natural and fundamental group unit of society and is entitled to protection by society and the State" (Article 16(3)) and "Parents have a prior right to choose the kind of education that shall be given to their children" (Article 26(3)).[24]

The hegemonic and deculturized conception (though actually culturally specific) of what is good, as held by symbolic liberal bureaucrats and politicians in Sweden, is further aggravated when it comes to ethnic minorities, as we currently witness with discourses from the (extreme) right-wing, even though we lack statistics. According to Hellblom Sjögren's letter to the Petition Committee of the European Parliament, statistics are

---

[23] Of course, this requires further qualification. Until after World War II, Sweden remained a highly socially stratified society, and since the 1800s, the dominant Protestant Christian faith had been diversified by the emergence of "free churches." From the 1950s onward, labor immigration from Southern Europe increased, followed by a surge in immigration from the Middle East, Africa, and Eastern Europe in the 1970s and 1980s, bringing with it significant religious diversity.

[24] See also UDHR Article 12: "No one shall be subjected to arbitrary interference with his privacy, family, home or correspondence, nor to attacks upon his honour and reputation. Everyone has the right to the protection of the law against such interference or attacks."

available elsewhere. For example, in Norway, a quarter of those in forced custody in 2014 were children whose mothers were born abroad (424 out of 1,663).[25]

Here I would like to raise three issues: 1. The collision between social services and security; 2. Orientalist social work; and 3. Discrimination against migrant families.

The Collision between Social Services and Security

The Swedish government defines terrorism broadly as a "threat to human rights and democratic values" presented as "our values" (Finch et al. 2022, 121). Like the UK's Prevent policy, this definition allows "a securitised turn in social policy, moving services such as social work, education and health away from the liberal, emancipatory origins towards a more sinister, intelligence gathering role on populations seen to be 'risky' or 'dangerous'" (Finch et al. 2022, 123). As Masoud Kamali (2015), professor of social work at Mid Sweden University, has argued, such narratives are more readily applied to Muslim populations in Western countries and operate as a vehicle to exaggerate concerns about the Muslim population, which, in turn, provides fertile ground for Islamophobia to grow.

Orientalist Social Work

Immigrants in Europe have often been scapegoated for much wider problems in the host society (domestic violence, unemployment, crime, etc.). Some Swedish scholars who have examined the scapegoating process have adopted a culturalist approach. For Jessica Jönsson, an associate professor of social work at Örebro University, social services use the concept of "cultural competency" to include "a stereotypical perception of people with immigrant backgrounds as essentially and culturally different from those considered 'Us'" (Jönsson 2013, 163). Gordon Pon argues that the discourse of cultural competence has become a form of new racism, which, instead of invoking

---

[25] I was deeply moved by Sagarika Chakraborty's memoir, *The Journey of a Mother* (2022), and recently watched the film *Mrs. Chatterjee vs. Norway* (2023), which was inspired by the book. It tells the story of a one-woman battle against the country of Norway and its social services system. The memoir reveals how cultural differences – such as hand-feeding children (perceived by social workers as force-feeding) and using Indian homeopathic medicine – contributed to the decision to remove two children from their family. I am amazed by how a mother's deep emotional connection to her children is often interpreted as irrational and even held against her, leading to perceptions of her being an "unfit mother."

race and biology, highlights cultural differences and hierarchies, calling for its abandonment (Pon 2009).

While some scholars conceptualize honor-related violence (HBV) uncritically,[26] others find it problematic, particularly in how it is understood by social services. Based on interviews with 16 prison clients convicted in Sweden of a crime related to HBV, Grip and Dynevall write that the participants

> explained the crimes as driven by emotions and impulses. Almost all refused what may be termed the cultural narrative and label and did not want to be associated with honour culture. Several characteristics of the perpetrators of relevance for the violent crimes were found, such as a history of normalisation of violence, past antisocial behaviour and a lack of prosocial coping and problem-solving skills. (Grip and Dynevall 2024, 12)

Based on in-depth interviews with 20 social workers in three different Swedish municipalities, Barzoo Eliassi, then a professor in social work at Linnaeus University, unfolds what is assumed to be a Swedish social workers' discourse of color-blindness and universalism. This discourse does not only see cultural differences but also construes these differences as central when they frame, assess and formulate interventions of these workers: "Muslim men are intrinsically viewed as 'oppressors' and Muslim women as 'victims' since they have direct consequences for social work practices and interventions" (Eliassi 2015, 566). For him,

> If inappropriate child-rearing and gender inequality among minoritized families are viewed as rooted in their cultural background, then social policy is encouraged to target and combat their culture. Consequently, in order to solve these problems, their cultures need to be contained, governed, fought, and excluded. An assimilationist social policy thus becomes a disciplinary means to "normalize" what are believed to be deviant and pathologized Muslim fathers, brothers, and families with immigrant backgrounds. (Eliassi 2013, 36)

In this conception, women are seen as oppressed Orientals subjected to honor violence. Nyamko Sabuni, who later became the Minister of Integration in Sweden, appeared in Swedish media following the murder of

---

[26] See, for instance, Thörn and Norberg (2020).

Kurdish girl Fatima Sahindal by her father in 2001. She claimed that the murder was part of a foreign "immigrant culture" that forces the wearing of the veil and the acceptance of the father's authority under the threat of death. She generalized the murder as part of the culture of all Muslim groups (Kamali 2015, 81).

Of course, this stereotype means that social services officials will consider Muslim families as a "family home" for placing youths with Swedish backgrounds. According to Eliassi,

> This prejudiced pattern of placement indicates that Muslim families are understood to be inappropriate places for nurturing and raising young people. Hence, class, ethnicity, and religion become important considerations when social workers assess their interventions and plan sanctions against families who do not adhere to the routines and the rule systems of social services. (Eliassi 2013, 42)

Findings by Keith Pringle (2010) concur with both Eliassi and Kamali, but he makes different assessments depending on the field of intervention. For him,

> the Swedish welfare system may be far less benign in challenging racism and ethnic discrimination than it is when assessed along more "mainstream" comparative measures associated with poverty alleviation or issues of work in the labour market and home. ...Similar findings occur when gendered violence to women and children is placed in focus rather than ethnicity. (Pringle 2010, 30)

Discrimination Against Migrant Families

African migrant children are much more likely (17.5 times) than others to be taken away from their homes and placed in foster care (Kubai and Mtetwa 2021, 335). Most African parents are shocked by this experience. They see it as an attempt or plan "to destroy" their families, as they "see children being turned against their parents" (338).

When it comes to the religion, Kubai and Mtetwa's two Christian informants said that social workers dismissed their concerns about children being placed in the care of Muslim families.

The two cases illustrate the ambiguities of the place of religion in the investigation and assessment of families to determine the placement of children in foster care. This attitude to religion can be attributed to the prevailing notion that, in Sweden, religion is a private matter (Kubai and

Mtetwa 2021, 339), and not important for the conception of the good for the biological families.

Kubai and Mtetwa also describes how social workers reported to the court what happened at a pastor's home during Bible study, and how he addressed his son. The pastor

> felt that though both their Christian faith and their specific African cultural orientation regard homosexuality as unnatural, they were tolerant of values that the Swedish society upholds. However, social services officials claimed that the family home was unsafe for the children and that the parents showed gross deficiency in parenting and building a family in Sweden. (Kubai and Mtetwa 2021, 346)

The attitude of these officials violate the principle that religion is a private matter. Family as a private setting is naturally a site of religious socialization by parents.

Beyond the academic research, there are Swedish, European and UN reports that provide critiques of interventionist Swedish social services. A 2009 UN Children's Committee Report raised criticism against the Swedish social service, and denounced the abuse in its system, including for migrants:

> The Committee reiterates its previous concern that, despite the adoption of legislative guarantees, including the new Anti-Discrimination Act, the principle of non-discrimination is not fully respected in practice, and it is particularly concerned about de facto discrimination against and xenophobia and racist attitudes towards children of ethnic minorities, refugee and asylum-seeking children and children belonging to migrant families. (para. 25)[27]

A 2013 Report to the European Parliament Petitions Committee on child removal cases in Denmark, Finland, Norway and Sweden, stated:

> From our professional experiences, it appears that mostly young, sole parent families, economically and educationally weaker families, families with health challenges and **immigrant parents** are targeted by the social services in Sweden, Norway, Denmark and Finland. Also, parents with religious and philosophical beliefs, which do not seem to

---

[27] "Committee on the Rights of the Child, Fifty-first session, Consideration of Reports Submitted by States Parties under Article 44 of the Convention." 2009. www2.ohchr.org/english/bodies/crc/docs/co/CRC-C-SWE-CO-4.pdf.

be politically accepted, are often deemed as unsuitable parents, which invariably leads the social councils, acting upon the advice of the social workers, to remove the children from their families and place them in foster homes. (my emphasis)[28]

Projekt Rågsved[29] – a Swedish social initiative aimed at addressing social inequality and promoting integration, particularly in the Rågsved area of southern Stockholm – produced a 7,000-word report, "Is LVU Legal Safe for Everyone?" written by Michaela Sjögren Cronstedt in 2022.[30] She showed the discrimination against migrant-background residents based on a survey of 867 individuals (84 percent of the respondents had experienced their own children being placed by social services into foster care). Cronstedt provided 5 scientific references. Here are some excerpts (my emphases):

- Children of parents born in countries other than Sweden in general and in Muslim countries in particular are taken into compulsory care more often than other groups by the social service under the Care of Young People Act (LVU). **This has long been noted by researchers.**

- The National Board of Health and Welfare, and Statistics Sweden, produced statistics for the news department of Sveriges Radio (Swedish Radio), where it appears that **twice as many children of foreign-born parents are taken into care compared to children of Swedish-born parents.**

- The Ombudsman for Discrimination has been able to establish in a recent survey of social workers, that many people experience discrimination when in contact with social services.

- In many of the cases into which we have had more detailed insight, **children have been taken into care based on ignorance, misinterpretation, speculation and sometimes pure prejudice.** We have also been able to see direct and illegal errors in the handling of various cases. ...This has had **disastrous consequences for children and parents**.

- From the aforementioned survey, 87 percent of parents believe that their case was not handled correctly; 84 percent believe that they discovered

[28] Report to the European Parliament Petitions Committee, "Child Removal Cases in Denmark, Finland, Norway and Sweden," 16.
[29] "Children and Young People in Care." www.projektragsved.com/.
[30] No longer available on their website in English, but see https://projektragsved.com/rapporten#.

specific errors in the handling of their case; 57 percent answered that they were not allowed to see their children after they were taken into care; 73 percent have appealed the social welfare board's decision; 63 percent of respondents stated that they were not born in Sweden.

- Social services are perceived consistently to have very little knowledge about what religious affiliation can mean in practice. In their handling of cases, they demonstrate **an obvious tendency to automatically link Muslim heritage with oppression, fundamentalism and activism**.

- There are **expert whistleblowers who are afraid of reprisals**, such as ostracism, bullying, dismissal, assignments being interrupted or having their duties curtailed.

- The right to appeal to the Administrative Court or to the Court of Appeal offered to parents and families is without real legal certainty (only 3 percent of judgments are in favor of the parents).

- We believe that the social welfare board and responsible officials within the social services have violated the Convention on the Rights of the Child, Article 8 (right of the child to preserve his or her identity), 12 (right to be heard and respected), 14 (right to freedom of religion and faith), 20 (given due regard to ethnic, religious, cultural and linguistic background).

- We can state that, unfortunately, as citizens of Sweden in 2022 we are not equal before the actions of the authorities or the law. Families and parents from other countries in general and with a Muslim background in particular are easily denounced as fundamentalists who oppress their children.

- **Is it ignorance and preconceived notions, or xenophobia, that drives so many investigations and decisions?** We understand the legitimate concerns of many children and parents regarding this issue. For social services to build trust, they must meet high standards, ensuring legal certainty and transparency. Investigations should be conducted by officials who are competent in their field, open to different perspectives, and not influenced by their own biases. If children require care outside the home, they must, of course, receive that protection. Likewise, children should not be separated from their parents without a legitimate and well-founded reason.

In an interview, Siv Westerberg, founder of the Nordic Committee for Human Rights (NCHR) and an internationally recognized lawyer who has won eight cases at the European Court of Human Rights against Swedish social services, provides the following observations: "They are kidnapping Muslim children. ...They don't accept that they have other ways to live. ... It is big business (in Sweden) taking away children from their mothers. It is a very big business in Sweden." She points out that foster homes are given too much money by the social services. "If you get a foster child in your home, you will get 25,000 (Swedish krona) (roughly $2,500) a month, and you need not pay any tax for that."[31] This naturally means that financial reward is an incentive to maximize the number of children fostered out.

In the 20-page 2013 Report to the European Parliament Petitions Committee, "Child Removal Cases in Denmark, Finland, Norway and Sweden," Thorbjørn Jagland, criticized "the foster home industry," showing many international studies which argued that,

> a child's separation from its parents increases the risk that the child, often well into adulthood, will experience severe depression, psychosis or other mental and physical ailments, 2–3 times more often than persons without similar experiences. Separation from parents is therefore just as harmful to the child as another "adversity" and it falls even under the term "neglect."[32]

This report was signed by 92 Swedish lawyers, judges, psychologists, university professors and medical doctors. The current director, lawyer Ruby Harrold-Claesson, informed me that the thrust of this report is still valid today.[33]

Discussion

So far, I have attempted to show that there is resistance to changing the status quo of Sweden's social system regarding compulsory child removal. Despite evidence of the system's dysfunctionality, as documented by social work scholars, as well as Swedish, European and UN human rights reports, this issue has not been adequately addressed by sociologists, academia in general (except for some social work scholars) or the Swedish media. Bo Edvardsson, who has extensive experience training social workers at various universities in Sweden, raises critical questions such as: "Are these really in the best

---

[31] "Experts, Families Say Sweden's Social System Mistreats Muslim Children."
[32] Report to the European Parliament Petitions Committee, "Child Removal Cases in Denmark, Finland, Norway and Sweden," 16.
[33] Communication with Ruby Harrold-Claesson, December 2023.

interests of the children?" or "Is a 'hunting the monster theory' influencing social work decisions?" (Edvardsson 2010). According to Edvardsson, the "monster" is the parent, whom Swedish social services conceptualize as far worse than they actually are. To understand why, Edvardsson formulated a set of hypotheses:

- Parents are dangerous monsters.

- Persecution is legitimate. If the investigator has the inner image of the biological parents as monsters it will be legitimate for her/him to attack, persecute, lie and make up stories or even psychically crush them in order to save the alleged victims, i.e., the children. Forged investigative documents seem acceptable.

- Informants that are loyal to the theory are used.

- Contradictory informants and contradictory information are avoided.

- Investigative reports should be persuasive and not objective.

- In a child-protection case, hunting the monster theory should be diffused in order to increase the hunting.

- The existence of "the theory" will produce support for it. Data that seems to support "the monster hypothesis" will be generated and reported to the social service organization by the believers in the monster theory. Leading and repeated questioning of the children can also lead to answers that are interpreted as support.

- Persuasive strategies are thought out and used.

- Dangerous parent monsters should be hunted after placement of the children.

- A monster cannot obtain redress. The social services seldom or never acknowledge errors in social work. It seems to be next to psychologically impossible for the social services to admit deficiencies. (Edvardsson 2010)

Erik Gandini's documentary film, *The Swedish Theory of Love* (2015) heavily criticizes Swedish *statsindividualism* ("statist individualism"), a term coined by Lars Trägårdh. This has seemingly produced widespread consensual collectivism, particularly in public policy discourse, where state authorities – including their entrepreneurial subsidiaries in the child care business – enforce a hegemonic conception of the good shaped by cultural majoritarianism. Despite the efforts of sociologist Hans Zetterberg, the leader of the

"Social State" project, who advocated for embracing "communitarian ideas like human dignity, self-help, personal responsibility, and civil society as an alternative to both state- and market-provided welfare" (Ervik and Kildal 2015, 15), statist individualism remains the dominant Swedish paradigm.

Conclusion: Social Policy and Dialogue

The objective of this chapter is not only to highlight the stark contrast between the theory and practice of the Swedish child protection system but also to explore explanations for this discrepancy. It is crucial to demonstrate the extent of intolerance in current debates on the importance of family. Equally important is addressing how critiques of the system have been met with claims of a conspiracy by "violent Islamist organizations." Additionally, the debate in the Arab and Muslim world is highly emotional, with many perceiving events in Sweden and other Nordic countries as acts of Islamophobic child abduction.

From the outset of this chapter, I propose the hypothesis that Swedish symbolic liberals in social services – supported, whether consciously or unconsciously, by the silence or justifications of the media, academia and the political sphere – are imposing their hegemonic (and deculturized) conception of the good onto society. This has reached the point where reputable lawyers have taken legal action against Swedish social services in the European Court. Historically, Sweden has functioned much like a religious community, with authorities regulating not only public but also private moral life. This has resulted in a social contract that maintains a complex relationship with religion – viewing it as a source of public morality while simultaneously rejecting it as a legitimate foundation for public action or claims-making (Mårtensson 2014). Even in today's secular Sweden, traces of this cultural legacy persist, creating alienation for those who hold alternative communitarian conceptions of the good in an increasingly multiethnic society.

I do not argue that all instances of compulsory child removal undermine pluralism in Swedish society's conception of the good. There are certainly justified cases involving systematic violence in some Swedish families. However, as Sarah Schulman asserts in her book, *Conflict Is Not Abuse* (2016), there is a tendency to exaggerate harm.

Has child removal truly been used as a last-resort intervention? Is the high number of child removals a consequence of Sweden's particularly low threshold for intervention regarding drug use, alcohol abuse and domestic violence? Why does the Swedish state not consider alternative punitive measures, such as fines or imprisonment for abusive parents, instead of coercively placing children in foster care?

As I previously argued, academic resistance to this issue exists, but it primarily comes from scholars in the field of social work rather than from sociologists. I briefly addressed the Swedish case in my presidential address at the International Sociological Association's Congress in Melbourne in July 2023 to illustrate how family authority is undermined by symbolic liberals. I later published this as an article (Hanafi 2023), which prompted an angry letter from Swedish sociologists denying the severity of the child removal issue and its disproportionate impact on migrant communities. Some of their criticisms were certainly valid, and I acknowledged them – for instance, I had cited a source that misrepresented the number of compulsory child removals. In this chapter, I am not only interested in critiquing symbolic liberalism as it manifests in the practice of child removal, but also in addressing it as a scientific controversy and demonstrating how Dialogical Sociology can foster meaningful debates among scholars and the public. Before doing so, however, I will first discuss two key points: the collaboration and dialogue between sociology and other disciplines, and sociology's critical role in this discourse.

First, Ramón Flecha, in *The Dialogic Society* (2022), calls for greater collaboration in the social sciences. He rightly highlights that up to 60 percent of articles in the social sciences are already co-authored and that most research groups include gender and ethnic diversity. However, he advocates for more co-authorship with researchers from other disciplines. For him, dialogic social science, conducted in collaboration with different disciplines, can achieve a much higher intellectual and scientific level than theories and methods developed in isolation. Should we expect the same if sociologists and social work scholars collaborate to challenge the "monster hunting" theory in the social welfare system?

Second, sociology appears to be largely absent from discussions on compulsory child removal, leaving this topic primarily to social work scholars, often in collaboration with psychologists. As Eva Illouz (2019) has meticulously argued in her work on love relationships, there is a pressing need for a sociological – not merely psychological – analysis of how children have become the focal point of excessive individualism. In this framework, symbolic liberals and emotional capitalists undermine and, in some cases, "destroy" family authority. Under the guise of promoting extreme autonomy, children can now "choose" their family with the assistance of social services. This phenomenon cannot be fully understood without examining how certain elites (symbolic liberals) have long sought to impose their particular conception of the good life on all communities within a country like Sweden.

Childhood education is fundamentally a domain where conceptions of the good are shaped and should remain so. However, this cannot be framed as a matter of justice unless there is a clear violation of the *Universal Declaration of Human Rights*, which must be understood in an abstract sense while also contextualized within cultural, social, and historical trajectories. If Sweden, like many Euro-American countries, seeks to reduce the rates of sexual harassment, sexual violence, drug use, and other social problems among children and youth, it must collaborate with families rather than undermine their moral authority. Sociology should strive to balance collective and communitarian rights with individual rights within the broader framework of political liberalism.

For Slimane Amansag (2024), Sweden could look to models like the "Community Partnership Programs" in the United States, where social services collaborate with local communities to co-develop and implement child welfare services. This will bring trust to these services rather than fear.

Sociologists, particularly, in the footsteps of Foucault, have long been interested in looking at the question of power and in identifying social groups benefiting from a specific social policy. Yet rare are those in the scholarly community who have conducted such analyses. What about the political economy of abuses of the social services? Bo Edvardsson (2010) highlighted clearly

> The data in the investigations come mostly from persons whose employment or economic wellbeing is dependent on the social service organization, e.g., day care personnel, home therapists, paid psychologists, and families who are paid to have children in their home as compulsory placements. This means that most of the information comes from challengeable witnesses. They have their own, economical, interests to deliver biased data, the kind of data that the social service organization wants.

Against market triumphalism, Michael Sandel (2013) points out how the market economy transformed into a market society by its expansion (as forcer and value) into spheres of life where they don't belong. What are the implications when social services were partly privatized and neoliberalized in the hands of the "market," and in the hands of those who profit from human vulnerability and suffering? At a time when the conservative government recruited the sociological skills of Hans Zetterberg to help dismantle the

Swedish Popular Social Welfare Model, should sociology rationalize the debate over this model?

Should sociologists be concerned with discrimination against migrants by social workers and municipal social welfare committees in a country like Sweden, where Islamophobia, among other factors, has contributed to the rise of populist political parties currently in power? Should they question why the first alarm was raised by human rights organizations rather than academia, highlighting the stark contrast between Sweden's highly regarded child protection system and its actual implementation in cases of compulsory child removal? Should they investigate who funds research on social services and whether this funding influences the extent to which critiques of social services are "softened"? It is worth examining who "dares" to expose certain abuses and who refrains from doing so.

I reiterate my appreciation for the critical scholarship I have encountered among Swedish social work scholars and in human rights reports. As someone deeply engaged in studying the Arab–Israeli conflict, I am aware that Israeli human rights organizations often report on brutal colonial practices in the Palestinian territories more quickly than Israeli academia. In Chapter 4, I discussed how cancel culture affects university campuses, making some topics nearly impossible to debate due to their taboo nature. I wonder whether compulsory child removal is one such topic. In my correspondence with a Swedish sociologist in December 2023, he remarked, "Here, there are only two sacred things: God and Swedish social services." These issues should be central to Dialogical Sociology, and I hope my chapter contributes to this discussion.

In essence, I believe that in the neoliberal age, the family remains a vital social structure for protecting individuals from both state and market coercion. It provides not only material support but also essential emotional support. Alain Touraine (2007; 2013), in his analysis of late modernity as the end of society and the social, underestimates the enduring significance of the family – an oversight that is critical not only in the Global South but also in the Global North, albeit to varying degrees. The neoliberal state's use of its authority – along with that of schools and social services – to override rather than complement family authority is deeply problematic. Of course, not all family authority is being eroded; the impact depends on factors such as nationality, migration status, and urban versus rural settings. What I critique is the way in which extending individual rights to children has come to mean protecting them *from* their families (state individualism) rather than *with* their families.

This is particularly relevant in a time when Sweden, struggling to manage youth and gang-related crime, is considering lowering the age of criminal responsibility. It coincides with the decline of Swedish exceptionalism, marked by the rise of the Sweden Democrats and the Tidö Agreement between conservative and liberal parties, as well as the broader shift from hospitality to what Derrida (Stocker 2007) calls *hostipitality*.

More broadly, this excessive individualism and disregard for family weaken filial love, as theorized by Scribano (2019, 2), who describes it as arising from family ties: "Love in a family context involves multidirectional links: parents to children, children to parents, siblings to each other, as these complex bonds generate the special energy needed to build collective practices." Through his extensive work in Latin America, Scribano demonstrates how filial love serves as a major source of struggle and resistance against oppression and violence. Numerous organizations have emerged to channel this collective action, including *Mothers for Equality* (Brazil), the *Association of Parents of Special Young People of Bella Unión* (Uruguay), *Relatives and Friends Against Delinquency and Kidnapping* (Guatemala), and *Mothers for Life* (Argentina), a network of families supporting one another in dealing with drug-related issues among their children. These groups exemplify generosity as a form of emotional investment.

Finally, when I presented a paper based on this chapter at the 6th International Conference of the Parental Alienation Study Group (PASG) in Oslo in September 2024, I received reactions from academics, lawyers and practitioners who noted that the issues I address are also prevalent in other Western countries, particularly Germany and Norway. However, what gives me hope is the growing awareness of the crisis in how child welfare systems handle family conflicts. Some speakers argued against a rigid rights-based approach to children, and instead called for a more flexible system of counseling and conflict resolution before resorting to legal action. I see this perspective as aligning with the principles of Dialogical Sociology.

CHAPTER 8

Conclusion

> There are only two ways to organize human relationships: dialogue
> or violence.
>
> Ramón Flecha, *The Dialogic Society* (2022)

This book began by exposing certain pathologies of late modernity, and I showed how some are related to flawed implementations of the political liberal project and others to its fundamental Rawlsian variation. A critical assessment of both is necessary. I do not fetishize any particular conception, but I seek to engage humanity in a conversation about universal concepts and values that converge. This (global sociology) book aims to contribute to that dialogue.

I consider certain cultural elements intrinsic to liberalism – such as libertarian and individualistic tendencies – that must be exposed and redressed. However, I find it crucial to treat political liberalism as a "thin theory" – justice as fairness, with its two egalitarian and difference principles, and its distinction between the conception of justice and pluralistic conceptions of the good. This framework has the potential to unleash the emancipatory promise of liberalism while directly confronting its authoritarian tendencies. This serves as the foundation of my global sociological reflection before delving into the cultural and historical analysis of specific social phenomena in particular societies. This (liberal) starting point, as I show in this book, cannot function without being supplemented by a rationality enriched by passions, a concept central to Elina Pulcini. Society does not need justice alone; it also requires care – care for the private, social, and global Other; care for future generations; care for the world; and care for the Earth itself.

The reader would be acquainted now with not only my positionality but also my preferences. I define myself as liberal in politics, socialist in economics and heterodox in culture. By heterodox in culture, I mean that I defend modernity and its values without the sense of linear progressivism, and I defend the idea of preserving some aspects of tradition as I see them as a source of social cohesion. They are there because of their anthropological roots in our society and humanity, but without reifying them or essentializing culture. In brief, there is fetishism neither for tradition nor for social change. My affinity to Moral Foundations Theory is to convince the liberal left that their moral intuitions based on fairness, care and loyalty to their [subculture] identity group are not sufficient to understand how people base their moral reasonings influenced by also loyalty (to their broader groups), authority and purity (what is accepted culturally), and there is a sore need to factor that when gauging evidence. About my (democratic) socialism, I question some of Rawls's liberalism by giving more space to the principle of difference and to positive liberty (political participation of lower strata of society) and I envisage alternative avenues for productive and egalitarian affective investments that counter the immense social and psychic power of neoliberalism.

If Rawls's political liberalism is the turning point of modern political philosophy, it has little underpinning in empirical sociological research. These conceptions are thin in their abstract form, but they become thick when each society has the freedom and capacity to debate them in light of its own circumstances. This is what I call "soft universalism." By "soft" I do not mean absolute relativism, which can lead to the mythology of uniqueness and exceptionalism as I see it in some Arab and Israeli sociological productions. Differentiating between "thick" and "thin" moral terms is very important. Michael Walzer (2019) argues that a *thin* set of universal principles should be adapted or elaborated *thickly* to historical circumstances in order to give sense to what we mean by specific principles (e.g., social democracy) in a given context where other thick principles (e.g., distributive justice) are in play. In this meaning, these thick moral arguments often are more legitimate and useful ones. Yet this minimal thin morality is very important, both for the sake of *criticism* and for the sake of *international solidarity*.

Not to confuse philosophical narratives on the one hand with the socio-economic-political on the other, as if philosophical doctrines are reliable indicators of everyday life, in this book I have sought to provide some socio-economic-political narratives on how symbolic liberals, being classical liberalism but politically illiberal, distort the definition of justice. This is by deflating the concept of social justice and inflating the conception of the universality of human rights and accepting only one possible conception of the good as being the conception of justice. They have also privatized the conception of the good for autonomous individuals, leaving no possibility for the common good and shared culture. Pushed to the margin by many electorates in liberal democracies and other countries, these symbolic liberals will be the contemporary "bobo" ("bourgeois-bohemian") living the paradox of being the tolerance-inspired leftists (some conservatives as well) but who have lost contact with the real life of common people whose "carefree lightness ignored the tragedy of the epoch, but with whom history will catch up sooner or later," echoing the words of Alexandre Devecchio (Botz-Bornstein 2019, 211).

To overcome this trend, I proposed the Dialogical Liberal Project, with some features that can be summarized as the following:

First, the primacy of the just over the good is important for addressing the question of social inequality.

Second, taking seriously the environmental destruction and ecological crisis highlighting particularly the fact that the excess of immediate enjoyment through consumption should not remain as a privatized conception of the good but should be upgraded to become part of the environmental justice so society should agree on how to regulate it (heavy taxation, penalty to polluters, public awareness; nudges, etc.). This is what the Indian environmental scholar and activist Vandana Shiva calls *Earth Democracy* (Bhattacharyya 2025).

Third, enhancing spaces of dialogue. Dialogue does not mean only ad hoc forums for discussion; it is living together in shared habitats and common urban and cultural spaces. Otherwise, it will be dialogue-washing.

Fourth, factoring in the power from Above and Below. Dialogue cannot operate without a minimum of a balance of power and political representation of lower-status sectors of society. The Dialogical Political Liberal Project seeks to circumvent the conservative critique of individual freedom and the libertarian view that freedom trumps all other values. For Dialogical Sociology, liberties are not only negative ones (no interference with the equal sharing of basic liberties by individuals) but also positive liberties (the possibility of political participation and utilization of capabilities). This is not possible as long as the rich are funding political parties and the media. Yet, power does not mean authority. It is also how social love and rehabilitating the fluidity of moral argumentations in society (instead of using excessive medical and rights talk language), including how individuals and communities exercise Montesquieu's "doux commerce" in their societal everyday interactions and establish good neighborhoods. Remember Paul Ricœur's teleological conception of the desire for a good life, living not only *with* others but also *for* others. Rawlsian justice, supplemented with ethics of hospitality and care (based on love, compassion and generosity) will mobilize emotions that become part of the *"solution"* of the problematic of power and life in common, instead of being only the *problem*.

Fifth, we need to distinguish between the universality of the *Universal Declaration of Human Rights* and the cultural particularity of each *system of human rights*. The right to culture is an inherent part of this declaration and should be balanced with the promotion and protection of all human rights and fundamental freedoms. Culture will shape the pluralistic conceptions of the good, and the Dialogical Political Liberal Project will thus rehabilitate such plurality against the hegemonic conception of the good by being attentive to how people conduct their moral deliberations. Thus, the Dialogical Political Liberal Project is rather a *compass* that connects sociology to moral and political philosophy (Hanafi 2021a). It considers values that sociology, as science with normative claims, defends as sociological, not accepting exclusively philosophical themes that stand alone. It means that these values cannot be reasoned independently of how we experience them (Bamyeh 2019).

Finally, the Dialogical Political Liberal Project accommodates culture and communities, not only autonomous individuals. It starts not from metaphysical assumptions or abstract ideals but from the world as it operates. People in all societies express significant support for religion, family and community, as well as individual liberty and equality. However, there are tradeoffs between these values. Different societies strike different balances between values, and these balances can shift over time. The Dialogical Political Liberal Project thus echoes Frédéric Vandenberghe (2023), that the moral and political presuppositions of sociology in its critiques of social injustices, agonistic feature of society and social pathologies basically adhere to the repertoire of "liberal communitarianism." Sometimes it veers more toward the communitarian pole of identity and authenticity, at other times toward the liberal pole of autonomy and justice. Community, family, responsibility, duty and the ethic of care and sustainability are values at least as worthy of protection as autonomy, self-reliance and individualism.

The Dialogical Political Liberal Project, as a process-oriented, slow and artisanal endeavor, relies on the synergy of multiple actors – from urban planners restructuring cities to accommodate diverse socio-economic classes and cultural groups, to social scientists, journalists and artists creating spaces for meaningful encounters. It cannot function without the support of Dialogical Sociology. As mentioned in Chapter 3, Dialogical Sociology builds on previous scholarship, most notably Michael Burawoy's *Public Sociology* (2021), which advances the engagement with diverse public(s).

Sociology will be dialogical when it disentangles its commitment to civil society at two levels: the level of mediation, or soft normativity, and the level of strong normativity. At the first level, sociology provides scientific research that is important for public reason debates and social movements. It is a moment of soft normativity, as the very scientific questions themselves carry moral "presuppositions," as Max Weber reminds us. It entails the possibility of providing knowledge to governments or organizations whose actions we don't always agree with. This sociology believes that despite the incommensurability of some modes of reasoning and political, cultural and religious traditions, actors can engage with each other through a dialogue and reach sometimes overlapping consensus. This is not only in line with the theories of Rawls and Habermas, but also with Durkheim's vision of a sociology that promotes social cohesion, or what he terms social solidarity. The mediation level always operates within the framework of universal social justice, including the principles enshrined in the *Universal Declaration of Human Rights* and social welfare rights.

The second level is *strong normativity*, where sociology not only engages with civil society and the civil sphere but also takes a position in favor of marginalized groups against hegemonic power, and defends those values dear to sociology.

I am worried when sociology analytically conflates the two levels or offers no distinction between providing scientific knowledge/critical thinking and position-taking or policy formulation – or worse, neglects the first level and becomes incapable of engaging with all strata of society.

In Part II of this book, I selected four themes to show how they have been addressed by symbolic liberals and how the Dialogical Political Liberal Project can mitigate their effects.

In Chapter 4, on societal intolerance in general and specifically in relation to academic freedom, I show how political polarization and cancel culture as political silencing are exercised by both symbolic liberals and conservatives. Each group becomes rigid and dogmatic. This results in a sharp increase in politically motivated dismissals of faculty, in the number and success of politically motivated attempts to stop invited speakers from speaking, and in politically motivated disciplinary measures against students; as well as in a chilling effect on lecturers and institutions that may lead to complete avoidance of sensitive topics. More than that, this induces a normative transformation, as political silencing and persecution are increasingly viewed as worthy and legitimate. What is very alarming is how campuses, a locus of liberal arts, have moved into illiberal positions under the effect of the eroding of their autonomy and the extreme polarization among faculty and students with the "safetyism" of (new managerial) administrators. While stepping down from his position as the Director of the Ford Foundation, Darren Walker wrote:

> Increasingly, I worry that well-intentioned boards of directors are selecting rising leaders for safety, appointing executives who have assiduously avoided controversy rather than those most adept at managing it. ...Trustees and directors tell their executives: *Just keep your head down. The prevailing attitude says: Speaking out will cost you more than it buys. Better to say as little as possible, to protect yourself and your reputation, to exhibit neutrality for the purpose of self-preservation.*[1]

I spell out a dilemma of academic freedom in the time of symbolic liberalism and excessive identity politics. Here, clearly, there is a tension between academic freedom and "diversity, equity and inclusion" (DEI). The issue is how to make the mission of sociology and related sciences to investigate marginalized people and historic injustices without excessive identity politics and disinvitation campaigns. The latter makes campuses vulnerable to attacks from both politicians of symbolic liberalism and the populist Right against their autonomy. Sometimes these politicians will use their power in government or parliament to pass illiberal bills, such as the 2021 Danish bill damning "excessive activism in research environments" (Aaltonen 2024).

Symbolic liberals' secularism, discussed in Chapter 5, becomes a religion against other religions (usually foreign religions such as Islam, in Europe). Here, I am thinking more particularly about how symbolic liberals' France deals today with the "Muslim problem" and how these citizens who refuse to be assimilated provide French society with a mirror. A crooked, passion-laden mirror in which to see a reflection of its own identity and societal problems, and its tough conception of secularism. Instead of taking France as a paradigmatical model for secularism, I proposed a soft/multicultural secularism that is not so divisive and would be necessary and even indispensable to each society. The new framework of the relationship between religion and state in a post-secular society allows a certain permeability between what has been dissociated for so long: religion and state, ethics and politics and religious and secular arguments in the public sphere. This is a multi-secularism that cannot be set up as an end in itself, sacralized and blind to the conditions

---

[1]   Walker Darren, "There Is No Leadership Without Risk: Guest Essay." *New York Times.* 20 October 2024.

under which it is implemented in each national or communal context.[2] Secularism is merely a mechanism – albeit one largely capable of effectively affirming the values of the Dialogical Liberal Project in society.

In Chapter 6, I distinguished between embracing gender diversity – accepting, tolerating, and refraining from discrimination – versus celebrating it, which involves actively campaigning for it and considering it beneficial to society. This distinction is not anecdotal; it is a strategic approach to advancing the rights and societal recognition of vulnerable sexual and gender groups. I observe how individuals in Western democracies shift toward the Right when they feel that symbolic liberals impose gender fluidity and a sex spectrum as fundamental principles for reorganizing society, framing them as a conception of justice (i.e., non-discrimination against LGBTQ individuals). The Dialogical Political Liberal Project seeks to contextualize sexuality and gender identity within cultural frameworks while adhering to the minimum standards of human rights established by the *Universal Declaration of Human Rights* and other international human rights conventions. It operates through a process of disentangling gender discourse – addressing both gender fluidity and anti-gender campaigns – by distinguishing between justifications based on conceptions of justice and those rooted in the plurality of conceptions of the good. The project advocates for keeping the debate open on how to reconcile the perspectives of those who wish to express their sexuality in the public sphere with those who prefer to confine it to the private sphere. While the Dialogical Political Liberal Project acknowledges the critical role feminist and LGBTQ movements have played in advancing the rights of women and sexual minorities, it also calls for greater tolerance of diverse feminist perspectives. In this regard, Elina Pulcini's engagement with feminist political thought is notable. Her feminism, grounded in an anti-essentialist and anti-naturalist interpretation of feminine selfhood as the result of reflexive choices, contrasts with other strands of feminism that, as Spini (2021, 301) describes, begin "with the stark and paralyzing view of those who reify 'difference' to the temptations of an uncritical mimetism towards the male subject."

---

[2] Both the concepts of post-secularism and multi-secularities have been subjects of intense critical scrutiny. While I find them highly useful in addressing the problematic use and misuse of the concept of secularization (see the work of the Leipzig-based multi-secularities project, including Darwish (2021), Wohlrab-Sahr and Burchardt (2012), and more recently Zemmin et al. (2024)), some scholars, such as Kchaou (2024b), remain skeptical about their utility. Nonetheless, there is broad consensus that secularism itself should not be discarded along with its critiques.

Finally, in Chapter 7, I continue in my critique of the attempt of symbolic liberals to undermine family authority by demonstrating how the Swedish state and its symbolic liberals violate their ideals by forcibly removing children from supposedly abusive parents. I make it clear that I have no nostalgia for the traditional family, but I don't think in this neoliberal world we can leave individuals to be devoured by the market or the state, whether democratic, populist or authoritarian.[3] However, I do believe that because we are in the neoliberal age, the family is a salient social structure for protecting individuals vis-à-vis the coercion of the state and the market and for providing material and also emotional support for their offspring. The way in which the neoliberal state uses its authority and that of the school/social service *over* the family's authority, instead of complementing it, is problematic. Being "seedbeds of virtue," (Griffiths 2021), we should not undermine the family (at least in level 1 of our commitment to civil society). The family has traditionally been a force for stability, socialization and the nurturing of moral behavior. I do not believe that the growing gap between generations can be celebrated by any intellectual tradition, especially as children spend less time talking with their parents and even less with their grandparents. Nor do I see intrinsic value in the trend of erasing social boundaries – whether in terms of gender or the distinction between children and adults. These boundaries have an anthropological depth that can, of course, be negotiated across political, cultural and generational contexts. Filial love is not only crucial in the face of state and societal violence but also serves as an essential force for collective action, linking the politics of sensibilities with social conflict, as Adrian Scribano (2019) shows us in Latin America. Some of my friends who advocate for "decolonizing" knowledge hesitate to raise similar questions, as if concepts related to family authority, parent–child interaction and gender fluidity had become universally accepted and unquestionable.

In my oral presentation of some of these chapters, I occasionally encountered unease and sometimes a fierce resistance to what is seen by some scholars coming from several intellectual quarters about how the Dialogical Liberal Project should accommodate the plurality of conceptions of the good (including those conceptions that we don't like, whether too conservative or too radical) and have a more robust conception of social justice. Again, let me be clear, the Dialogical Political Liberal Project does not undermine the critical energy of approaches like Marxism, feminism, race studies, critical

---

[3]   Even in Middle Eastern countries such as Egypt, where kinship relations were destroyed by the authoritarian state, unless these relationships were part of state–society patronage networks. See Hani Awad (2022).

theory and intersectionality, but is a call for more situated criticism; one that, while criticizing powers, is also able to simultaneously open up a dialogue with the very forces it critiques. Those who know my scholarship on the Palestinian–Israeli conflict, know how I can strongly criticize the current Israeli settler colonial project in the Palestinian territories and its genocide in Gaza, but also engage in dialogue with Israeli scholars. Here the question of power is very important. You cannot dialogue with a powerful group/entity if you don't have a minimal weight. Social movements, resistance and even revolution are necessary before the dialogue.

Should we engage in dialogue with illegal settlers in the West Bank or far-Right populists? The answer is both yes and no. It depends on the context of this dialogue and the minimum rules for debating in the public sphere. It is interesting to note that some of those we labeled far-Right received the majority of seats in parliament. Should we remove the word "far" and admit that there is something wrong with our measurement? In the same vein, is the request for cooperatives and a solidarity-based economy with very restrictive measures against the financialization of the economy far-Left? This form of socialism – or at least a social economy – is not truly far-Left but rather a version of the Left that deserves serious consideration. After half a century of failed "trickle-down economics," built on the flimsy philosophies of Hayek, Friedman and Nozick, is it not time to explore alternatives?

In brief, it is not acceptable any more to exclude from debate and dialogue those who don't agree with our social vision because of their religiosity, conservatism or nationalism, as symbolic liberals used to do. For a long time, and by allying with civil society, radical criticism preempts our scholarship to establish a dialogue with the broader civic sphere. This means it is not enough simply to support those who have liberal democratic ideals. We also need to listen attentively to those who refuse to embrace, partially or totally, these ideals. Let us remember the excellent work of Arlie Russell Hochschild (2016) on rural white Americans in Louisiana. Many became Trump supporters, voicing their discontent with globalization and their lived experiences of social inequality. Similarly, before rushing to judgment, we should listen to those who fear the arrival of Syrian and African migrants and refugees in Europe. Even if some, like Steinhoff (2022), frame their arguments in a utilitarian, universalist liberal framework, this can serve as a starting point for introducing concepts central to the Dialogical Political Liberal Project – Mauss's logic of the gift, fraternity, care for the world, compassion and reciprocity. All the while, the social sciences will provide empirical insights into demography, labor markets, crime and other relevant factors.

While our sociological endeavor may provide salient knowledge on topics such as poverty, social inequality or forced migration, it should also mobilize emotions and moral impulses, compassion, altruism, fraternity, solidarity and activism. As Vandenberghe puts it, we need "a minimal morality (*minima moralia*), a moral baseline that sets forth the fundamental principles (universalism, pluralism, and individualism) and fundamental procedures (democracy, dialogue, and discussion) that allow for the formulation of the most basic rules of a reasonably [rather than rationally] ordered society that makes social life possible" (Vandenberghe 2018, 90). The goal is not merely to describe and critique social life but to construct an intellectual framework for a communicative society – one that incorporates all its citizens while respecting all forms of pluralism, without pushing the "others" into assimilation to cultural majoritarianism.

Ultimately, this book is filled with hope and possibility – a galvanizing alternative to the cynicism that pervades contemporary politics. I have proposed some alternatives and measures, but I trust that readers will conceive of others. This requires searching for common ground and building bridges between polarized and divided groups. It also demands embracing a complex, multidimensional and multilayered theorization of the pathologies and uncertainties of our late modernity.

References

Aaltonen, Sofie. 2024. "Islamophobia and Danish Academic Knowledge Production." Lund University Student Papers. http://lup.lub.lu.se/student-papers/record/9157176.

Abboud, Hosn. 2019. "How Islamic Feminism Can Be an Effective Part of Islamic Studies." In *Towards the Reconstruction of Islamic Studies*, ed. Al-Sayyed Radwan, Sari Hanafi and Bilal Orfali. Beirut: Arab Scientific Publishers, 223–52.

Abou El Fadl, Khaled. 2014. *Reasoning with God: Reclaiming Shari'ah in the Modern Age*. Lanham, MD: Rowman & Littlefield.

Acharya, Amitav, Antoni Estevadeordal and Louis W. Goodman. 2023. "Multipolar or Multiplex? Interaction Capacity, Global Cooperation and World Order." *International Affairs* 99(6): 2339–65. https://doi.org/10.1093/ia/iiad242.

Achcar, Gilbert. 2020. "On the 'Arab Inequality Puzzle': The Case of Egypt." *Development and Change* 51(3): 746–70.

———. 2022. *The People Want: A Radical Exploration of the Arab Uprising*. London: Saqi Books.

———. 2023. *Israel's War on Gaza*. Amsterdam: Resistance Books.

Adelkhah, Fariba. 2024. *Prisonnière à Téhéran*. Paris: Editions Seuil.

Adloff, Frank. 2023. "Ontology, Conviviality and Symbiosis or: Are There Gifts of Nature?" *MAUSS International* 3(1): 154–75.

Al Azmeh, Zeina, and Patrick Baert. 2025. "Stop the Performance! Cancel Culture in the Contemporary Academy." In *Dramatic Intellectuals*, ed. Javier Pérez-Jara and Nicolás Rudas. London: Palgrave Macmillan.

Alatas, Syed Farid, and Vineeta Sinha. 2017. *Sociological Theory beyond the Canon*. London: Palgrave Macmillan.

Albitar, Rim. 2024. "Examining the Impact of Gender Curriculum on Alienation: An Assessment of Implementation in Norwegian Educational Institutions." Master's thesis, American University of Beirut.

Aldrin, Philippe, Pierre Fournier, Vincent Geisser and Yves Mirman, eds. 2022. *L'enquête en danger: Vers un nouveau régime de surveillance dans les sciences sociales*. Paris: Armand Colin.

Alexander, Jeffrey. 1990. "Introduction: Understanding the Relative Autonomy of Culture." In *Culture and Society: Contemporary Debates*, ed. Alexander Jeffrey and Steven Seidman. New York: Cambridge University Press, 15–39.

———. 2008. *The Civil Sphere*. 1st ed. Oxford: Oxford University Press.

Al-Gharbi, Musa. 2024. *We Have Never Been Woke: The Cultural Contradictions of the New Elite*. Princeton, NJ: Princeton University Press.

Allen, Danielle. 2023. *Justice by Means of Democracy*. Chicago: University of Chicago Press.

Allen, Lori. 2020. *A History of False Hope: Investigative Commissions in Palestine*. 1st ed. Stanford, CA: Stanford University Press.

Al-Taher, Hanna, and Anna-Esther Younes. 2023. "Lebensraum, Geopolitics and Race – Palestine as a Feminist Issue in German-Speaking Academia." *Ethnography* 25(2): 1–27.

Amansag, Slimane. 2024. "Child Removal among Minority Children in Sweden: An Analysis Using the Ecological Systems Theory." Term paper, King's College London.

Anderson, Elizabeth. 2019. *Private Government: How Employers Rule Our Lives*. Princeton, NJ: Princeton University Press.

An-Na'im, Abdullahi Ahmed. 1992. *Human Rights in Cross-Cultural Perspectives: A Quest for Consensus*. Philadelphia: University of Pennsylvania Press.

———. 2013. "From the Neocolonial 'Transitional' to Indigenous Formations of Justice." *International Journal of Transitional Justice* 7(1–2): 197–204.

Asad, Talal. 2003. *Formations of the Secular: Christianity, Islam, Modernity*. Stanford, CA: Stanford University Press.

Atallah, Devin G. 2017. "A Community-Based Qualitative Study of Intergenerational Resilience with Palestinian Refugee Families Facing Structural Violence and Historical Trauma." *Transcultural Psychiatry* 54(3): 357–83.

Awad, Hani. 2022. *The Dilemma of Authoritarian Local Governance in Egypt*. Edinburgh: Edinburgh University Press.

Bacevic, Jana. 2024. "What Is Social Science If Not Critical?" *British Journal of Sociology*. https://doi.org/10.1111/1468-4446.13142.

Baert, Patrick. 2012. "Positioning Theory and Intellectual Interventions." *Journal for the Theory of Social Behaviour* 42(3): 304–25.

Bahlul, Raja. 2003. "Toward an Islamic Conception of Democracy: Islam and the Notion of Public Reason." *Critique: Critical Middle Eastern Studies* 12(1): 43–60.

Bamyeh, Mohammed A. 2019. *Lifeworlds of Islam: The Pragmatics of a Religion*. Oxford: Oxford University Press.

Baubérot, Jean. 2014. *La laïcité falsifiée*. Paris: La Découverte.

———. 2017. *Les sept laïcités françaises: Le modèle français de laïcité n'existe pas*. Paris: Éditions de la Maison des sciences de l'homme.

Bauman, Zygmunt. 1993. *Postmodern Ethics*. 1st ed. Oxford: Wiley-Blackwell.

———. 2003. *Liquid Love: On the Frailty of Human Bonds*. 1st ed. Cambridge: Polity Press.

Baxi, Upendra. 2002. *The Future of Human Rights*. 3rd ed. Oxford: Oxford University Press.

Beeker, Timo, China Mills, Dinesh Bhugra, Sanne te Meerman et al. 2021. "Psychiatrization of Society: A Conceptual Framework and Call for Transdisciplinary Research." *Frontiers in Psychiatry* 12: 645556.

Bennett, Marlyn, and Cindy Blackstock. 2005. *A Literature Review and Annotated Bibliography Focusing on Aspects of Aboriginal Child Welfare in Canada*. Winnipeg, MB: John Thompson.

Bennett, Steven. 2016. "Secrets and Lies Inside Barnevernet." www.barnefjern. org/secrets-and-lies-inside-barnevernet/.

Ben-Porath, Sigal. 2023. *Cancel Wars: How Universities Can Foster Free Speech, Promote Inclusion, and Renew Democracy*. Chicago: University of Chicago Press.

Bergeaud-Blackler, Florence. 2023. *Le Frérisme et ses réseaux: L'enquête*. Paris: Odile Jacob.

Berger, Peter L. 2014. *The Many Altars of Modernity: Toward a Paradigm for Religion in a Pluralist Age*. Boston: de Gruyter. https://doi. org/10.1515/9781614516477.

Berle, Adolf A., and Gardiner Means. 1932. *The Modern Corporation and Private Property*. 2nd ed. London: Routledge.

Bernstein, M. 2023. "Knowledge Machines: A Complex Web of History and Technology." In *Routledge Handbook of Academic Knowledge Circulation*, ed. Wiebke Keim, Leandro Rodriguez Medina et al. New York: Routledge, 288–95.

Bezuidenhout, Andries, Sonwabile Mnwana and Karl von Holdt, eds. 2022. *Critical Engagement with Public Sociology: A Perspective from the Global South*. Bristol: Bristol University Press.

Bhambra, Gurminder K. 2014. *Connected Sociologies*. London: Bloomsbury Academic.

Bhambra, Gurminder K., and John Holmwood. 2021. *Colonialism and Modern Social Theory*. 1st ed. Cambridge: Polity Press.

Bhargava, Rajeev. 2019. "Reimagining Secularism: Respect, Domination, and Principled Distance." In *Freedom of Religion, Secularism, and Human Rights*, ed. Nehal Bhuta. Oxford: Oxford University Press. https://doi. org/10.1093/oso/9780198812067.003.0002.

Bhattacharyya, Satadru. 2025. "Seeds of Change: South Asian Ecology and Vandana Shiva's Legacy." In *Theory Reimagined: Voices of Sociologists From Around the World*, ed. Rianka Roy, Anjana Narayan, Melanie Heath and Bandana Purkayastha. London: Frontpage Publications, 78–89.

Biesel, Kay, Judith Masson, Nigel Parton and Tarja Pösö, eds. 2020. *Errors and Mistakes in Child Protection: International Discourses, Approaches and Strategies*. 1st ed. Bristol: Policy Press.

Bishara, Azmi. 2013. *Religion and Secularism in Historical Context* [Arabic]. vol. 1. Beirut: Arab Network for Research and Publishing.

———. 2015. *Religion and Secularism in Historical Context* [Arabic]. vol. 2. Beirut: Arab Network for Research and Publishing.

———. 2021. *Understanding Revolutions: Opening Acts in Tunisia*. London: I.B. Tauris.

———. 2023a. "On Comprehensive Liberalism, Political Liberalism, and Ideology." *Global Dialogue* 13(2).

———. 2023b. "Political Culture and Democratic Transition: A Reassessment." *Al-Muntaqa* 6(3): 8–30.

———. 2023c. *The Question of the State: Philosophy, Theory, and Context.* [Arabic]. Doha: Arab Center for Research and Policy Studies.

———. 2024. "Moral Issues in Hard Times." [Arabic]. *Tabayyun* 47: 7–40.

Blix, Bodil H., Vera Caine, D. Jean Clandinin and Charlotte Berendonk. 2021. "Considering Silences in Narrative Inquiry: An Intergenerational Story of a Sami Family." *Journal of Contemporary Ethnography* 50(4): 580–94.

Bob, Clifford. 2019. *Rights as Weapons: Instruments of Conflict, Tools of Power*. Princeton, NJ: Princeton University Press.

Bohman, M., and S. Sigvardsson. 1980. "A Prospective Longitudinal Study of Children Registered for Adoption: A 15-year Follow-up." *Acta Psychiatrica Scandinavica* 61(4): 339–55. https://doi.org/10.1111/j.1600-0447.1980.tb00586.x.

Boltanski, Luc. 1999. *Distant Suffering: Morality, Media and Politics*. Trans. Graham D. Burchell. Cambridge: Cambridge University Press. https://doi.org/10.1017/CBO9780511489402.

Boltanski, Luc, and Eve Chiapello. 2018. *The New Spirit of Capitalism*. London: Verso.

Boltanski, Luc, and Laurent Thévenot. 1991. *De la justification: Les économies de la grandeur*. Paris: Gallimard.

Botz-Bornstein, Thorsten. 2019. *The New Aesthetics of Deculturation: Neoliberalism, Fundamentalism and Kitsch*. London: Bloomsbury Academic.

Brahimi, Mohamed Amine. 2020. "The Trusteeship Paradigm in the Social Sciences: Moral Agency as an Islamic Ethical Turn." In *Islamic Ethics and the Trusteeship Paradigm: Taha Abderrahmane's Philosophy in Comparative Perspectives*, ed. Mohammed Hashas and Mutaz al-Khatib. Leiden: Brill, 218–32.

Braunstein, Ruth. 2017. *Prophets and Patriots: Faith in Democracy across the Political Divide*. 1st ed. Oakland: University of California Press.

Brown, Wendy. 2002. "Moralism as Antipolitics." In *Materializing Democracy: Toward a Revitalized Cultural Politics*, ed. Russ Castronovo and Dana D. Nelson. Durham, NC: Duke University Press, 368–92.

———. 2008. *Regulating Aversion: Tolerance in the Age of Identity and Empire*. Princeton, NJ: Princeton University Press.

Burawoy, Michael. 2005. "For Public Sociology." *American Sociological Review* 70(1): 4–28.

———. 2008. "Rejoinder: For a Subaltern Global Sociology?" *Current Sociology* 56(3): 435–44. https://doi.org/10.1177/0011392107088237.

———. 2015. "Facing an Unequal World." *Current Sociology* 63(1): 5–34.

———. 2021. *Public Sociology: Between Utopia and Anti-Utopia.* Cambridge: Polity Press.

Burdge, Hilary, Shannon Snapp, Carolyn Laub, Stephen T. Russell and Raymond Moody. 2013. "Implementing Lessons That Matter: The Impact of LGBTQ-Inclusive Curriculum on Student Safety, Well-Being, and Achievement." San Francisco, CA: Gay–Straight Alliance Network/Tucson, AZ: Frances McClelland Institute for Children, Youth, and Families at the University of Arizona.

Burgat, François. 2008. *Islamism in the Shadow of Al-Qaeda.* Texas: University of Texas Press.

———. 2016. *Comprendre l'islam politique: Une trajectoire de recherche sur l'altérité islamiste, 1973–2016.* Paris: La Découverte.

———. 2020. "L'islamophobie sanctionnée par l'Etat français est la plus grande menace pour la république." *Middle East Eye* [blog]. 25 November.

Burns, Kenneth, Tarja Pösö and Marit Skivenes. 2016. *Child Welfare Removals by the State: A Cross-Country Analysis of Decision-Making Systems.* Oxford: Oxford University Press.

Caillé, Alain. 2015. *Le convivialisme en dix questions.* Lormont: Le Bord de l'eau.

Castro, Lucia Rabello de. 2020. "Why Global? Children and Childhood from a Decolonial Perspective." *Childhood* 27(1): 48–62.

Cataldi, Silvia. 2020. "Un concept karstique de la sociologie: l'amour comme socialité." *Sociétés* 149(3): 15–30.

Chakrabarty, Dipesh. 2007. *Provincializing Europe: Postcolonial Thought and Historical Difference (New Edition).* Princeton, NJ: Princeton University Press.

———. 2019. *The Crises of Civilization: Exploring Global and Planetary Histories.* New Delhi: Oxford University Press.

Chakraborty, Sagarika. 2022. *The Journey of a Mother.* Pune: Vishwakarma Publications.

Chancel, L., T. Piketty, E. Saez, G. Zucman et al. *World Inequality Report 2022.* World Inequality Lab. https://wir2022.wid.world/www-site/uploads/2023/03/D_FINAL_WIL_RIM_RAPPORT_2303.pdf.

Chandler, Daniel. 2023. *Free and Equal.* New York: Allen Lane.

Chauvel, Louis. 2023. "Squeezing the Western Middle Class: Precarization, Uncertainty and Tensions of Median Socioeconomic Groups in the Global North." In *Handbook of Post-Western Sociology: From East Asia to Europe,* ed. Laurence Roulleau-Berger, Peilin Li, Seung Kuk Kim and Shujiro Yasawa. Leiden: Brill, 495–509.

Christou, Fanny. 2019. "Ecologies of Integration: Palestinian Socio-Cultural Activism in Sweden." *Sociétés plurielle* 3: 3–34.

Cipriani, Roberto. 2017. *Diffused Religion: Beyond Secularization*. London: Palgrave Macmillan.

Connell, Raewyn. 1994. "The Sociology of Gender in Southern Perspective." *Current Sociology* 62(4): 550–67.

Connolly, William. 1995. *Ethos of Pluralization*. Minneapolis: University of Minnesota Press.

Convivialist International. 2020. "The Second Convivialist Manifesto: Towards a Post-Neoliberal World." *Civic Sociology* 1: 12721. https://doi.org/10.1525/001c.12721.

Cooke, Maeve. 2005. "Avoiding Authoritarianism: On the Problem of Justification in Contemporary Critical Social Theory." *International Journal of Philosophical Studies* 13(3): 379–404. https://doi.org/10.1080/09672550500169182.

———. 2007. "A Secular State for a Postsecular Society? Postmetaphysical Political Theory and the Place of Religion." *Constellations* 14(2): 224–38.

Crenshaw, Kimberlé. 1989. "Demarginalizing the Intersection of Race and Sex: A Black Feminist Critique of Antidiscrimination Doctrine, Feminist Theory and Antiracist Policies." *University of Chicago Legal Forum* 1989(1): 139–67.

Cudd, Ann E. 2019. "Harassment, Bias, and the Evolving Politics of Free Speech on Campus." *Journal of Social Philosophy* 50(4): 425–46.

Cunneen, Chris, and Terry Libesman. 2000. "Postcolonial Trauma: The Contemporary Removal of Indigenous Children and Young People from Their Families in Australia." *Australian Journal of Social Issues* 35(2): 99–115. https://doi.org/10.1002/j.1839-4655.2000.tb01088.x.

Dabashi, Hamid. 2024. "Thanks to Gaza, European Philosophy Has Been Exposed as Ethically Bankrupt." *Middle East Eye*. 18 January. www.middleeasteye.net/opinion/war-gaza-european-philosophy-ethically-bankrupt-exposed.

Dalacoura, Katerina. 2014. "Homosexuality as Cultural Battleground in the Middle East: Culture and Postcolonial International Theory." *Third World Quarterly* 35(7): 1290–306.

Darwish, Hossam El-Din. 2021. *On Thick Normative Concepts: Secularism, (Political) Islam, and the Renewal of Religious Discourse*. Beirut: Arab Network for Research and Publishing.

Davie, Grace, and Nancy T. Ammerman. 2018. "Religions and Social Progress: Critical Assessments and Creative Partnerships." In *Rethinking Society for the 21st Century: Report of the International Panel on Social Progress*. Cambridge: Cambridge University Press, 641–76.

Davis, Kathy, and Helma Lutz. 2023. "Intersectionality as Travelling Theory: Possibilities for Dialogues." In *The Routledge International Handbook of Intersectionality Studies*, ed. Kathy Davis and Helma Lutz. London: Routledge, 3–13.

Dewey, John. 1922. *Human Nature and Conduct*. New York. Holt.

DiResta, Renée. 2023. "The New Media Goliaths." *Noema*. 1 June. www.noemamag.com/the-new-media-goliaths.

Dolgon, Corey. 2024. "Introduction: What the Philosophers (and Sociologists) Have and Haven't Done." In *The Oxford Handbook of Sociology for Social Justice*, ed. Corey Dolgon. Oxford: Oxford University Press. https://doi.org/10.1093/oxfordhb/9780197615317.013.2.

Dosse, François. 2024. *La saga des intellectuels français*. vol. 1. *À l'épreuve de l'histoire, 1944–1968*. Paris: Folio histoire.

Downs, Anthony. 1957. "An Economic Theory of Political Action in a Democracy." *Journal of Political Economy* 65(2): 135–50.

Dreyer, Jacob. 2024. "China in 2035." *Noema*. 11 June. www.noemamag.com/china-in-2035.

Duara, Prasenjit. 2014. *The Crisis of Global Modernity: Asian Traditions and a Sustainable Future*. New York: Cambridge University Press.

Dubet, François. 2020. "Le retour de la société." *Revue du MAUSS* 56: 49–76.

Dufoix, Stéphane. 2021. "For Another World History of Sociology." *MAUSS International* 1(1): 215–26.

Dupret, Baudouin, and Jean-Noël Ferrié. 2024. "Islam, frérisme et autres chimères: Réflexion à partir de débats français oiseux et pernicieux." *Mouvements* [blog]. 13 January. https://mouvements.info/islam-frerisme-et-autres-chimeres-reflexion-a-partir-de-debats-francais-oiseux-et-pernicieux/.

Dworkin, Roland. 1998. "We Need a New Interpretation of Academic Freedom." In *The Future of Academic Freedom*, ed. Louis Menand. Chicago: University of Chicago Press, 181–213.

Edvardsson, Bo. 2010. "Child Protection Investigations in the Swedish Social Services: Are They Really Children's Best Interests? Is a 'Hunting the Monster Theory' Influencing Social Work and Decisions?" University of Örebro, School of Law, Psychology and Social Work. https://shorturl.at/B6Djm.

Eidelson, Roy J. 2023. *Doing Harm: How the World's Largest Psychological Association Lost Its Way in the War on Terror*. Montreal: McGill-Queen's University Press.

El-Affendi, Abdelwahab. 2003. "What Is Liberal Islam? The Elusive Reformation." *Journal of Democracy* 14(2): 34–39.

———. 2024. "Gaza and the Dilemmas of Genocide Scholars." *Al Jazeera* [blog]. 2024. www.aljazeera.com/opinions/2024/2/3/gaza-and-the-dilemmas-of-genocide-scholars.

El Amine, Adnan. 2018. "Arab Universities and the Challenges of Social Change." [Arabic]. *Omran* 26: 61–85.

El Amine, Loubna. 2015a. *Classical Confucian Political Thought: A New Interpretation*. Princeton, NJ: Princeton University Press.

———. 2015b. Review of *Confucian Democracy in East Asia: Theory and Practice*, by Sungmoon Kim, *Notre Dame Philosophical Reviews*. https://ndpr.nd.edu/reviews/confucian-democracy-in-east-asia-theory-and-practice/.

———. 2021. "Political Liberalism, Western History, and the
   Conjectural Non-West." *Political Theory* 49(2): 190–214. https://doi.
   org/10.1177/0090591720927802.
El Karoui, Hakim. 2016. "A French Islam Is Possible." Paris: Institute
   Montaigne.
Elias, Norbert. 2000. *The Civilizing Process*. Oxford: Blackwell.
Eliassi, Barzoo. 2013. "Orientalist Social Work: Cultural Otherization of
   Muslim Immigrants in Sweden." *Critical Social Work* 14(1): 33–47.
———. 2015. "Constructing Cultural Otherness within the Swedish Welfare
   State: The Cases of Social Workers in Sweden." *Qualitative Social Work*
   14(4): 554–71.
Elsadda, Hoda. 2024. "Humanities in the Arab World in Times of Conflict
   and Change." Beirut: Arab Council for the Social Sciences. www.theacss.
   org/pages/fourth_assr.
Ervik, Rune, and Nanna Kildal. 2015. *New Contractualism in European
   Welfare State Policies*. Farnham: Ashgate.
Esmili, Hamza. 2024. "Who Is Still Liberal? Islamophobia and Anti-Racism in
   Authoritarian Times." In *Race Politics and Colonial Legacies: France, Africa
   and the Middle East*. New York: Pomeps Studies, 71–76.
Espvall, Majen. 2018. "Professional Strategies and Neoliberal Challenges in
   Swedish Social Work Practice." In *Neoliberalism, Nordic Welfare States
   and Social Work: Current and Future Challenges*, ed. Masoud Kamali and
   Jessica Jönsson. London: Routledge, 131–67.
Etzioni, Amitai. 1993. *The Spirit of Community: Rights, Responsibilities and the
   Communitarian Agenda*. New York: Crown.
Fadel, Mohammad. 2022. "Muslim Modernism, Islamic Law, and the
   Universality of Human Rights." *Emory International Law* 36(4): 712–40.
———. forthcoming. "Beyond Liberal Zionism: International Law, Political
   Liberalism and the Possibility of a Just Zionism." *Transnational Law
   and Contemporary Problems*. https://papers.ssrn.com/sol3/papers.
   cfm?abstract_id=4997224.
Faridi, Afreen. 2023. "What Palestine Teaches Teachers of Politics
   and Law." *The Leaflet* [blog]. 29 October. https://theleaflet.in/
   what-palestine-teaches-teachers-of-politics-and-law/.
Finch, Jo, Jessica H. Jönsson, Masoud Kamali and David McKendrick. 2022.
   "Social Work and Countering Violent Extremism in Sweden and the UK."
   European Journal of Social Work 25(1): 119–30.
Fish, Stanley. 2014. *Versions of Academic Freedom: From Professionalism to
   Revolution*. Chicago: University of Chicago Press.
Flecha, Ramón. 2022. *The Dialogic Society: The Sociology Scientists and
   Citizens Like and Use*. Barcelona: Hipatia Press.
Frankfurt, Harry G. 1971. "Freedom of the Will and the Concept of a Person."
   Journal of Philosophy 68(1): 5–13.
Fraser, Nancy. 2016. "Contradictions of Capital and Care." *New Left Review*
   100. https://newleftreview.org/issues/ii100/articles/nancy-fraser-
   contradictions-of-capital-and-care.

Freeman, Mark. 2023. "First Principles: The Need for Greater Consensus on the Fundamentals of Polarisation." Barcelona: Institute for Integrated Transitions. https://ifit-transitions.org/wp-content/uploads/2023/05/First-Principles-The-Need-for-Greater-Consensus-on-the-Fundamentals-of-Polarisation-Final.pdf.

Fricker, Miranda. 2009. *Epistemic Injustice: Power and the Ethics of Knowing.* Oxford: Oxford University Press.

Fukuyama, Francis. 1989. "The End of History?" *National Interest* 16: 3–18.

Furedi, Frank. 2002 [1997]. *Culture of Fear: Risk-Taking and the Morality of Low Expectation.* London: Continuum.

Gauthier, François. 2020. *Religion, Modernity, Globalisation: Nation-State to Market.* London: Routledge.

———. 2021. *Religion, Modernity, Globalisation.* New York: Routledge.

———. 2023. "Introduction." *MAUSS International* 3: 3–12.

Gerards, Janneke. 2024. "Protect the Safety of Researchers." *Science* 385: 915. www.science.org/doi/10.1126/science.ads6586.

Gergen, Kenneth J. 1997. "Social Construction and the Transformation of Identity Politics." In *A New Developmental Way of Learning*, ed. Fred Newman and Lois Holzman. New York: Routledge.

———. 2000. *The Saturated Self: Dilemmas of Identity in Contemporary Life.* New York: Basic Books.

Giddens, Anthony. 2013. [1992]. *The Transformation of Intimacy: Sexuality, Love and Eroticism in Modern Societies.* Cambridge: Polity Press.

Gill, Michael B. 2023. "Of Racist Philosophers and Ravens." *Journal of Controversial Ideas* 3(1): 2. https://doi.org/10.35995/jci03010002.

Glendon, Mary Ann. 1998. *Rights Talk: The Impoverishment of Political Discourse.* New York: Free Press.

Global Witness. 2023. "Global Hating: How Online Abuse of Climate Scientists Harms Climate Action." *Global Witness.* www.globalwitness.org/en/campaigns/digital-threats/global-hating/.

Gordon, Neve. 2023. "On Antisemitism and Human Rights." *International Journal of Human Rights* 28(4): 1–20.

Graeber, David. 2016. *The Utopia of Rules: On Technology, Stupidity, and the Secret Joys of Bureaucracy.* London: Melville House Publishing.

Griffiths, Brian. 2021. "Challenges for Post-Liberalism: Can We Have a Politics of Virtue with God on the Bench?" In *After Liberalism? A Christian Confrontation on Politics and Economics*, ed. Martin Schlag and Giulio Maspero. Cham: Springer, 47–61.

Grinberg, Lev. 2024. "Israeli-Palestinian Murderous Escalation in Context." *Global Dialogue.* 9 February. https://globaldialogue.isa-sociology.org/articles/israeli-palestinian-murderous-escalation-in-context.

Grindheim, Jan Erik. 2019. "Why Right-Leaning Populism Has Grown in the Most Advanced Liberal Democracies of Europe." *Political Quarterly* 90(4): 757–71.

Grip, Lina, and Marcus Dynevall. 2024. "Honour-Based Violence in Sweden: An Offender Perspective." *Nordic Journal of Criminology* 25(1): 1–17.

Gudynas, Eduardo. 2011. "Buen Vivir: Today's Tomorrow." *Development* 54(4): 441–47.

Guénif-Souilamas, Nacira, and Eric Macé. 2004. *Les féministes et le garçon arabe*. La Tour d'Aigues: Editions de l'Aube.

Habermas, Jürgen. 2006. "Religion in the Public Sphere." *European Journal of Philosophy* 14(1): 1–25.

———. 2023. *A New Structural Transformation of the Public Sphere and Deliberative Politics*. Cambridge: Polity Press.

Habib, Claude. 2021. *La question trans*. Paris: Gallimard.

Hage, Ghassan. 2013. "Arab Social Sciences: Between Two Critical Traditions." [Arabic]. *Bidayyat* 6.

Haidt, Jonathan. 2013. *The Righteous Mind: Why Good People Are Divided by Politics and Religion*. New York: Vintage.

Haidt, Jonathan, and Craig Joseph. 2004. "Intuitive Ethics: How Innately Prepared Intuitions Generate Culturally Variable Virtues." *Daedalus* 133(4): 55–66.

Hajjat, Abdellali. 2021. "Islamophobia and French Academia." *Current Sociology* 69(5): 621–40.

Halwani, Raja. 2023. "Sex and Sexual Orientation, Gender and Sexual Preference." *Journal of Controversial Ideas* 3(2): 1–23.

Hamouchene, Hamza, and Katie Sandwell. 2023. "Introduction: Just in Time – The Urgent Need for a Just Transition in the Arab Region." In *Dismantling Green Colonialism: Energy and Climate Justice in the Arab Region*, ed. Hamza Hamouchene and Katie Sandwell. London: Pluto Press, 1–25.

Hanafi, Sari. 2013. "Explaining Spacio-Cide in the Palestinian Territory: Colonization, Separation, and State of Exception." *Current Sociology* 61(2): 190–205.

———. 2019. "Global Sociology Revisited: Toward New Directions." *Current Sociology* 68(1): 3–21.

———. 2020. "A Cognitive Arab Uprising? Paradigm Shifts in Arab Social Sciences." In *The Oxford Handbook of the Sociology of the Middle East*, ed. Armando Salvatore, Sari Hanafi and Kieko Obuse. Oxford: Oxford University Press, 28–48.

———. 2021a. "Connecting Sociology to Moral Philosophy in the Post-Secularity Framework." *MAUSS International* 1(1): 243–63.

———. 2021b. "The Pen and the Sword: The Narrow Margin of Academic Freedom in the Arab World." *TRAFO. Blog for Transregional Research*. 2021. https://trafo.hypotheses.org/28464.

———. 2022. "Social Love as an Approach: Notes from the Field." In *Social Love and the Critical Potential of People*, ed. Silvia Cataldi and Gennaro Iorio. London: Routledge, 89–100.

———. 2023. "Toward a Dialogical Sociology: Presidential Address – XX ISA World Congress of Sociology 2023." *International Sociology* 39(1): 123–45.

———. 2024a. "From 'Spacio-cide' to Genocide: The War on Gaza and Western Indifference." *Institute of Palestine Studies* [blog]. https://www. palestine-studies.org/en/node/1654923.

———. 2024b. *Studying Islam in the Arab World: The Rupture between Religion and the Social Sciences.* London: Routledge.

———. 2024c. "The Transformation of the Discourse on Secularism/The Civil State in Arab Academic Writings Post Arab Spring." *Filozofija i drustvo* 35(3): 625–44. https://doi.org/10.2298/FID2403625H.

———. forthcoming. "Introduction." In *Religion in Public Life in Jordan, Lebanon, Egypt, and Tunisia*, ed. Zaid Eyadat. London: Palgrave Macmillan.

Hanafi, Sari, and Azzam Tomeh. 2020. "Beyond Religion and Secularism: Gender Equality in the Inheritance Debate in Tunisia and the Formation of Non-Authoritarian Reasoning." *Omran* 8(32): 71–94.

Hanafi, Sari, and Rigas Arvanitis. 2015. *Knowledge Production in the Arab World: The Impossible Promise.* London: Routledge.

Hanafi, Sari, and Zhao Tingyan. 2024. "The Tianxia System and Smart Democracy: An Interview with Zhao Tingyan." *Global Dialogue* 14.1: 3–9.

Haraway, Donna. 1988. "Situated Knowledges: The Science Question in Feminism and the Privilege of Partial Perspective." *Feminist Studies* 14(3): 575–99. https://doi.org/10.2307/3178066.

Harper's Magazine. 2020. "A Letter on Justice and Open Debate." *Harper's Magazine.* 7 July. https://harpers.org/a-letter-on-justice-and-open-debate/.

Hartley, Christie, and Lori Watson. 2022. "Against Convergence Liberalism: A Feminist Critique." *Canadian Journal of Philosophy* 52(6): 654–72.

Hashas, Mohammed. 2023. "Towards a Civilizational Ethos: From the Homo Moralis to the Homo Ethicus." In *Islam and the Drive to Global Justice: Principles of Justice Beyond Dominant Ethnic and Religious Communities*, ed. Louay M. Safi. New York: Lexington Books.

Hashas, Mohammed, and Mutaz al-Khatib. 2020. "Introduction: Modern Arab–Islamic Scholarship on Ethics." In *Islamic Ethics and the Trusteeship Paradigm: Taha Abderrahmane's Philosophy in Comparative Perspectives*, ed. Mohammed Hashas and Mutaz al-Khatib. Leiden: Brill, 1–31.

Hauchecorne, Mathieu. 2019. *La gauche américaine en France: La réception de John Rawls et des théories de la justice.* Paris: CNRS éditions.

Haydar, Bashar. 2024. "The Unity of the Oppressed...in Discussion with Al-Jumhuriya in Response to a Post Entitled 'Despotism and Occupation Are One.'" *Aljumhuriya.Net* [blog]. 13 June. https://aljumhuriya.net/ar/2024/06/13/.

Heath, Melanie. 2023. *Forbidden Intimacies Polygamies at the Limits of Western Tolerance.* Stanford, CA: Stanford University Press.

Heerwig, Jennifer, and Brian J. McCabe. 2022. "Broadening Donor Participation in Local Elections. Results from the Seattle Democracy Voucher Program in 2021." Washington, DC: Georgetown's McCourt School of Public Policy and Piper Fund.

Heilinger, Jan-Christoph. 2019. *Cosmopolitan Responsibility: Global Injustice, Relational Equality, and Individual*. Berlin: de Gruyter.

Heinich, Nathalie. 2004. *La sociologie de l'art*. Paris: La Découverte.

Helliwell, J.F., R. Layard, J.D. Sachs, J.-E. De Neve et al. 2022. "World Happiness Report 2022." New York: Sustainable Development Solutions Network.

Hermassi, Abdel Latif. 2012. *On the Islamic Religious Heritage: A Sociological–Historical Reading*. [Arabic]. Cairo: Dar al-Tanwir.

Hervieu-Léger, Danièle. 2001. *La religion en miettes ou la question des sectes*. Paris: Calmann-Lévy.

Hibou, Béatrice. 2012. *La bureaucratisation du monde à l'ère néolibérale*. Paris: La Découverte.

Hill, Samantha. 2023. "Hannah Arendt Would Not Qualify for the Hannah Arendt Prize in Germany Today." *The Guardian*. 12 December. www.theguardian.com/commentisfree/2023/dec/18/ hannah-arendt-prize-masha-gessen-israel-gaza-essay.

Hobbes, Thomas. 2003. [1651]. *Leviathan: A Critical Edition*, ed. G.A.J. Rogers and Karl Schuhmann. 2 vols. London: Continuum.

Hochschild, Arlie Russell. 2016. *Strangers in Their Own Land: Anger and Mourning on the American Right*. New York: The New Press.

Hodder, Ian. 1986. *Reading the Past: Current Approaches to Interpretation in Archaeology*. Cambridge: Cambridge University Press.

Höjer, Staffan, and Torbjörn Forkby. 2011. "Care for Sale: The Influence of New Public Management in Child Protection in Sweden." *British Journal of Social Work* 41(1): 93–110.

Höjer, Staffan, and Inger Kjellberg. 2020. "The Political-Administrative and the Professional Approach to Errors and Mistakes in Swedish Child Protection." In *Errors and Mistakes in Child Protection: International Discourses, Approaches and Strategies*, ed. Kay Biesel, Judith Masson, Nigel Parton and Tarja Pösö. Bristol: Policy Press, 135–50.

Horowitz, Mark, William Yaworsky and Kenneth Kickham. 2019. "Anthropology's Science Wars: Insights from a New Survey." *Current Anthropology* 60(5): 674–98. https://doi.org/10.1086/705409.

Hourani, Albert. 1983. *Arabic Thought in the Liberal Age, 1798–1939*. 2nd ed. New York: Cambridge University Press.

Hovde, Amanda. 2022. "Maintaining and Protecting the Cultural Identity of Sami Children in Progressive Nordic Countries: The Laws of Sweden and Its Past and Current Implications on Sami People," *Children's Legal Rights Journal* 42(2): 145–80.

Illouz, Eva. 2007. *Cold Intimacies: The Making of Emotional Capitalism*. Cambridge: Polity Press.

———. 2019. *The End of Love: A Sociology of Negative Relations*. New York: Polity Press.

———. 2022. *Les émotions contre la démocratie*. Paris: Premier Parallèle.

———. 2024. "Antisemitismus an Den Universitäten: Euer Hass Auf Juden," *Süddeutsche Zeitung*, 17 May 2024. https://tinyurl.com/vetf26bv.

Iorio, Gennaro. 2016. *Sociology of Love: The Agapic Dimension of Societal Life*. Wilmington, DE: Vernon Press.

Jamieson, Lynn. 1998. *Intimacy: Personal Relationships in Modern Societies*. Cambridge: Polity Press.

Join-Lambert, Hélène, and Gilles Séraphin. 2020. "Dysfunctions in French Child Protection." In *Errors and Mistakes in Child Protection: International Discourses, Approaches and Strategies*, ed. Judith Masson, Kay Biesel, Nigel Parton and Tarja Pösö. Bristol: Bristol University Press, 193–214. https://doi.org/10.46692/9781447350927.011.

Jönsson, Jessica H. 2013. "Social Work beyond Cultural Otherisation." *Nordic Social Work Research* 3(2): 159–67.

Jureidini, Ray. 1979. "The Industrial Producer Co-Operative in a Capitalist Economy." BA (Hons) thesis, Flinders University of South Australia.

———. 2006. "Sexuality and the Servant: An Exploration of Arab Images of the Sexuality of Domestic Maids Living in the Household." In *Sexuality in the Arab World*, ed. Samir Khalaf and John H. Gagnon. London: Saqi.

Kamali, Masoud. 2015. *War, Violence and Social Justice: Theories for Social Work*. London: Routledge.

Kandil, Feriel. 2020. "Ricœur, Rawls and the Aporia of the Just." In *The Ambiguity of Justice: New Perspectives on Paul Ricœur's Approach to Justice*, ed. Geoffrey Dierckxsens. Leiden: Brill, 169–205. https://doi.org/10.1163/9789004424982_010.

Kanelos, Pano. 2021. "We Can't Wait for Universities to Fix Themselves." *Cornell Free Speech Alliance* [blog]. 8 November. https://cornellfreespeech.com/we-cant-wait-universities-fix-themselves-common-sense-11821.

Karam, Jeffrey G., and Rima Majed, eds. 2022. *The Lebanon Uprising of 2019: Voices from the Revolution*. London: I.B. Tauris.

Kassab, Elizabeth Suzanne. 2009. *Contemporary Arab Thought: Cultural Critique in Comparative Perspective*. New York: Columbia University Press.

———. 2019. *Enlightenment on the Eve of Revolution: The Egyptian and Syrian Debates*. New York: Columbia University Press.

Kassem, Ali. 2024. *Islamophobia and Lebanon: Visibly Muslim Women and Global Coloniality*. London: I.B. Tauris.

Kaufman, Stuart J. 2017. "Symbolic Politics as International Relations Theory." In *Oxford Research Encyclopedia of Politics*. Oxford: Oxford University Press. https://doi.org/10.1093/acrefore/9780190228637.013.323.

Kaufmann, Eric. 2021. "Academic Freedom in Crisis: Punishment, Political Discrimination, and Self-Censorship." Center for the Study of Partisanship and Ideology. Report No. 2. www.cspicenter.com/p/academic-freedom-in-crisis-punishment.

———. 2022. "Born This Way? The Rise of LGBT as a Social and Political Identity." Center for the Study of Partisanship and Ideology. Report No. 6.

Kazemipur, Abdolmohammad. 2022. *Sacred as Secular: Secularization under Theocracy in Iran*. Montreal: McGill-Queen's University Press.

Kchaou, Mounir. 2007. *Le juste et ses normes: John Rawls et le concept du politique*. [Arabic]. Tunis: FSHST.

———. 2016. "The Secularization of Morality and the Emergence of Conscience: A Comparison between the Western and Arab Contexts." *Tabayyun* 18: 7–21.

———. 2019. "Liberalism and the Problem of Political Theology." [Arabic]. *Al-Bab* 13: 46–89.

———. 2023. "Liberalism and Freedom of Expression: The Philosophical Background of a Legal and Political Debate." [Arabic]. *Tabayyun* 11(43): 13–35.

———. 2024a. "From the Ethics of the Act to the Ethics of the Agent: Debating Consequentialism, Deontology and Virtue Ethics in Contemporary Moral Philosophy." *Tabayyun* 47: 120–53.

———. 2024b. "Secularism Revisited: Implications in the Relationship Religious with Politics." In *Islam, Christianity, and Democracy: Comparative Studies from East and West*, ed. Mounir Kchaou. Beirut: Arab Center for Research and Policy Studies, 89–125.

Keim, Wiebke. 2010. "The Internationalization of Social Sciences: Distortions, Dominations and Prospects." In *World Social Science Report, 2010*. Paris: Unesco, 169–70.

Kenworthy, Lane. 2024. "The Good Society." https://lanekenworthy.net/.

Khan, Muqtedar. 2019. *Islam and Good Governance: A Political Philosophy of Ihsan*. New York: Palgrave Macmillan. https://doi.org/10.1057/978-1-137-54832-0.

Kim, Hee-Kang. 2007. "Locating Feminism beyond Gender and Culture: A Case of the Family-Head System in South Korea." *Tamnon 201* 10(1): 245–90.

Kim, Sungmoon. 2015. "Public Reason Confucianism: A Construction." *American Political Science Review* 109(1): 187–200.

———. 2023. *Confucian Constitutionalism: Dignity, Rights, and Democracy*. New York: Oxford University Press.

Kirk, Russell. 1955. *Academic Freedom: An Essay in Definition*. Chicago: Henry Regnery Company.

Kiwan, Dina. 2023. *Academic Freedom and the Transnational Production of Knowledge*. Cambridge: Cambridge University Press.

Kocsis, Tiffani. 2019. *A Critical Analysis of Sexuality Education in the United States: Toward an Inclusive Curriculum for Social Justice*. London: Routledge.

Konings, Martijn. 2015. *The Emotional Logic of Capitalism: What Progressives Have Missed*. Stanford, CA: Stanford University Press.

Kostić, Ivan Ejub. 2024. "Political Empowerment: The Role of Party Politics in the Future of European Muslim." *Filozofija i drustvo* 35(3): 607–24. https://doi.org/10.2298/FID2403607E.

Kristof, Nicholas. 2016. "A Confession of Liberal Intolerance." *New York Times* [blog]. 7 May. www.nytimes.com/2016/05/08/opinion/sunday/a-confession-of-liberal-intolerance.html.

Kubai, Anne, and Ezekiel Mtetwa. 2021. "'Our Children Are No Longer Ours': Child Social Welfare Services and Diminished Parental Authority Amongst African Migrant Families in Sweden." In *Law, Religion and the Family in Africa*, ed. M. Christian Green and Faith Kabata. Stellenbosch: Sun Press, 333–65.

Laborde, Cécile. 2017. *Liberalism's Religion*. Cambridge, MA: Harvard University Press.

Lalmi Abderrahmane, Yasmina. 2023. "La ética del cuidado: El caso de Argelia." Ph.D. thesis. Valencia: Universitat de València.

Lama, Fadi. 2023. *Why the West Can't Win: From Bretton Woods to a Multipolar World*. Atlanta, GA: Clarity Press.

Larzillière, Pénélope. 2013. *La Jordanie contestataire: Militants islamistes, nationalistes et communistes*. Arles: Actes Sud.

Lawford-Smith, Holly. 2022. *Gender-Critical Feminism*. Oxford: Oxford University Press.

Lefebvre, Rémi, and Frédéric Sawicki. 2006. *La société des socialistes: Le PS aujourd'hui*. Bellecombe-en-Bauges: Editions du Croquant.

Levey, Geoffrey Brahm. 2018. "The Bristol School of Multiculturalism." *Ethnicities* 19(9): 200–26.

Li, Chunling. 2023. "Wealthization and Housing Wealth Inequality in China." In *Handbook of Post-Western Sociology: From East Asia to Europe*, ed. Laurence Roulleau-Berger, Peilin Li, Seung Kuk Kim and Shujiro Yasawa. Leiden: Brill, 487–94.

Li, Peilin, M.K. Gorshkov and Celi Scalon, eds. 2013. *Handbook on Social Stratification in the BRIC Countries: Change and Perspective*, ed. Peilin Li, M.K. Gorshkov, Celi Scalon and K.L. Sharma. Hackensack, NJ: World Scientific Publishing Company.

Lipovetsky, Gilles. 2005. *Hypermodern Times*. Trans. Sebastien Charles. Cambridge: Polity Press.

Losego, Philippe, and Rigas Arvanitis. 2008. "Science in Non-Hegemonic Countries." *Revue d'anthropologie des connaissances* 2(3). https://doi.org/10.3917/rac.005.0343.

Lukianoff, Greg, and Jonathan Haidt. 2018. *The Coddling of the American Mind: How Good Intentions and Bad Ideas Are Setting Up a Generation for Failure*. Illustrated ed. New York: Penguin Press.

Lutard-Tavard, Catherine. 2014. "Être à la barre, être accusé(e)." *Socio. La nouvelle revue des sciences sociales* 3: 63–78. https://doi.org/10.4000/socio.578.

Macé, Eric. 2018. "From Patriarchy to Composite Gender Arrangements? Theorizing the Historicity of Social Relations of Gender." *Social Politics: International Studies in Gender, State & Society* 25(3): 317–36.

———. 2020. *Après la société: Manuel de sociologie augmentée*. Paris: Le Bord de l'Eau.

———. 2024. "Towards An Augmented Sociology: A Non-Hegemonic Approach As A Condition For Shared Sociological Reasoning." In *An Invitation to Non-Hegemonic World Sociology*. Lanham, MD: Rowman & Littlefield, 144–67.

McGrath, John J., Ali Al-Hamzawi, Jordi Alonso, Yasmin Altwaijri et al. 2023. "Age of Onset and Cumulative Risk of Mental Disorders: A Cross-National Analysis of Population Surveys from 29 Countries." *Lancet Psychiatry* 10(9): 668–81.

MacIntyre, Alasdair. 1988. *Whose Justice? Which Rationality?* Notre Dame, IN: University of Notre Dame Press.

MacKinnon, Catharine. 1989. *Toward a Feminist Theory of the State.* Cambridge, MA: Harvard University Press, 1989.

Maffettone, Sebastiano. 2011. "Sen's Idea of Justice versus Rawls' Theory of Justice." *Indian Journal of Human Development* 5(1): 119–32.

Magout, Mohammad. 2024. "Sari Hanafi: Secularism and Its Types (2021)." In *Global Secularity: A Sourcebook*, vol. 2, *The Middle East and North Africa*, ed. Florian Zemmin, Neguin Yavari, Markus Dressler and Nurit Stadler. Boston: de Gruyter, 251–61.

Mahama, Ruhia, Rikard Eriksson and Pål Ellingsen. 2024. "African Immigrants in Sweden Experiencing the Threat of Forced Child Removal." *European Journal of Social Work* 27(2): 222–32.

Mahmood, Saba. 2011. *Politics of Piety: The Islamic Revival and the Feminist Subject*. Princeton, NJ: Princeton University Press.

Majed, Rima. 2022. "'Sectarian Neoliberalism' and the 2019 Uprisings in Lebanon and Iraq." In *The Lebanon Uprising of 2019: Voices from the Revolution*, ed. Jeffrey G. Karam and Rima Majed. London: I.B. Tauris, 76–88.

Mallat, Chibli. 2015. *Philosophy of Nonviolence: Revolution, Constitutionalism, and Justice beyond the Middle East*. New York: Oxford University Press.

Mang, Franz. 2023. "Perfectionism, Public Reason and Excellences." *Analysis* 83(3): 627–39. https://doi.org/10.1093/analys/anad023.

MAP (Movement Advancement Project). 2024. "LGBTQ Curricular Laws." www.lgbtmap.org/equality-maps/curricular_laws.

Marsault, Elsa Deck. 2023. *Faire justice: Moralisme progressiste et pratiques punitives dans la lutte contre les violences sexistes*. Paris: Fabrique.

Marsili, Lorenzo. 2024. "Austerity and Immigration No Longer Explain the Far Right's Rise in Europe." *Al Jazeera* [blog]. 13 July. www.aljazeera.com/opinions/2024/7/13/ austerity-and-immigration-no-longer-explain-the-far-rights-rise-in-europe.

Mårtensson, Ulrika. 2014. "Introduction: 'Public Islam' and the Nordic Welfare State: Changing Realities?" *Scandinavian Journal of Islamic Studies* 8(1): 4–55.

Massad, Joseph A. 2008. *Desiring Arabs*. Illustrated ed. Chicago: University of Chicago Press.

Mbembe, Achille. 2001. *On the Postcolony*. Berkeley: University of California Press.

———. 2023. *La communauté terrestre*. Paris: La Découverte.

Mearsheimer, John J. 2018. *The Great Delusion: Liberal Dreams and International Realities*. Cambridge, MA: Yale University Press.

Meghji, Ali. 2020. *Decolonizing Sociology: An Introduction*. Cambridge: Polity Press.

Mejcher-Atassi, Sonja. 2024. *An Impossible Friendship: Group Portrait, Jerusalem Before and After 1948*. New York: Columbia University Press.

Meter, Karl Van, and Jean-Pierre Pagès. 2023. *Débat public: Le jeu des valeurs et des symboles: L'approche Agoramétrie*. Paris: L'Harmattan.

Michéa, Jean-Claude. 2018. *Le loup dans la bergerie: Droit, libéralisme et vie commune*. Paris: Flammarion.

Milanovic, Branko. 2024. "The Three Eras of Global Inequality, 1820–2020 with the Focus on the Past Thirty Years." *World Development* 177:106516. https://doi.org/10.1016/j.worlddev.2023.106516.

Milbank, John, and Adrian Pabst. 2016. *The Politics of Virtue: Post-Liberalism and the Human Future*. Lanham, MD: Rowman & Littlefield.

Mishra, Pankaj. 2024. "Memory Failure." *London Review of Books*, 4 January.

Modood, Tariq. 2022a. "Bristol School of Multiculturalism as Normative Sociology." *Civic Sociology* 3(1): 57379.

———. 2022b. "Resolving the Tension between Academic Freedom and EDI." *The Loop* [blog]. https://theloop.ecpr.eu/resolving-the-tension-between-academic-freedom-and-edi/.

Modood, Tariq, and Thomas Sealy. 2024. *The New Governance of Religious Diversity*. Cambridge: Polity Press.

Mohammed, Hossameldeen, and Ray Jureidini. 2022. "Umma and the Nation-State: Dilemmas in Refuge Ethics." *Journal of International Humanitarian Action* 7(17): 1–25.

Mongiardo, Melissa, and Marco Palmieri. 2024. "Opposite Universes. A Focus on the Ideological Polarisation of the Italian Electorate." *Partecipazione e Conflit* 3(17): 661–81.

Moorhead, Laura. 2018. "LGBTQ+ Visibility in the K-12 Curriculum." *Phi Delta Kappan* 100(2): 22–26.

Mourad, Sara. 2022. "Appearing as Women." In *The Lebanon Uprising of 2019: Voices from the Revolution*, ed. Jeffrey G. Karam and Rima Majed. London: I.B. Tauris, 140–51.

Moustakbal, Jawad. 2023. "The Moroccan Energy Sector: A Permanent Dependence." In *Dismantling Green Colonialism: Energy and Climate Justice in the Arab Region*, ed. Hamza Hamouchene and Katie Sandwell. London: Pluto Press, 220–31.

Nakissa, Aria. 2021. "Cognitive and Quantitative Approaches to Islamic Studies: Integrating Psychological, Socioeconomic, and Digital-Cultural Statistics." *Religion Compass* 15(12): e12424.

Nassar, Nassif. 2003. *Freedom Gate: When Being Is Doing*. Beirut: Dar al-Tali'a.

———. 2022. *Ishtar's Book on Clothing and the Body*. [Arabic]. Beirut: Center for Arab Unity Studies.

Nesvetailova, Anastasia, and Ronen Palan. 2020. *Sabotage: The Hidden Nature of Finance*. New York: PublicAffairs.

Neves, Catarina. 2023. "Between Charity and Entitlement: Unconditional Basic Income as a Gift." *Mauss International* 3(1): 220–43.

Nitzan, Jonathan, and Shimshon Bichler. 2002. *The Global Political Economy of Israel*. London: Pluto Press.

Noelle-Neumann, Elisabeth. 1974. *The Spiral of Silence*. Chicago: University of Chicago Press.

Norberg, Johan. 2023. *The Capitalist Manifesto*. London: Atlantic Books.

Norris, Pippa. 2020. "Closed Minds? Is a 'Cancel Culture' Stifling Academic Freedom and Intellectual Debate in Political Science?" Harvard Kennedy School Faculty Research Working Paper Series. www.hks.harvard.edu/publications/closed-minds-cancel-culture-stifling-academic-freedom-and-intellectual-debate.

———. 2023. "Cancel Culture: Heterodox Self-Censorship or the Curious Case of the Dog-Which-Didn't-Bark." HKS Working Paper No. RWP23-020. Harvard Kennedy School. https://ssrn.com/abstract=4516336.

Norris, Pippa, and Ronald Inglehart. 2019. *Cultural Backlash: Trump, Brexit, and Authoritarian Populism*. New York: Cambridge University Press.

Nussbaum, Martha. 2009. *Hiding from Humanity: Disgust, Shame, and the Law*. Princeton, NJ: Princeton University Press.

Nyhagen, Line. 2017. "The Lived Religion Approach in the Sociology of Religion and Its Implications for Secular Feminist Analyses of Religion." *Social Compass* 64(4): 495–511.

Oberlin, Christophe. 2020. "Cour Pénale Internationale: face aux Palestiniens, Badinter défend Netanyahou." https://blogs.mediapart.fr/christophe-oberlin/blog/200220/cour-penale-internationale-face-aux-palestiniens-badinter-defend-netanyahou.

O'Connor, Alan. 1989. *Raymond Williams, Writing, Culture, Politics*. Oxford: Blackwell.

Odhav, Kiran, and Jayanathan Govender. 2023. "Conclusion." In *Handbook on Sociology of Inequalities in BRICS Countries*, ed. Kiran Odhav and Jayanathan Govender. London: Frontpage Publications, 345–52.

Olson, Glen W., and Terry Lee Brussel-Rogers. 2022. *Fifty Years of Polyamory in America: A Guided Tour of a Growing Movement*. Lanham, MD: Rowman & Littlefield.

Orwell, George. 2020. [1938]. *Homage To Catalonia*. London: Penguin Books.

Özyürek, Esra. 2023. *Subcontractors of Guilt: Holocaust Memory and Muslim Belonging in Postwar Germany*. Stanford, CA: Stanford University Press.

Parker, Richard. 2009. "Sexuality, Culture and Society: Shifting Paradigms in Sexuality Research." *Culture, Health & Sexuality* 11(3): 251–66.

Parodi, Katharine B., Melissa K. Holt, Jennifer Greif Green, Michelle V. Porche et al. 2022. "Time Trends and Disparities in Anxiety among Adolescents, 2012–2018." *Social Psychiatry and Psychiatric Epidemiology* 57(1): 127–37.

Patel, Sujata, ed. 2009. *International Handbook of Diverse Sociological Traditions*. London: Sage.

Paternotte, David, and Roman Kuhar. 2017. "Gender Movement: Introduction." In *Anti-Gender Campaigns in Europe: Mobilizing against Equality*, ed. Roman Kuhar and David Paternotte. Lanham, MD: Rowman & Littlefield, 1–22.

Phoenix, Ann. 2023. "European Trajectories of Intersectionality." In *The Routledge International Handbook of Intersectionality Studies*, ed. Kathy Davis and Helma Lutz. London: Routledge, 14–27.

Piketty, Thomas. 2014. *Capital in the Twenty-First Century*. Trans. Arthur Goldhammer. Cambridge, MA: Belknap Press.

Pleyers, Geoffrey. 2020. "Interconnected Challenges of the 21st Century." *Global Dialogue*. 21 February. http://globaldialogue.isa-sociology.org/interconnected-challenges-of-the-21st-century/.

———. 2024. "For a Global Sociology of Social Movements: Beyond Methodological Globalism and Extractivism." *Globalizations* 21(1): 183–95.

Plumwood, Val. 2002. *Environmental Culture: The Ecological Crisis of Reason*. London: Routledge.

Polanyi, Karl. 1983. [1944]. *La grande transformation: Aux origines politiques et économiques de notre temps*. Paris: Gallimard.

Pollet, Thomas V., and Tamsin K. Saxton. 2019. "How Diverse Are the Samples Used in the Journals 'Evolution & Human Behavior' and 'Evolutionary Psychology'?" *Evolutionary Psychological Science* 5(3): 357–68. https://doi.org/10.1007/s40806-019-00192-2.

Pon, Gordon. 2009. "Cultural Competency as New Racism: An Ontology of Forgetting." *Journal of Progressive Human Services* 20(1): 59–71.

Port, Andrew I. 2023. *Never Again: Germans and Genocide after the Holocaust*. Cambridge, MA: Belknap Press.

Pringle, Keith. 2010. "Swedish Welfare Responses to Ethnicity: The Case of Children and Their Families." *European Journal of Social Work* 13(1): 19–34.

Puar, Jasbir. 2007. *Terrorist Assemblages: Homonationalism in Queer Times*. Illustrated ed. Durham, NC: Duke University Press Books.

Pulcini, Elena. 2017. "What Emotions Motivate Care?" *Emotion Review* 9(1): 64–71.

Purkayastha, Bandana. 2024. "Human Rights and Humanitarianism." In *Handbook on Humanitarianism and Inequality*, ed. Silke Roth, Bandana Purkayastha and Tobias Denskus. Cheltenham: Edward Elgar Publishing, 92–107.

Qing, Jiang. 2012. *A Confucian Constitutional Order: How China's Ancient Past Can Shape Its Political Future*, ed. Daniel A. Bell and Ruiping Fan. Trans. Edmund Ryden. Princeton, NJ: Princeton University Press.

Quijano, Aníbal. 1992. "Colonialidad y Modernidad/Racionalidad." In *Los Conquistados: 1492 y la Población Indígena de las Américas*, ed. H. Bonilla. Quito: FLACSO/Ediciones Libri Mundi, 437–49.

Rawls, John. 1971. *A Theory of Justice*. Cambridge, MA: Harvard University Press.

———. 1993. *Political Liberalism*. New York: Columbia University Press.

———. 1999. *The Law of Peoples: With "The Idea of Public Reason Revisited."* Cambridge, MA: Harvard University Press.

———. 2001. *Justice as Fairness: A Restatement*. 2nd ed. Cambridge, MA: Harvard University Press.

Riggs, A., and B.S. Turne. 1997. "The Sociology of the Postmodern Self: Intimacy, Identity and Emotions in Adult Life." *Australian Journal on Ageing* 16(4): 229–32. https://doi.org/10.1111/j.1741-6612.1997.tb01061.x.

Rončević, Borut. 2024. *Sociologies in Post-Socialist Transformations in Eastern Europe: A Cultural Political Economy Approach*, ed. Borut Rončević and Tamara Besednjak Valič. Cham: Springer.

Rosa, Hartmut. 2019. *Resonance: A Sociology of Our Relationship to the World*. Medford, MA: Polity Press.

Rougier, Bernard. 2022. "Préface: La France face à une menace multiforme." In *Les territoires conquis de l'islamisme*, ed. Bernard Rougier. Paris: J'AI LU, 2–12.

Roy, Olivier. 2022. *L'Aplatissement du monde: La crise de la culture et l'empire des normes*. Paris: Seuil.

Sabbagh-Khoury, Areej. 2023. *Colonizing Palestine: The Zionist Left and the Making of the Palestinian Nakba*. Stanford, CA: Stanford University Press.

Sadek, Karim. 2014. "Maṣlaḥa and Rachid Al-Ghannushi's Reformist Project." In *Maqāṣid Al-Sharīʿa and Contemporary Reformist Muslim Thought: An Examination*, ed. Adis Duderija. New York: Palgrave Macmillan, 151–75. https://doi.org/10.1057/9781137319418_7.

Safi, Louay M. 2021. *Islam and the Trajectory of Globalization: Rational Idealism and the Structure of World History*. London: Routledge.

———, ed. 2023. *Islam and the Drive to Global Justice: Principles of Justice Beyond Dominant Ethnic and Religious Communities*. New York: Lexington Books.

Saleh, Rasheed al-Haj. 2023. "Reflections on Contemporary Arab Moral Thought: An Investigation of the Relationship between Ethics and Politics." *Tabayyun* 46: 7–47.

Saleh, Yassin al-Haj. 2011. *Other People's Myths: Criticism of Contemporary Islam and Critique of Its Critique*. Beirut: Dar al-Saqi.

———. 2021. *The Atrocious and Its Representation: Deliberations on Syria's Destroyed Form and Its Laborious Formation*. Beirut: Dar al-Jadid.

Sandel, Michael J. 2013. *What Money Can't Buy: The Moral Limits of Markets*. New York: Farrar, Straus and Giroux.

Sapiro, Gisèle. 2020. *Peut-on dissocier l'oeuvre de l'auteur ?* Paris: Seuil.

Sartori, Andrew Stephen. 2014. *Liberalism in Empire: An Alternative History.* Oakland: University of California Press.

Schaumburg-Müller, Sten. 2011. "In Defense of Soft Universalism: A Modest, Yet Presumptuous Position." *Cuadernos Constitucionales de La Cátedra Fadrique Furió Ceriol* 62/63: 113–26.

Schulman, Sarah. 2016. *Conflict Is Not Abuse: Overstating Harm, Community Responsibility, and the Duty of Repair.* Vancouver: Arsenal Pulp Press.

Schwarzmantel, John, ed. 2014. *The Routledge Guidebook to Gramsci's Prison Notebooks.* London: Routledge.

Scott-Baumann, Alison, Mathew Guest, Shuruq Naguib, Sariya Cheruvallil-Contractor and Aisha Phoenix. 2020. *Islam on Campus: Contested Identities and the Cultures of Higher Education in Britain.* Oxford: Oxford University Press.

Scribano, Adrian. 2019. *Love as a Collective Action: Latin America, Emotions and Interstitial Practices.* New York: Routledge.

Seidman, Steven. 2003. *The Social Construction of Sexuality.* New York: W. W. Norton & Company.

Sen, Amartya. 2011. *The Idea of Justice.* Cambridge, MA: Belknap Press.

Shahrokni, Nazanin. 2019. *Women in Place: The Politics of Gender Segregation in Iran.* Oakland: University of California Press.

Sharma, Ruchir. 2024. *What Went Wrong with Capitalism.* New York: Simon & Schuster.

Shestack, Jerome J. 1998. "The Philosophic Foundations of Human Rights." *Human Rights Quarterly* 20(2): 201–34.

Shiva, Vandana. 1993. *Monocultures of the Mind: Perspectives on Biodiversity and Biotechnology.* London: Zed Books.

SIECUS (Sex Ed for Social Change). 2023. "Sex Ed State Legislative Mid-Year Report 2023." https://siecus.org/wp-content/uploads/2023/08/Mid-Year-Report-2023-SIECUS-1.pdf. Routledge, 237–64.

Singh, Bhrigupati. 2024. "Teaching Social Theory under Repressive Regimes: Traversals between Arab, Indian and Other Sociologies." *Contributions to Indian Sociology* 58 (2): 186–94.

Singh, Suzanne. 1996. "Contradictory Knowings & Women's Sexuality." *Youth Studies Australia* 15(3): 33.

Sjögren, Lena Hellblom. 2013. *The Child's Right to Family Life: 25 Swedish Case Studies of Parental Alienation.* 2nd ed. https://avskildabarn.se/2016/03/30/the-childs-right-to-family-life-25-swedish-case-studies-of-parental-alienation/.

Smith, Carole. 2002. "The Sequestration of Experience: Rights Talk and Moral Thinking in 'Late Modernity.'" *Sociology* 36(1): 43–66. https://doi.org/10.1177/0038038502036001003.

Snapp, Shannon D., Hilary Burdge, Adela C. Licona, Raymond L. Moody and Stephen T. Russell. 2015. "Students' Perspectives on LGBTQ-Inclusive Curriculum." *Equity & Excellence in Education* 48(2): 249–65.

Soler Gallart, Marta. 2017. *Achieving Social Impact: Sociology in the Public Sphere*. Cham: Springer.

Spini, Debora. 2021. "Elena Pulcini. The Time to Think of the Good." *Rivista Italiana Di Filosofia Politica* 1 (December), 287–305.

Spitz, Jean-Fabien. 2023. "La laïcité dévoyée." AOC (Analyse Opinion Critique). 17 April. https://aoc.media/analyse/2023/04/16/la-laicite-devoyee/.

Steinhoff, Uwe. 2022. *Freedom, Culture, and the Right to Exclude: On the Permissibility and Necessity of Immigration Restrictions*. London: Routledge.

———. 2023. "Against the Harm Argument for Censorship: On the Abuse of Psychology and the Dismissal of Rights." *Controversial Ideas* 3(1): 1–16.

Stocker, Barry. 2007. "'Hostipitality.'" In *Jacques Derrida: Basic Writings*. London: Routledge, 237–64.

Sukarieh, Rana. 2024. "Political Imaginaries of Solidarity: The Boycott, Divestment, and Sanctions (BDS) in Toronto." *Social Movement Studies*. 23 February: 1–16. www.tandfonline.com/doi/full/10.1080/14742837.2024.2321132.

Svensson, Gustav, and Staffan Höjer. 2016. "Placing Children in State Care in Sweden: Decision-Making Bodies, Laypersons, and Legal Framework." In *Child Welfare Removals by the State: A Cross-Country Analysis of Decision-Making Systems*, ed. Kenneth Burns, Tarja Pvsv and Marit Skivenes. Oxford: Oxford University Press, 65–88. https://doi.org/10.1093/acprof:oso/9780190459567.003.0004.

Thörn, Mikael, and Katarina Norberg. 2020. "Amanda-kommissionen. Granskning av Göteborgs Stads arbete mot hedersrelaterat våld och förtryck 2017–2018. [The Amanda Commission: *Review of the City of Gothenburg's Work against Honour-Related Violence and Oppression, 2017–2018*]. City of Gothenburg. www.uu.se/centrum/nck/kunskapsbank-om-vald/publikation?query=2341.

Todd, Emmanuel. 2016. *Who Is Charlie? Xenophobia and the New Middle Class*. Cambridge: Polity Press.

Todorov, Tzvetan. 2011. "La tyrannie de l'individu." *Le Monde*. 18 March. www.lemonde.fr/idees/article/2011/03/26/la-tyrannie-de-l-individu_1498940_3232.html.

Touraine, Alain. 2007. *New Paradigm for Understanding Today's World*. Cambridge: Polity Press.

———. 2013. *La fin des sociétés*. Paris: Seuil.

Traboulsi, Fawwaz. 2014. *Social Classes and Political Power in Lebanon*. Beirut: Heinrich Böll Stiftung – Middle East. https://lb.boell.org/sites/default/files/2024-06/social-classes-in-lebanon-en-2014-.pdf.

Turner, Bryan S. 2011. "Religion in Liberal and Authoritarian States." In *Religion and the State: A Comparative Sociology*, ed. Jack Barbalet, Adam Possamai and Bryan S. Turner. London: Anthem Press, 25–43.

Vandenberghe, Frédéric. 2018. "Sociology as Practical Philosophy and Moral Science." *Theory, Culture & Society* 35(3): 77–97.

———. 2023. "Sociology as the Continuation of Moral Philosophy by Other Means." *Global Dialogue*. 16 June.

Viles, Dawn J. 2023. "Teachers' Perceptions of Policies and Practices of LGBTQ-Inclusive Curriculum in Rural Appalachian High School English Language Arts Classes." Washington, DC: Lincoln Memorial University.

Wagner, Peter. 2021. "The Bird in Hand Rational Choice – The Default Mode of Social Theorizing." *MAUSS International* 1(1): 164–82.

———. 2023. "The Triple Problem Displacement: Climate Change and the Politics of the Great Acceleration." *European Journal of Social Theory* 26(1): 24–47. https://journals.sagepub.com/doi/full/10.1177/13684310221136083.

———. 2024. *Carbon Societies: The Social Logic of Fossil Fuels.* Cambridge: Polity Press.

Walhof, Darren R. 2013. "Habermas, Same-Sex Marriage and the Problem of Religion in Public Life." *Philosophy and Social Criticism* 3(39): 225–42.

Walzer, Michael. 2019. *Thick and Thin: Moral Argument at Home and Abroad.* Notre Dame, IN: University of Notre Dame Press.

Warfield Rawls, Anne. 2021. "The Structure of Social Facts: Self, Objects and Action as Products of Reciprocity and Cooperation in Constitutive Practices." *MAUSS International* 1(1): 182–200.

Winlow, Simon, and Steve Hall. 2022. *The Death of the Left: Why We Must Begin from the Beginning Again.* Bristol: Policy Press.

Wohlrab-Sahr, Monika, and Marian Burchardt. 2012. "Multiple Secularities: Toward a Cultural Sociology of Secular Modernities." *Comparative Sociology* 11(6): 875–909.

Wright, Erik Olin. 2010. *Envisioning Real Utopias.* London: Verso.

Younes, Anna-Esther. 2020. "Fighting Anti-Semitism in Contemporary Germany." *Islamophobia Studies Journal* 5(2): 249–66.

Yuval-Davis, Nira. 2023. "The Analytical and the Political: Situated Intersectionality and Transversal Solidarity." In *The Routledge International Handbook of Intersectionality Studies*, ed. Kathy Davis and Helma Lutz. London: Routledge, 86–98.

Zapata-Barrero, Ricard, and Ibrahim Awad, eds. 2023. *Migrations in the Mediterranean: IMISCOE Regional Reader.* 2024 edition. Cham: Springer.

Zemmin, Florian, Neguin Yavari, Markus Dressler and Nurit Stadler, eds. 2024. *Global Secularity: A Sourcebook*, vol. 2, *The Middle East and North Africa.* Boston: de Gruyter.

Zerilli, Linda M.G. 2015. "Feminist Critiques of Liberalism." In *The Cambridge Companion to Liberalism*, ed. Steven Wall. Cambridge: Cambridge University Press, 355–80.

Zhao, Tingyang. 2012. "The Ontology of Coexistence: From Cogito to Facio." *Diogenes* 57(4): 27–36.

———. 2021. *All Under Heaven: The Tianxia System for a Possible World Order.* Oakland: University of California Press.

Zuber, Valentine. 2019. "La laïcité française, une exception historique, des principes partagés." *Revue du droit des religions* 7 (May): 193–205.

Index of Authors

Index

Countries & Regions

Key Concepts

www.ingramcontent.com/pod-product-compliance
Lightning Source LLC
Chambersburg PA
CBHW062347300326

41947CB00013B/1512

* 9 7 8 1 8 3 6 2 4 4 6 7 7 *